TRAUMATIZED

A LOVE STORY

©2025 Michael Stone

All rights reserved. No part of this book may be used or reproduced in any manner without written permission from the author.

Some names and identifying details have been changed to protect the privacy of individuals. This book is a story of portions of the author's life and is not intended as a substitute for medical recommendations of physicians, mental-health professionals, or other health-care providers. Rather, it is intended to offer a story and information to help the reader, if they choose, work with and consult physicians, mental-health professionals, and health-care providers in a mutual quest for well-being. We advise readers to carefully review and understand the ideas presented and to seek the advice of qualified professionals before attempting to follow or use them.

Published by Michael Stone June 2025

Printed in the United States of America

ISBN 979-8-9991538-0-7

TRAUMATIZED
A LOVE STORY

Healing the Wounds that Separate,
Alienate, and Marginalize Us

MICHAEL STONE

TRAUMATIZED: A LOVE STORY - MICHAEL STONE

READER ENDORSEMENTS FOR
TRAUMATIZED

"Michael Stone's *Traumatized: A Love Story* is a masterpiece of a memoir and a vitally important guide to healing. With heart and honesty, Stone shares the intimate story of layered trauma, including the ramifications and the blessings. This book is a must for anyone working to heal their own trauma and an important support for anyone in a personal or professional relationship with someone traumatized. In these pages, we find a steady hand held out in love and tools that are not concepts, but hard-earned experience transmuted. As Stone writes and demonstrates through his own healing journey: here is a pathway to alchemize grief into wisdom, longing into love, and separation into a sense of belonging."

Heather Ash Amara
Author of the *Warrior Goddess* Books and Trainings

"Michael Stone has gifted us with an amazing book on healing trauma. This is just not another book on trauma, but includes a very intimate autobiography about his own trauma and the trauma of his family. Through his own experience, he wrote Traumatized: A Love Story, which offers insight into the transformative practices and philosophies that have shaped his work as a trauma integration teacher, facilitator, and advocate. It explores the concept of post-traumatic healing—a journey not just of survival but of rediscovering wholeness, connection, and the completion of unfinished experiences from the past.

This book addresses the universal wounds of abandonment, loss, and betrayal with authenticity and compassion while providing actionable tools for embracing a life of loving awareness. *Traumatized: A Love Story* is more than a personal memoir—it's a call to action for individuals and communities to become trauma-informed and embrace the transformative power of post-traumatic healing.

Michael is a fantastic writer. He has this incredible ability to flesh out what we all need to learn, and he is so articulate and engaging. This is a brilliant book."

Sandra Ingerman, MA
International shamanic teacher and award-winning author of 13 books, including *Soul Retrieval: Mending the Fragmented Self*

"*Traumatized: A Love Story* by Michael Stone is a courageous and heartfelt account for those ready to meet their inner warrior and transform their lives. With honesty and compassion, Stone shares his deeply personal journey, offering powerful inspiration to move beyond pain and suffering. I highly recommend this essential and healing book."

Itzhak Beery
Author of *The Gift of Shamanism*, *Shamanic Transformations*, and *Shamanic Healing*. He is a leading ancestral medicine teacher, healer, speaker, and publisher of *Shaman Portal*.

CONTENTS

Introduction v

Chapter One: The Mother Wound 1

Chapter Two: The Father Wound 17

Chapter Three: Looking for Love in Levittown 31

Chapter Four: Severe Times 47

Chapter Five: Bourbon, My First Dog 59

Chapter Six: Military School 69

Chapter Seven: On The Road 87

Chapter Eight: Healing Journey Begins 105

Chapter Nine: Teachers & Awakenings 119

Chapter Ten: Death Wasn't All That Bad 143

Chapter Eleven: Sonia Romance & Reality 153

Chapter Twelve: Sonia - The Unimaginal 169

Chapter Thirteen: Marriage & Relationships 189

Chapter Fourteen: The Trial: Vindication & Healing 211

Chapter Fifteen: Holding Little Mickey:
        A Case Study in Trauma Healing 227

Chapter Sixteen: Relational Intimacy 241

Chapter Seventeen: Finding Our Purpose:
        A Journey Toward Wholeness 259

Chapter Eighteen: Ancestors 267

Chapter Nineteen: Collective Trauma, Technology,
        and Post-Truth 289

Chapter Twenty: The Light of A Dying Star 305

About the Author 315

TRAUMATIZED: A LOVE STORY – MICHAEL STONE

INTRODUCTION

How is Trauma a Love Story?

> *Trauma is not what happens to you; it's what happens inside you as a result of what happened to you. Trauma is that scarring that makes you less flexible, more rigid, less feeling, and more defended.*
>
> Gabor Maté

Trauma and love may seem like opposites, but I've come to see trauma healing as an evolutionary path—one that leads us, again and again, back to love. Not the soft, sentimental kind of love, but a fierce, embodied presence born in the heart of pain. A love that lives in the willingness to turn toward what once felt unbearable. A love that says, even this can be held and healed.

This book explores trauma not as a flaw or pathology, but as a form of intelligence—our nervous system's exquisite response to overwhelming situations. The tension, numbness, and pain stored in our bodies are not merely remnants of the past; they are living invitations to return to ourselves, to reclaim what was once exiled, and to remember who we are beneath the layers of defense.

We tend to view trauma as something broken inside us, something to conquer or fix. But trauma is not the event itself—it's the imprint that lives on in our body, psyche, and spirit. It's how we adapt when our environment becomes too much.

It fragments our sense of self, exiles our tenderness, and narrows our capacity to trust or connect—all in the name of protection. These aren't failures. They are expressions of a profound, often misunderstood love—our body's devotion to keeping us alive.

This book was born from a lifetime of searching—for freedom, for meaning, for something that made sense of all the pain. Along the way, I've come to see that suffering doesn't arise simply from what happens to us, but from the meanings we attach to those events, and from the resistance we develop to feeling what's buried beneath them. The stories we carry—judgments, interpretations, shame—keep us trapped in cycles of suffering and absence. But when we meet our pain with curiosity and compassion, those same stories can become portals to transformation, to coming home to our true selves.

Some of what I share here may be difficult to read. This is a story marked by suicide, murder, betrayal, addiction, abandonment, and deep loss. But it's also a story of healing, awakening, and the kind of love that is forged in the fire of adversity. I don't tell it to shock or burden you, but because I believe in the redemptive power of truth. When shared with vulnerability, our stories can become bridges—offering others a way through their own darkness.

I was born into war. Both of my parents, serving in the U.S. Army, were caught in the bombing of Pearl Harbor. That legacy of trauma seeped into my beginning. At just two and a half years old, I discovered my mother hanging—an image that shattered my world before I could even form words for what I saw. My father, already scarred by war and now devastated by her death, withdrew emotionally, leaving me to grow up in the hollow silence of unspoken grief. I longed for safety and love that never came.

Years later, a tragic accident took the life of my beloved dog—also by hanging—uncannily echoing my earliest trauma. And still later, my wife was murdered. I lived beneath a cloud of suspicion, slander, and fear for 42 years, until DNA evidence finally cleared my name in 2023.

These events could have broken me. At times, they nearly did. But something deeper kept pulling me forward—a stubborn, sacred instinct to make meaning and find healing out of the mess. Through decades of spiritual practice, therapy, and soul inquiry, I've come to believe that trauma, when met with presence, becomes a teacher. It shows us not just where we were hurt, but where love is most needed—and where it has always been trying to return.

Unhealed trauma doesn't just live in the mind. It resides in the nervous system, quietly shaping our thoughts, emotions, health, and relationships. Left unexamined, it numbs us, isolates us, and repeats itself—both in our lives and in the world around us. The crises we face—violence, addiction, inequality, ecological collapse—are not separate from our wounds. They are symptoms of disconnection from ourselves, each other, and the natural world.

Trauma is not just personal. It is familial, ancestral, and collective. It lives in our cells, our stories, and the human systems we've created. And yet—trauma is not a life sentence. Healing is possible. Not through force or perfection, but through a radical shift in how we relate to our pain.

When we stop running and start listening—when we learn to befriend the symptoms we once feared—something powerful begins to happen. The protective contractions of our body begin to soften. The frozen parts start to thaw. And the tender, exiled pieces of our being—long thought lost—begin to return home.

Healing, as I've come to know it, is not linear or simple. It asks for patience, courage, and a deep willingness to feel our bodies and emotions. It asks us to stop fighting ourselves and to embrace the very parts we've been taught to avoid. Throughout this book, I'll share the reflections, tools, and a four-step process that emerged from my own path—Presencing, Witnessing, Embracing, and Integrating—not as a prescription, but as a compass.

You may recognize yourself in these pages. You may feel your own hidden grief, your inherited burdens, or the quiet ache you've carried for too long. If so, let this be your reminder: you are not broken. You are not alone. The pain you carry is not a sign of failure—it is the doorway to healing.

This is not just a book about trauma—it's a book about transformation. It's about turning pain into insight, suffering into wisdom, and wounds into gateways to love. True love isn't born from ease or perfection; it arises through our willingness to meet what once felt unbearable with presence and compassion. It invites us to say yes to the parts of ourselves we've long hidden and suppressed, to gently hold what we once believed we couldn't survive. And in that courageous embrace, we begin to see that what we thought had broken us was, all along, guiding us back— to wholeness, to love, to home.

This is my story. This is your story. This is a love story—not in the romantic sense, but in the deepest sense. A story that begins in pain, but leads us back to joy, to connection, and to the sacredness of life itself.

I am aware that, in the greater scheme of global suffering, my pain may seem small. I write as a white, privileged male who, by birth and circumstance, had the time and access to explore what healing requires. And with that privilege comes responsibility.

The responsibility to turn toward the trauma embedded in our culture. To help release the inherited suffering of our ancestors. To contribute—however humbly—to the collective healing of our fractured world.

Each chapter in this book weaves together three threads: a story from my life, a reflection on its meaning, and a healing insight or practice for your own journey. It is my deep hope that these offerings will meet you where you are, and that they will support you in facing life's challenges with more compassion, resilience, and love.

Welcome. May your healing begin here.

> *"Transformative change is not coercive. It occurs naturally when you fully embrace what has happened in your life."*
>
> Michael Stone

CHAPTER ONE

The Mother Wound

The mother's image is the first that stamps itself on the unwritten page of the young child's mind.

David O. McKay

Shoes. I had been dreaming about the same pair for years. They were diminutive, moss green, 1940s-style, open-toed, peek-a-boo platform shoes with repeating leaf-like cutouts on the soft suede leather. The petite ankle bands, connected with two straps, resembled the curvaceous arch of a human spine and were attached to elevated cork heels. Crimson-colored toenails peeped through the small round openings at the front.

These tiny, delicate shoes often appear to me in my sleep, floating curiously in a dreamlike mist—silent witnesses to a story waiting to be told.

Before understanding my story, I needed to understand the world that shaped my parents. Both my mother and father were in the Army Air Corps, stationed in Hawaii, when the Japanese attacked Pearl Harbor on December 7, 1941. My father, Bill, was a fighter pilot, and my mother, Margaret, served in the Women's Air Force.

The attack came so quickly that they couldn't get planes off the ground at Hickam Field, Honolulu. With smoke, fire, death, and destruction everywhere, both my parents were right in the middle of it all. That day, the Japanese killed 2,403 U.S. personnel, including 68 civilians, and destroyed or damaged 19 U.S. Navy ships, including eight battleships.

I always considered my father a kind of Errol Flynn of the Royal Air Force's Dawn Patrol. But then, I never really knew him. World War II changed my parents, as wars change us all. Both of them left military service after the war with "shell shock"—what would be called PTSD today.

I was born on July 21, 1945, in a military hospital at the end of an Air Force runway in Bolling Field, Washington, DC—a mere two weeks before the first atomic bomb was dropped on Hiroshima, followed by Nagasaki three days later, just five weeks before the end of the war.

My mother never recovered from the bombing attack on Pearl Harbor. While she was under a doctor's care, therapy in the 1940s was just beginning to emerge amid much controversy. Being in the bombing of Pearl Harbor left her carrying a lot of stress and fear. The overwhelm of having a baby during wartime, plus financial and relational stresses, became too much for her fragile system.

Shortly after my mother and I moved in with my father's parents in New York, she began to show symptoms that all was not well in her tiny five-foot-tall body and brain. I was informed later that she had tried to kill me on numerous occasions—or perhaps she was just trying to stop me from crying. However, putting a pillow over a child's face is generally not advisable. Each time, she was either stopped or blacked out.

I'm not sure, but I think she must have been psychotic. Along with symptoms from the violence and shock of war, she also had what we would call postpartum depression today.

Now, decades later, I sit back on the well-worn leather couch in my therapist's office in Mill Valley, CA. Dr. Miller is an expert in Age Regression Therapy, a psycho-therapeutic process that aims to facilitate access to childhood memories, thoughts, and feelings.

He invites me to close my eyes and take some deep breaths. As I do, he asks me to imagine that I am floating gently downward through a fog and can see the shoes I have been dreaming about somewhere in that fog.

10, 9, 8, 7, 6… I feel a deep tension growing in my body and jaw. Fear spreads like octopus ink through my body, filling every pore and cell of my stiffening form.

5, 4, 3, 2… At first, there is nothing but inky blackness. Then, the image of those shoes and feet emerges from the haze, and suddenly, I remember it all.

It is January 8th, 1947. I am two and a half years old.

It was just after Christmas, and I had been thrilled to receive a Lionel train set from my grandparents. However, there were strict orders not to touch it without an adult present. That morning, I raced down the stairs into the kitchen, excited to play with my new train set. But instead of joy, I was met with my grandmother's angry, red face. Nonnie, as I called her, yelled at me for leaving the electric transformer on the night before. Her words cut through me: "You're going to burn the house down and kill us all!" A statement that would haunt me in later years.

Fear gripped me, and I started crying, wanting nothing more than to hide from her wrath.

Later that day, after things had settled down, Nonnie took me to Golden Gate Park, my favorite place to go and play. We lived nearby, and I loved to crawl into the bushes and feel the plants' protective embrace. This was a world where I felt safe from harm.

That afternoon, we returned to my grandparents' home, where my mother and I had lived for the past year. I ran up the stairs, eager to see my mother. As I rounded the corner of the staircase, heading straight for her room, I abruptly stopped.

And that's when I saw her shoes floating in the air.

I stopped running. Why was she hanging in the air like that?

Before I could take it all in, my grandmother screamed, yanked me by my right arm, and put her hands over my face.

That was the last time I saw my mother. There was no funeral, no goodbyes, no mother, and almost no mention of her from then on. It was as if she never existed.

"Begin to notice your breath, feel your fingers and toes…." I hear my therapist's compassionate voice breaking through the fog. "Just breathe deeply as you feel yourself coming back into your body. Take your time and just breathe. When you're ready, open your eyes."

Hearing the soothing sounds of my therapist's gentle voice brings me back into his dimly lit office. His heavy-set torso is leaning toward me. I can't see his face as the sun shines through the window behind him. Tears stream down my face. I am exhausted and yet, somehow, exhilarated at the same time. I can feel something has changed inside of me.

Before this hypnotic regression session, I had given my therapist some essential background information to understand my history. Both my parents were products of a world transformed by war—a world that left deep, invisible wounds.

CHAPTER ONE: THE MOTHER WOUND

The United States in the 1940s was a far different country from what it subsequently became. Nearly a third of Americans lived in poverty. A third of the country's homes had no running water, two-fifths lacked flushing toilets, and three-fifths lacked central heating. People were struggling to find work wherever they could find it.

My paternal grandparents were from Denmark and carried the stoic sternness of old-world reformation-style Lutheranism. There we were: my mother, my little self, and my old-world, lower-middle-class grandparents. My mother and I slept in the living room of their one-bedroom apartment. There always seemed to be a constant fear of not having enough money. I'm sure they felt we were an added financial burden they couldn't afford.

This new living arrangement must have shocked my mother, who had been raised in a wealthy, upper-middle-class country club lifestyle. She was the daughter of a Canadian banker who had come to the United States to help A.P. Giannini transform the Bank of Italy into the Bank of America. My grandfather served as Senior Vice President for 36 years and earned a high level of respect in banking and commerce.

Most of what I know about my mother, Margaret, I learned after her death. As I pieced together the fragments of her life, a fuller, more radiant picture began to emerge. She was a Stanford University graduate, a remarkable achievement for a woman in her time, and a straight-A psychology student with a keen mind and a compassionate heart.

The daughter of a banker, she carried both grace and depth, expressed through her love for Chopin and her gift as a concert pianist. Her delicate frame, standing under five feet tall and wearing size four shoes, belied a vibrant and magnetic presence.

Kind, sensitive, and brilliant, Margaret embodied a blend of creativity and warmth that shaped me in ways I never fully understood until much later. Though her life ended far too soon, she was the mother I had always longed for. Her essence, her brilliance, and her love live on in me.

But beneath her outward brilliance and charm, my mother struggled profoundly after the bombing. Her mental health deteriorated rapidly after the war, and her attacks on me became more frequent and severe.

Looking back, I believe my mother became deeply delusional, her fragile, sensitive nature shattered by the trauma she endured during the attack on Pearl Harbor. It was simply more than she could bear.

> *When early life experience is traumatic, the trauma lingers as a persistent state of high arousal. Unresolved, it becomes a nameless dread—a sense of impending doom that never dissipates.*
>
> Lawrence Heller

My whole life, I've longed for a mother. As a child, I envied those who had one, feeling shame and loneliness in her absence. I yearned to be seen, soothed, and held in a mother's love. I fantasized about living with another family, and as an adult, I sought mothering qualities in my partners—a longing that often complicated relationships. Even now, the void remains, an ache deep in my heart and stomach, a longing for something forever out of reach.

Lacking the nurturing I so desperately needed, I felt alone and afraid. I saw others as threats and withdrew into my thoughts, disconnected from my body and emotions. I craved connection, yet it terrified me.

As Dr. Peter A. Levine says, "The paradox of trauma is that it has both the power to destroy and the power to transform and resurrect." Over time, my trauma led me on a path of spiritual and personal evolution, teaching me compassion—first for myself, then for others. I saw that separation is an illusion; we are all interconnected through our suffering, reliance on nature, and the influence of those who have gone before.

Despite my grief, I never felt anger toward my mother. In my mind, she remained sacred, idealized, and untouchable. While my body held the trauma, fear, and unease, my mind protected her from blame. With no clear memories to challenge my longing, she became a saintly figure, remembered for love rather than complexity.

Instead, I directed my anger toward my father. He was present enough to be accountable yet distant enough to fuel my frustration. To my child's mind, he was responsible for my mother's absence, my loneliness, my pain. I clung to the illusion of my mother's perfection, fearing that I would lose the fragile hope that sustained me if I let go.

It took years to recognize the gifts my mother left me. Beyond life itself, I imagined she sacrificed hers to save mine—a belief that became central to my healing. This perspective softened the wounds of abandonment, helping me see that my sensitivity, compassion, and desire to make a difference in the world were also her gifts.

My work as a trauma integration facilitator is my way of honoring her and our family history—a way to transform pain into something meaningful.

Through therapy, meditation, and deep inner work, I have come to understand that my mother's struggles were not solely hers. They were the product of war, societal silence, and generational trauma. Her pain was not hers alone but part of a greater collective and ancestral wounding.

This realization brought a sense of responsibility in me to embody and share her gifts. My work in trauma healing is an extension of her legacy. Honoring her kindness and strength, I ensure that her beauty and brilliance are not lost to history. She is no longer just a figure of loss but an inspiration, a reminder that love and creativity endure beyond suffering.

Healing has not been immediate for me. It has unfolded over decades of therapy, contemplation, and transformational work. I have learned that trauma is not a disease but an intelligent response of the nervous system designed to protect us from overwhelming fear and pain.

Trauma is not defined by what happens to us but by how we internalize those experiences and how they shape our bodies, emotional responses, and minds. Without resolution and integration, these wounds perpetuate cycles of grief, fear, and shame being passed down through generations.

Context shapes the meaning we assign to trauma. My family's silence and shame surrounding my mother's death created a powerful narrative that defined me. Unable to grasp the complexities of mental illness and grief, I imagined her as a martyr, a sacred absence.

This story preserved her memory but left me with an unresolved ache, an invisible burden I had carried for decades.

Trauma is best processed in the presence of a caring witness—someone who listens, sees, and holds space for us. Without this, the pain lingers, disrupting our ability to repair, self-regulate, and connect. Left unprocessed, trauma can manifest as chronic illness, emotional distress, and dysfunctional relationships.

My nervous system's response to shut down was not a flaw but an act of survival. Honoring this intelligence allowed me to soften, heal, and reclaim the parts of myself that were frozen in time.

For much of my life, I was terrified of my anger. I believed that if I let it rise, it would erupt like an uncontrollable volcano, destroying everything in its path. It felt too vast, too volatile—something I had to suppress or risk being consumed by its destruction. But beneath the fury and grief lay something even more powerful: the universal longing for connection, love, and belonging. In confronting my shadow, I didn't lose myself—I found my way back home.

My father's absence shaped me as profoundly as my mother's. While her loss was overt, his presence—distant, unavailable—left its wound as well. Healing meant recognizing both wounds and understanding how they shaped my fears, relationships, and sense of self.

I did not feel nurtured, soothed, or protected as a child, but understanding this has helped me build the inner stability I once lacked. Looking back at photos of my mother gazing at me with caring, tender eyes, I now see what I could not before—I was truly loved. And in that love, I continue to heal.

> *From early infancy, our ability to regulate emotional states depends upon feeling that a significant person in our life is simultaneously experiencing a similar state of mind.*
>
> Dr. Daniel J. Siegel

Trauma can begin before birth, shaping a child's development while still in the womb. Research shows that prenatal trauma stems from many sources—maternal stress, substance use (both of my parents smoked and drank), exposure to violence, loss, or large-scale events like war. These experiences can disrupt fetal development, leading to long-term emotional and neurological challenges.

A child's struggle with trust, safety, or emotional regulation may be rooted in their earliest social and environmental conditions.

One key factor is cortisol, the stress hormone. Elevated maternal stress can alter a fetus's brain and nervous system, increasing sensitivity to stress, immune vulnerabilities, and neurodivergent traits. While brain development accelerates in utero, it continues exponentially through the first three years of life, making early nurturing and support essential for long-term well-being.

A caregiver's presence and responsiveness can help a child heal after birth. Infants need to feel safe, seen, soothed, and protected. Play, movement, drumming, rocking, singing, and bouncing can foster emotional regulation. Children need to feel loved to learn how to self-regulate their emotions and respond to triggered reactions.

Our nervous system has evolved over hundreds of thousands of years to keep us safe. When we feel unseen, unsafe, or unprotected, especially in childhood, our bodies interpret these experiences as threats to survival. Because our well-being depends on our caregivers, we can't afford to see them as the source of harm. Instead, we turn the blame inward, concluding, "Something is wrong with me." If the person who offers comfort is also a source of fear, the nervous system fragments, suppressing overwhelming emotions to protect us.

To make sense of pain, uncertainty, or fear, we instinctively create narratives and assume roles within the family system—roles such as the smart one, the helper, the black sheep, the fixer, or the one who always has it together. These identities emerge as adaptive strategies, allowing us to maintain a sense of safety and belonging. However, unless we raise awareness of these unconscious patterns, they will continue to shape how we perceive ourselves and respond to stress. What once ensured our survival can become a strength, a profession, or a compulsive drive, while unresolved trauma may linger in the body as chronic tension, numbness, or emotional overwhelm.

Healing begins when we fully feel, integrate, and bring awareness to the emotions, sensations, and experiences we once had to suppress. With awareness, the past can finally be released and returned to where it belongs: in the past.

Throughout my life, I've had a persistent feeling that something terrible is about to happen—what I call "awfulizing." I'll be driving and suddenly fear an accident. I'll worry my dog will run into the street and be hit, or war is on the brink of erupting. This looming sense of catastrophe feels ingrained and intergenerational.

In meditation and deep inner work, I've traced this fear back to the nine months I spent in my mother's womb, absorbing her terror of war, attack, poverty, abandonment, and alcohol abuse.

Epigenetic research confirms that prenatal stress can alter gene expression, impacting brain development and increasing the risk of behavioral disorders. Our earliest environment shapes us in ways we are only beginning to understand.

Psychologist Bethany Webster coined the term "Mother Wound" to describe the generational trauma passed from mothers to children within a patriarchal framework. Healing this wound means addressing inherited pain and breaking free from limiting patterns.

Mother energy is the essence of presence, flow, and nurturing. It embodies earthiness, receptivity, and creation. Our connection to Mother Earth is primal—she grounds us, nourishes us, and provides the foundation for our growth. She is the unseen force weaving together the many threads of our existence.

But what of the father? If the mother is the ground beneath us, what role does the father play in shaping who we become? Where was my father in all of this? And how did his presence—or absence—shape my evolution?

REFLECTIONS

Looking back, I understand that I wasn't just grieving the loss of my mother—I was mourning the loss of safety, of innocence, of belonging. For much of my life, I thought something was wrong with me. I now see that what I carried were the natural responses of a child overwhelmed by circumstances too big to put into words. There was never anything wrong with me—only unmet needs, unspoken truths, and a nervous system doing its best to protect me.

I've come to understand trauma not as a flaw or illness but as evidence of how deeply we are wired to survive—and how profoundly we are wired to love. My longing for my mother wasn't only about her absence; it revealed my innate capacity to attach, feel, and deeply care. Through the integration process, what once felt like a source of pain has become a source of strength.

For years, I lived in the shadow of a story I didn't have words for to express. When I spoke of my past, it was like telling someone else's story, someone walking beside me. But the body remembers, and eventually, the heart finds its way to meaning. What once felt like a void now feels like a sacred space that taught me how to listen, hold others, and show up with presence even when it's hard.

I used to think healing meant "fixing" my broken self." Now I know it means becoming more fully myself—reclaiming the parts of me I left behind, softening around the parts that once felt too painful to touch—and seeing myself through eyes of compassion.

The idealized image I held of my mother wasn't wrong—it was simply incomplete. With time and tenderness, I've made room for her humanity alongside her grace. She didn't abandon me;

she was overwhelmed by her own pain. And that pain, I now understand, wasn't hers alone—it was the echo of unhealed wounds passed down through generations.

My father's distance, too, makes more sense now. I can see the war in his eyes, the silence in his body, the numbness that once felt like rejection. I spent many years angry, longing for what he could not give. But as I healed, I stopped asking him to be someone he wasn't and started offering to myself what I had always needed.

Healing has given me something I never thought possible—gratitude, not for the trauma but for what it awakened in me: the capacity to hold space, the ability to sit with discomfort, the gift of empathy, and the unwavering belief that evolutionary transformation is always possible.

What once felt like a wound that defined me now feels like an opening door that continues to deepen me.

Love is no longer something I chase—it's something I remember.

EARLY ATTACHMENT STYLES

Our earliest experiences—especially with caregivers—profoundly shape how we connect, handle conflict, and regulate emotions in relationships. Attachment theory provides a powerful lens for understanding these formative patterns.

From the womb through early childhood, we begin developing our attachment style. This reflects how we seek connection, express needs, and adapt when those needs are unmet. Typically described as secure, anxious, avoidant, or disorganized, these styles are rarely fixed categories. Most people carry a unique blend that evolves.

Attachment styles are not destiny. They're dynamic and responsive to growth and upgrading. Through self-awareness, nurturing relationships, and intentional healing, we can transform our relationships with others and ourselves.

Secure Attachment develops when a caregiver consistently responds to a child's signals with attunement and care. The child learns to trust that their needs will be met, forming a foundation of emotional resilience, healthy self-regulation, and relational safety. Ruptures are inevitable. Still, when caregivers repair them with presence and love, the child integrates that repair as part of a secure bond.

Avoidant (dismissive) Attachment arises when caregivers are emotionally unavailable or unresponsive. Feeling unseen and unmet, the child learns to shut down their needs and rely only on themselves. They may internalize the message that needing connection is shameful or a sign of weakness. As adults, they often struggle with emotional intimacy, appearing distant or detached, despite longing for closeness.

Anxious (ambivalent) Attachment forms when care giving is inconsistent—sometimes attuned, sometimes absent. The child becomes hyper-vigilant, uncertain whether they can count on others. This creates a heightened need for reassurance and fear of abandonment. As adults, they may appear clingy or overly sensitive, craving connection but never fully trusting it.

Disorganized (chaotic) Attachment results when a caregiver is also a source of fear, through abuse, neglect, or chaos. The child has no safe strategy for connection, often dissociating or shutting down emotionally. Conflicted between the need for closeness and fear of it, they may grow up with emotional dysregulation, a fragmented sense of self, and difficulty forming stable relationships. Yet even this most painful style can be healed through understanding, safety, and compassionate support.

CHAPTER TWO

The Father Wound

Every father should remember one day, his son will follow his example, not his advice.

Charles Kettering

After my mother's suicide, everything blurred into what I can only describe as a whiteout period. My father vanished, consumed by grief. His absence wasn't entirely new—he had been missing for my first couple of years. Instead, my maternal grandfather, GP, became the central male figure in my world. Even after I was sent away from their home, he visited frequently, and our relationship endured.

Nonnie, my grandmother, was in no condition to care for me. Her constant fear, anxiety, and worry created a heavy atmosphere in a family that avoided confronting their pain. We lived in a household enshrouded in darkness, where emotions were buried beneath layers of silent shame and grief.

GP had long been Nonnie's protector. Her life was filled with anxiety, a constant fear that something terrible was about to happen. Like me, she tended to catastrophize. She was obsessed with fire, often making my grandfather turn the car around to check if she had turned the stove burners off—a classic sign of OCD (Obsessive-Compulsive Disorder). I can't help but wonder if a fire-related tragedy haunted her family history, as fears so often echo through generations. Yet, despite her worries, my grandfather always spoke of her with love, still calling her his bride after many decades of marriage.

I remember riding in my grandfather's gigantic, beige Lincoln Premier when Nonnie would suddenly say, "Oh, I think I might have left the stove on." GP would pull over and dutifully turn around with a loving smile and calm demeanor. He was always gracious, regardless of what she did. When she once scrubbed all his beloved pipes with soap and water, instead of being upset, he simply decided it was time to stop smoking.

Unable to care for me after my mother's death, I was taken in by the Porters, a neighboring family in San Francisco's Sunset district, just a block from my grandparents. I felt numb and remember little from that year. I've only been able to weave events together through therapy, meditation, and constant pecking for answers like a small bird scratching for scarce seeds. My discovery process has been like repairing an old, tattered tapestry retrieved from a dark, dusty attic.

The Porters took me in on the condition that my grandmother would have limited visiting rights. Reg Porter was a college professor, and his wife stayed home with their three children. When I met them years later, they told me I was happy with their family, though I suspect I was too disoriented and shocked to feel much of anything. Meanwhile, my father remained a distant figure in my life. He continued working on the East Coast selling whiskey.

One bright memory from this time was my friendship with Timmy Tarrentino, whose family owned a famous restaurant on Fisherman's Wharf. Our families often took us there for lunch, where we were treated like young princes in wooden highchairs with paper bibs. At three and a half, I acquired a taste for cracked crab that remains with me today. Tragically, Timmy died suddenly of leukemia. Already accustomed to people leaving unexpectedly, I felt something was wrong with me.

The next significant event was learning that my father was coming from New York to get me, having remarried his first wife, the mother of my half-brother, Peter, whom I had never heard of. My memories of my mother and this man whom people called my father had been suppressed. I was terrified of leaving the only family comfort I had known. The Porters later told me I threw a fiery tantrum at the airport, screaming and grasping the chain link fence that separated me from them. I shut down that memory for years. There had been so much change in my young life that rage and whiteout seemed better than the unknown with this stranger called my father.

My father and his sister Edith grew up in a traditional Danish household defined by strictness and emotional austerity, reminiscent of the movie Babette's Feast. My paternal grandfather's mantra, "Children are to be seen and not heard," stifled any joy in my childhood. Men were expected to be tough, and women confined to domestic roles. Their house was cold, damp, and musty, and visiting filled me with dread. My only warm memories were of my grandmother baking Danish Christmas cookies and my grandfather helping me plant a garden when I was five.

My father's most notable attribute was his absence. Even when physically present, he wasn't truly there. From my interactions with my Danish grandfather, I doubt my father ever received much love or attention growing up.

I yearned for his affection as a boy, but he remained distant, aloof, and often absent due to work and chronic drinking. Later in life, I ironically tried connecting with him by mirroring his behaviors—drinking and womanizing became unconscious attempts to bridge that divide. Watching other boys spend time fishing or playing ball with their fathers filled me with envy. At summer camp, I gravitated toward counselors because I craved the nurturing they offered. When other kids shared stories about their fathers, I often made up tales, claiming mine was a fighter pilot and a war hero. While rooted in truth, these stories felt disconnected, as if describing someone I'd only seen in a movie.

My father was indeed a fighter pilot in the Army Air Corps stationed at Hickam Field in Hawaii. Dashing and charismatic, always impeccably dressed—a consummate ladies' man. Yet beneath his charm lay harsh misogyny. He criticized women for their weight, appearance, and driving, making remarks like "female-type driver" or "brainless beauties." His dual nature embarrassed and fascinated me; I longed to be like him. Desperate for his approval, I became a troublemaker when I realized nothing I did would ever please him.

My father met Peggy Hepburn, his first wife, while stationed in Hawaii after fighter pilot school in the early '40s. He quickly married this uber-wealthy alcoholic whose family had somehow acquired the Hawaiian Islands' water rights—colonialism at its best. My half-brother once proudly showed me a bill of sale for selling water to King Kamehameha.

Despite his taste for extravagance—fine dining, expensive clothes, and endless drinks—my father was always anxious about money. Peggy provided luxury and a built-in babysitter, first for my half-brother Peter and later for me. Their marriage revolved around alcohol and wealth. Rumor had it that she bought him a yacht when they got married.

Years later, I envied Peter when he inherited a massive trust fund after Peggy's alcoholism took her life. He never had to work, spending his days sailing and traveling. But as I got to know him, my jealousy turned to sadness. He was angry and miserable, treating people as if he were royalty. Though I always tried to connect, he never shared my desire for a brotherly bond. As adults, whenever we reunited, he either criticized me, much like our father, or tried to get me to take whatever drug he was using at the time. After conquering alcohol, he fell into painkillers, psychedelics, and mood-altering drugs. I suspect he was terrified of being exploited, especially after losing his mother at nineteen. However, he married a loving woman who cared for him until the end of his days, even after their divorce. I doubt he ever truly felt loved in spite of her commitment to him.

Before Pearl Harbor, my father met Margaret (Margie) Louise Yealland, assistant to General George Martin, commander of the U.S. Air Corps. Swept up in love, he quickly divorced his first wife, Peggy, and married Margie. But less than a year after my mother's tragic death, he went back to Peggy—not, I imagine, out of love, but out of necessity. He needed financial support and someone to care for me, his second son.

At three and a half, I boarded a Pan Am Clipper bound for Honolulu, leaving behind the comfort of the Porters' home. I felt a mix of fear and excitement about flying on such a magnificent aircraft. The Clipper was a floating palace with a bar, beds, and dressing rooms. A striking brunette stewardess, who spent much of the flight chatting with my father, brought me Coca-Cola and pinned a pair of shiny Pan Am wings to my shirt. Her kindness briefly distracted me from the unease churning inside me. My father, in rare form, entertained us with stories of flying, sparking a fleeting dream in me of becoming a pilot someday. But as the plane descended, my anxiety returned.

Peggy's house sat high above Honolulu, overlooking Diamond Head and the vast Pacific Ocean. People called the street Kalawahini Drive, also known as "Rich Lady Drive" in Hawaiian. Her mansion looked like something out of Architectural Digest, but inside, it was a house of horrors. My father dropped me off and disappeared, leaving me to navigate a world of loneliness, cruelty, and chaos.

Peggy's alcoholism ruled the household. Her rage was relentless, turning home into a battleground of screaming, flying objects, and shattered glass. One night, she hurled a bottle at the TV, and the screen exploded in sparks. I froze as the acrid smell filled the air. These violent outbursts were routine, leaving me in constant fear. I was always to blame, no matter what happened, and Peter used that to his advantage.

Once, while we bathed in the grand sunken marble tub, he pooped in the water and told Peggy I had done it. Her fury descended on me like a storm. I only remember sobbing myself to sleep in my dark, musty room. Another time, while playing with Christmas present trucks, Peter filled a large toy gasoline tanker with real gas from the lawnmower. The next thing I knew, the hillside was nearly burned down. Fire engines flooded the street. Somehow, that was my fault. I was told I was a bad influence and became the scapegoat for everything that went wrong.

Desperate for kindness, I befriended Peggy's Japanese gardener. One day, he called me behind the garage, where he had a rat, a bucket of water, and a plank. With glee, he forced the creature to "walk the plank" into the water. The rat clawed desperately at the tin, screeching in terror. I ran away before it drowned, sickened by his laughter. That was the end of my only friendship at the big house. I saw myself in that struggling rat, drowning in an island paradise that had become my prison.

Despite everything, I idolized my father, constantly yearning for his love and attention. But an unspoken tension existed between us—one I felt, but couldn't name. I was the child conceived by the woman he left Peggy for, a truth that cast a long shadow. Though never directly addressed, it shaped every interaction.

As a child, that silence was both confusing and terrifying. I saw it in his eyes, his tone, and his actions. The past formed a barrier I couldn't cross. I longed for him to see me, to truly connect—but instead, I carried the burden of a story I never asked to be part of.

Although it felt like I'd been at the Big House for years, it had only been eight or nine months before they sent me to live with Reg and Ruth Schofield, my father's friends from his time stationed on the island. Reg was a surfer and would take me out on his board, perched on his shoulders. I was relieved, even happy, to escape the chaos of the Big House. I don't remember much from that time, but almost anything felt better than Peggy's constant yelling and abuse, especially when she drank, which was often.

My father reappeared after about a year in Hawaii and took me away. He must have sensed how miserable I was. At the time, I thought I was being cast out for all the trouble I'd caused—but even that felt like a relief compared to the Big House of Horrors. I had only been with the Schofields for a month or so, and I suspect I had also become a burden there. I was scared but relieved and hopeful to finally be with my father.

I barely knew him, yet I felt a mix of nervous excitement. Dashingly handsome and strong, he had always left me crying during my brief early visits. Still, I imagined him as a superhero, swooping in to rescue me. To my surprise, what followed was the happiest time of my life, though it didn't last long.

After separating from Peggy for the second time, my father bought into the Lane Club, a stylish bar tucked away on Maiden Lane, just off Union Square in San Francisco. Every evening, the place was packed with fancy people. My father held court behind the bar, mixing drinks and charming the ladies with his fighter pilot charisma. I was in heaven. Not yet five years old, I soaked up the hugs and kisses from women who doted on me. Looking back, I see it now, they weren't there for me, but for him. I was a cute accessory, more appealing than a dog. Still, I felt special. I felt loved. Living in that bar, I felt at home for a little while.

One Christmas, my father's girlfriend, a beautiful young brunette artist, took over decorating the club and made the entrance into a giant Santa. The mouth became the doorway, and the red carpet into the restaurant was his tongue. It was so cool! It was the best Christmas ever. She told me she made it just for me. I loved her, but like most women in my life, she wasn't around for long.

The Asian chef also took care of me, always ensuring I had food. I often slept in the back of the bar on one of the dining room benches. Sometimes, I would stay with my father in his small apartment in Parkmerced. When he cooked, I would sit on the counter and watch him. That's probably why I enjoy cooking and creating meals. Over the years, people have said cooking is my way of showing love. It's true!

Being in San Francisco meant opportunities to see my grandparents and Aunt Billie. They had a summer home in Los Altos, and sometimes, on weekends, I would take the train with my grandfather to spend time with them. I loved the countryside and the 158 oak trees my grandfather had counted on the land. There were also apricot trees all around. I would climb up and eat apricots until I got sick. I loved this country setting and being away from the city and noisy bar. Life was good, and I was happier than I had ever been!

Then, shortly after my fifth birthday, my father sat me down. His face was unreadable, but something about his voice felt different—like something big was about to happen.

"I've sold my share in the Lane Club," he said. "I've been offered a commission to return to the Air Force. We're leaving for New York in a week, so start packing your things."

The words didn't make sense at first. Leaving? New York? I stared at him, waiting for the punchline, the part where he'd laugh and tell me it was all a mistake. But he didn't. His decision was already made.

A cold weight settled in my chest. I felt I would lose everything—Aunt Billie, my grandparents, my friends at the bar. The only real happiness I had ever known was being ripped away, and I could do nothing to change his decision. I cried for seven days straight. I begged, pleaded, and clung to the people I loved, but it didn't matter. My father had spoken. And when he decided it was time to go, we went.

The next thing I knew, we were on another plane heading East.

REFLECTIONS

Loneliness and fear followed me through childhood and well into adulthood. Looking back, I see how much I absorbed from my father in our brief time together in San Francisco. I remember riding the bus with him, standing proudly beside him on the seat, when I noticed a beautiful Black man sitting behind us. Innocently, I asked, "Daddy, why is that man's face black?" My father stiffened, shushed me, and shrank away. But the man—he beamed love toward me. That moment left an imprint: the tension between my father's fear and a stranger's kindness. I know now that I internalized my father's unease, his biases woven into me before I ever had the awareness to question them. It took years to unravel them.

Like him, I sought refuge in movement and distraction, anything to escape my fear of abandonment. He loved women, and I suspect sex and conquest numbed his grief. I followed suit. Growing up in the sexual revolution of the '60s, I confused lust with love, mistaking fleeting passion for authentic connection. Beneath the chase was a desperate longing to be seen, to belong, to be held in love. My short-lived relationships mirrored the wounds I hadn't yet faced.

I became skilled at masking my fear, burying it under a busy schedule. By my twenties, I was drinking heavily, smoking three packs a day, taking speed, and downing two pots of coffee daily. I threw myself into selling real estate, college, and running a candle-making business—anything to outrun the emptiness. When I tried Rolfing, a deep-tissue bodywork therapy, my practitioner, Dub Lee, told me, "Michael, you're the first person I've ever worked with who doesn't realize he has a body." That struck me. I had spent my life running from myself, detached from the body that carried me through the world.

But where did all this fear come from? I believe I carried my mother's terror—the anxiety and horror she absorbed from witnessing the bombing of Pearl Harbor. I bore my father's shame, his unspoken inadequacy. These weren't just personal wounds; they were ancestral. My father never recovered from losing my mother, and perhaps my resemblance to her only deepened his pain. I idolized him, believing that I might finally be enough if I mastered his world—drinking, charming women, chasing success. But I never was. No matter how hard I tried, he couldn't see me. I felt invisible.

I've understood this as the Father Wound—a deep imprint left by emotional or physical absence, criticism, neglect, or detachment. Traditionally seen as providers, many fathers remained distant, leaving profound marks on their children's self-worth, relationships, and emotional resilience. As one of my mentors, Gabrielle Roth, wisely noted, "The masculine must be grounded in the feminine, or we end up being abusive fathers to ourselves and each other."

Unresolved father wounds often manifest as anxiety, depression, difficulty setting boundaries, or cycles of addiction and unhealthy attachments. Both Father and Mother Wounds shape how we experience intimacy and vulnerability. My fear of abandonment led me to push others away, even as I longed for connection. As a man, my Father Wound surfaced as unresolved grief, anger, and struggles with emotional expression.

The Adverse Childhood Experiences (ACEs) study by the CDC and Kaiser Permanente found that early trauma significantly impacts long-term health, linking high ACE scores to increased risks of depression, substance abuse, and chronic disease. I scored seven out of ten. Yet, these are statistics, not destinies.

I saw myself through the lens of these wounds for much of my life. However, healing has shown me that fear can be a guide rather than an enemy when met with awareness and understanding. I spent decades in therapy, transformational programs, and psychedelic journeys, constantly circling the same precipice: the belief that if I fully felt my fear, I would die. It wasn't just psychological—it was primal, preverbal, ancestral. Yet, over time, I stopped running. I began to recognize fear as a protective force, heightening my awareness and intuition. But when left unchecked, it distorts reality, trapping us in cycles of anxiety and reactivity.

Instead of rejecting my fear, I leaned into it. Yoga, dance, running, and meditation became my anchors, helping me reintegrate what had long been fragmented. Slowly, I reconnected with some of my childhood innocence. I saw how my adult self had fused with my wounded inner child, reacting to ancient, undigested pain. Learning to pause and ask whether my wise adult or wounded child was responding changed everything. When overwhelmed, I reached out to those who could hold space for me without dismissing or trying to fix my pain. I realized you can't heal what you won't feel.

Over time, I saw my father in a different light. He, too, was shaped by unhealed wounds. His childhood had been stripped from him, his ability to love stunted by forces beyond his control. Seeing this, I found compassion where there was once resentment. I no longer needed to carry the pain of my past. Letting go has freed me from the story of suffering and blame that once defined my life.

Healing is possible. Understanding our past, breaking generational cycles, and reclaiming our sense of worth can transform inherited wounds into hard-earned wisdom. Though the work is ongoing, I've discovered something I once thought unreachable—a sense of home within myself.

In the chapters ahead, I'll continue to share my journey—how trauma shaped me from the womb onward, and how, through decades of searching, breakdowns, and breakthroughs, I've begun to reclaim my wholeness. You'll see how healing unfolds not all at once, but layer by layer—through relationships, spiritual encounters, bodywork, therapy, and the slow courage of facing what was once too painful to name.

We'll explore how the wounds of absence, criticism, neglect, and abuse don't begin in isolation. They are often rooted in the unseen legacy of ancestral trauma, passed down, unspoken, through generations.

These next chapters follow not just the pain, but the repair. This is the deeper terrain of transformation, where personal healing becomes ancestral healing, and where the possibility of belonging, connection, and inner peace begins to take root.

ADVERSE CHILDHOOD EXPERIENCES (ACES)

The original ACEs study, conducted in 1995 by the CDC and Kaiser Permanente, identified ten types of childhood adversity—emotional, physical, and sexual abuse, along with household dysfunction such as violence, addiction, mental illness, incarceration, and divorce. These early experiences were found to have lasting effects on the nervous system, immune response, and overall development.

ACEs are strongly linked to serious health conditions later in life, including heart disease, autoimmune disorders, substance abuse, depression, and even early death. The higher your ACE score, the greater the risk. For example, adults with an ACE score of 4 or more are 12 times more likely to attempt suicide and over 10 times more likely to use injected drugs. I scored 7 out of 10.

You can take the short ACEs quiz here: https://americanspcc.org/take-the-aces-quiz.

But remember—these are statistics, not life sentences. I'm living proof that transformation is possible. With awareness, love, and support, healing can happen. The impact of early trauma can be softened—and even rewritten.

CHAPTER THREE

Looking for Love in Levittown

The greater a child's terror, and the earlier it is experienced, the harder it becomes to develop a strong and healthy sense of self.

Nathaniel Branden

Levittown, Long Island, America's first modern suburb, built in 1947, was a vision of post-war conformity. Rows of identical houses stretched endlessly across a barren landscape, each with its standard floor plans, neatly trimmed lawn, and white picket fences, embodying the American dream. This was where we landed after my father sold his interest in the Lane Club and took a commission in the Air Force. I was happy to be moving with him, but I deeply missed my friends, family, and the golden days at the bar.

As it turned out, I still didn't see much of my father. He was often away on military business, and once again, I was left in the care of others—babysitters, neighbors, whoever happened to be available. My father had a talent for arranging caregivers, but rarely showed up.

Nights were the hardest. Not knowing where I'd sleep or who would be watching over me gnawed at my nervous system. The uncertainty made it nearly impossible to rest. I cried myself to sleep many nights, often in a stranger's home, aching for the scent and softness of a mother's arms.

One of the few bright spots in Levittown was the brief visit from my Danish grandfather. He helped me plant a garden in our backyard, fertile land once a potato and onion farm. With his quiet patience, he showed me how to plant seeds, tend to them, and nurture their growth. Watching those tiny green sprouts break through the soil was pure magic, a rare moment of connection and stability.

Every morning, when I was at home, I rushed to check on my garden, thrilled by each new leaf and bud. It was a source of joy, a small sanctuary where I felt grounded and safe, like crawling through the bushes in Golden Gate Park as a child. But like my father, my grandfather soon disappeared. The pattern was undeniable: like father, like son.

That summer, my little garden earned me a moment of recognition. The local newspaper came to take my picture, a young boy standing proudly beside a three-foot-long zucchini, nearly as tall as I was. I beamed, holding up the fruits of my labor, unaware that this moment of triumph would soon be overshadowed by losses I could not yet understand.

One of my caregivers, Mary Hart, was a beautiful blonde woman with a soft southern accent and the scent of jasmine emanating from her skin. She brought me presents, smothered me in hugs and kisses, and made me feel wanted in a way I rarely experienced. I was always thrilled when she came to stay with me while my father was away.

Bath time with Mary was eagerly anticipated. She would play with me, read to me, and then wrap me in a warm towel. After that, she would touch me. She would tickle me, play with my pee-pee, and make me laugh. It felt warm and safe, a balm against the loneliness of sleepless nights. I think that's when I started touching myself and pressing my body into the mattress when fear, loneliness, and isolation closed in.

I never thought of it as something wrong. How could it be when it felt so comforting? I believed this was what all loving mothers did to soothe their children, ease their fears, and show loving tenderness. I adored Mary. I wanted her to be my mother, and my father to marry her, so she would never ever leave.

But she was already married. Her husband was away on overseas duty, and then one day, he came back. Just like that, she was gone.

On the day she came to say goodbye, she brought me gifts—books, a junior chemistry set, and treasures meant to soften the blow. I clung to her like a puppy on a pant leg, my small hands gripping her dress, refusing to let go. She cried, too, but it didn't lessen the pain of yet another loss, another love slipping through my fingers.

I remember the frantic beating of my heart, the question searing through me: Why does love always leave? And a darker thought, whispered in the spaces where no one could hear:

What's wrong with me that nobody wants to stay with me?

The bombshell dropped without warning—my father was getting married again. I hadn't met her, hadn't even heard of her before. One day, she simply existed. I was five years old, still reeling from the chaos of my father's second divorce from Peggy, and now here he was, marrying a stranger. It all happened so fast. Change had become the only constant in my life.

Her name was Jean Severe—Dickens himself couldn't have invented a better name for an evil stepmother. Her rigid red hair looked like it had been starched to withstand a hurricane.

Her jaw could crack walnuts. Her body was stiff as a soldier at attention. And her dark, forbidding eyes seemed to hold secrets I never wanted to uncover. To this day, she remains the coldest, most tightly wound, and relentlessly critical woman I have ever encountered.

Every interaction with her sucked the air from the room. She carried herself like a fortress—stiff, unyielding, as if constantly bracing for battle. Her sharp words held an undercurrent of contempt, and even as a child, I felt the weight of her disapproval. Good choice, Dad. And don't even get me started on that overpowering French perfume that made me gag. I couldn't imagine this woman being remotely interested in playing with my pee-pee!

A week later, they got married, just like that. I stood in my little suit, watching them, like a gift wrapped in fancy paper but empty inside. Instead of rice, they had tapioca at the wedding. I hurled mine at them with all the strength I could muster, hoping it might kill them both. Maybe I could find new parents, return to the Porters, or my grandparents and Aunt Billie. As they rode off in a black limousine, the guests cheered, except for one small boy crying in the corner, feeling abandoned, again.

That night, Jean Severe's parents took me home with them. Her father, seeing my confusion, did his best to comfort me. We played gin rummy, watched TV, and he tried to distract me with small kindnesses. But nothing could fill the hollow space inside me, the infinite void that seemed to grow with every loss.

They were on their honeymoon for two weeks, and when they returned, my father dropped the real bomb. He had received a new assignment in Japan. He would be gone for two years, leaving me behind.

I pleaded, "No, Daddy, please, I want to go with you."

He knelt down and placed a firm hand on my shoulder. "I'm sorry, son. This is military business. You must be a good little soldier and care for your new mother."

My new what?

Everything went foggy white again.

Why was everyone always leaving me? What had I done to make them go? It had to be my fault. I must just be unlovable, a broken boy without a mother.

My father left for Japan immediately after the wedding and honeymoon, and I was dropped into the chaos of the Severe family home in Rockville Centre, New York.

Unlike Levittown's treeless uniformity, this neighborhood had towering chestnut trees lining the streets, their thick canopies casting long shadows. In the fall, the ground was blanketed in chestnuts, and I watched Asian families walk through with baskets, gathering them by the basketful. I never liked the taste, but throwing them became an outlet for my rage. Each tree became my father or Jean Severe, and I hurled chestnuts at their trunks, imagining I could hurt them the way they had hurt me.

The Severe house was big, bustling, and filled with noise. The backyard had a swing set, my only refuge from the endless chatter. While climbing on it one afternoon, my finger got caught in the moving seesaw. A sharp snap of pain shot through me, and suddenly, there was blood everywhere. I ran screaming into the house, my nearly severed finger gushing onto the kitchen floor. They wrapped it in Vaseline and rushed me to the hospital. Miraculously, they sewed it back on. It took a long time to heal, and to this day, the crooked little finger aches—a permanent reminder of mostly unhappy times.

Jean Severe was the middle of three sisters. She was, by far, the least friendly. Doris, the youngest, was flighty and excitable. Elizabeth, the eldest, was the kindest. Despite my resistance, I gradually warmed up to the Severe parents. They were strict but kind, and they treated me better than Jean ever did.

Her father, Raymond—Ray—Severe, was a boisterous, cigar-smoking Scot with an eye for the ladies. He had made his fortune in real estate and drove an enormous Cadillac convertible. He liked having a boy around to balance out all the chatty women in the house, and I liked the attention. We played gin rummy and watched Arthur Godfrey and Ed Sullivan on TV. Sometimes, he took me for drives with the top down, wind whipping through my hair. That feeling—the rush of speed and the open air's wild freedom—stayed with me. In later years, I was drawn to motorcycles and sports cars, always chasing that same exhilaration.

Ray owned several properties, including a motel in a nearby town. I loved visiting, but what I loved most was the black workers who gathered there, singing during their breaks. Their voices lifted into harmonies, blending gospel with the sounds of Fats Domino, Chuck Berry, Aretha Franklin, Little Richard, Diana Ross, and James Brown. The rhythm, the joy—it was magnetic. I wanted to clap my hands, stomp my feet, and lose myself in the music.

Ray disapproved. "That's not a place for you," he warned.

I didn't understand why. It was a haven of pure joy hidden in a darker world. That music stayed with me, igniting a lifelong passion for movement and rhythm. Years later, I would dance with Gabrielle Roth and the 5Rhythms® community for over fifty years. I believe, in some way, that dance saved my life.

Ray owned property on Fire Island, one of the barrier islands along the South Coast of Long Island. On Saltaire Bay, they had a lodge, a small grocery store, and an ice cream shop. We stayed at their beach house that first summer, perched on a beautiful boardwalk above the sand. The air smelled of salt and sun-warmed wood, and the rhythmic crash of the waves became my lullaby.

I loved it there. I spent my days riding my bike along the endless wooden pathways, the wind whipping through my hair, the sea always in sight. The beaches were pristine—miles of soft, white sand stretching into the horizon. Beyond them, ancient maritime forests whispered in the breeze, their twisted branches telling stories older than time itself.

Despite the magic of the island, my happiness was never complete. I always wanted more ice cream than they would let me have. And no amount of sun, sand, or boardwalk adventures could erase the ache inside me. I missed my father. I missed our time in San Francisco, the little moments of connection we had shared. He called a few times from Tokyo, but the distance was unbearable. I counted down the days until his return.

I spent two summers there, yet I do not remember Jean Severe being around. It was as if she had disappeared entirely from my life during those months, a ghost hovering on the edges of my awareness. Ray and his wife, Elizabeth, watched over me.

That year passed quickly. Despite my initial resistance to school, I secretly enjoyed it, though I kept to myself. The deep sadness and loneliness I carried made it hard to connect with other children. I felt like an outsider, an observer in a world I didn't quite belong to.

The teachers told Jean, "He has good potential but needs help." I didn't know what that meant, and I didn't care. What mattered was that my father would be coming home soon. Someone had told me he would return from Japan in a few months, and I clung to that hope like a lifeline.

But months stretched into a year. And then another. Time seemed to forget I was waiting.

The Severes kept me busy, distracting me from the ever-present question I kept asking: When is my daddy coming home? But no distraction could quiet the sadness at night. Lying alone in the stuffy bedroom, I cried into my pillow, the smell of Ray's cigar smoke mingling with the varied scents of the women in the house. Each had a different energy and presence, but none felt safe. The most repulsive was Jean, my so-called stepmother, a woman I would never accept as my mother.

When fall came, the Severes informed me it was time to start school. I didn't care about school. I only wanted to go to Japan to be with my father. But they assured me he would be home soon. Soon, it always felt like never.

Ray and Elizabeth, who were progressive for their time, enrolled me in the New York Waldorf School, founded by Rudolph Steiner. His education philosophy focused on learning through play, creativity, and hands-on experience, especially in early childhood.

First grade was held on the campus of New York City College. The sprawling, busy campus felt intimidating, and I resisted going, but Ray convinced me it would be fun.

And, to my surprise, it was.

We swam in the campus pool, painted, sang, and spent time in nature. I learned to play the recorder and even started speaking French and Spanish. One of the most unusual aspects of Waldorf education was Eurythmy, a movement-based practice where we danced while speaking, supposedly to synchronize the body and mind. I didn't fully understand it at the time, but I loved it. It was my first authentic taste of the power of movement and music—something that would shape my life for decades to come.

Then, one day, the news I had been waiting for finally arrived.

My father was coming home from Japan.

The moment I heard, I could barely contain my excitement. I bounced up and down like a kangaroo, my whole body buzzing with anticipation.

After what felt like an eternity, he was finally coming back.

But would we return to California?

REFLECTIONS

Looking back, Looking back, I'm grateful to my paternal grandfather for introducing me to the soil. Gardening—tending to plants, nurturing the earth, watching life emerge—became one of the most fantastic therapies I've ever known. Yet, my grandfather carried a deep darkness, an ancestral "hand-me-down" I now recognize. Still, his simple act of teaching me to garden reminds me that even those who bring fear and criticism into our lives can also offer love and guidance in unexpected ways.

Mary taught me something different—how the body can become a source of comfort, a refuge when love and tenderness are absent. Learning to connect with myself physically helped me feel more present and grounded. Our bodies hold wisdom, offering self-soothing in moments of anxiety, fear, or insecurity. However, self-soothing can also become compulsive—such as biting nails or sucking a thumb—an escape rather than genuine comfort. For me, it eventually spiraled into struggles with sex, lust, and pornography, numbing the ache of loneliness that had followed me since childhood. Even now, those echoes still surface.

My father's marriage to Jean Severe felt like a betrayal—one that, as the reader will see, extended beyond their deaths. When he left again, he uttered the exact same devastating words: "Take care of your new mother."

I didn't want to take care of her—I barely knew her. I wanted someone to take care of me. I longed for love, for safety, for the father I kept losing over and over again. Instead, I was handed responsibilities far beyond my years, forced to navigate an unstable and unkind world.

Loneliness and fear became my constant companions. I lived in the shadow of uncertainty, afraid my father might never return.

For most children, childhood is a time of innocence, wonder, and security. For me, it was survival.

I remember the Severe woman trying to teach me cursive. I resisted. She gave up after one try. She must have sensed my hatred for her from the moment we met. No wonder she was so cold toward me, though, in hindsight, I suspect that was simply her nature. She was a childless, unhappy woman, never loved by me or, I believe, by my father. That must have been painful for her. How many generations of suffering had lived through her, shaping her into someone incapable of warmth?

But as a child, I couldn't see her pain. In my eyes, she was simply the woman who had stolen my father. Of course, he had made that choice, choosing distance over facing his grief, loss, and unresolved trauma. Leaving was easier than looking inward.

Yet, despite everything, I am grateful to my father. He gave me life, and that is no small thing. Now, I understand that my healing is not just for me—it's for my ancestors, my daughter, and for the spirit of life itself. Life has a will to thrive, push forward, and express itself through us, just as it has for millennia; it's how we evolve.

Losing my mother and enduring my father's repeated absences left me with deep feelings of shame, guilt, and unworthiness. Studies confirm what I lived firsthand—losing a parent in childhood increases the risk of emotional struggles. No matter how hard I tried to be seen, I always felt invisible. No matter what I did to prove my worth, I always felt unlovable.

By the time I started school, I had learned to numb myself completely. Outwardly, I expressed fear, anger, and rage. Inwardly, I felt nothing—a somatic black out.

Through years of therapy, movement practices, and plant medicine, I've learned that trauma isn't healed through words and a cognitive approach. It lives in the body, frozen in time, waiting to be acknowledged and felt in the light of our awareness. Healing requires a somatic approach, one that meets the parts of ourselves that have been frozen and silenced, bringing light to what was once hidden. And because trauma is formed in relationships, it is best healed in relationships. That is why I started doing trauma healing circles.

Facilitating trauma integration work has shown me the power of collective healing. People open up in a safe, supportive space, sharing their stories in trauma-awareness circles. As we witness one another's truths, the isolating grip of trauma begins to loosen. A deep resonance occurs when someone feels seen, heard, and understood. That shared recognition fosters connection and compassion for others and, perhaps most importantly, ourselves. It's in this sacred witnessing that true healing begins.

That said, group healing isn't always the first step—and it's not for everyone. Trauma can shatter our sense of safety, making it difficult or even re-traumatizing to share in a group. For many, the healing journey must begin in the safety of one-on-one support. Working with a skilled somatic therapist can help rebuild a foundation of self-trust and support nervous system regulation, creating the inner stability needed before engaging in more profound relational or collective healing.

One of the most challenging parts of my journey has been finding empathy for Jean Severe. When I first wrote about her, my words reflected my raw emotions: anger, hurt, hatred, and resentment. But time has softened those edges.

I now see that pain is inherited, passed down through generations, shaping us in ways we often don't fully understand. Jean was a product of her familial suffering, just as I was a product of mine. Recognizing this doesn't erase the wounds but allows me to hold her humanity alongside my own. True healing, I've learned, requires more than confronting our pain—it asks us to open our hearts, even to those who hurt us.

My ability to regulate emotions was shaped by early loss and trauma. As a child, I needed a steady, caring presence to see me, soothe me, and help me feel safe. Like all children, I needed coregulation to learn how to self-regulate. Instead, I was met with chaos, abandonment, and fear.

Without that foundation of attuned support, I grew up unanchored, dysregulated, anxious, and unsure how to navigate my inner world. My nervous system became wired for survival, not connection. It's taken years of healing to slowly untangle these patterns and rediscover what safety feels like—intellectually and in my body.

That healing is still unfolding. One thing I know for sure: trauma doesn't heal in the mind alone. It heals in the body, through the heart, and in safe, relational spaces where we can be felt and seen.

PATHWAYS TO EMOTIONAL SELF-REGULATION

Emotional regulation—our ability to manage how we experience and express emotions—is foundational to mental health and meaningful connection. It begins in early childhood, through coregulation: when caregivers lovingly mirror, soothe, and guide us, helping us internalize a sense of calm and trust.

But when that attunement is missing—due to trauma, neglect, or inconsistent care—our nervous systems often remain stuck in dysregulation. Without early coregulation, we adapt by surviving alone, often through numbing, withdrawal, hyper-vigilance, or emotional shutdown.

How to Heal and Build Self-Regulation:

1. **Understand Your Nervous System.** Dysregulation is not a flaw; it's an adaptive intelligence. The first step is learning to recognize states of hyperarousal (tension, anxiety, anger) or hypoarousal (numbness, freezing, and dissociation).

2. **Create Internal Safety.** Practices such as slow breathing, grounding, and gentle movement signal to the brain that shifting out of survival mode is safe.

3. **Borrow Regulation Through Relationships.** Healing relationships—whether with a therapist, partner, or a caring friend—can offer the coregulation you may have missed. Consistent, attuned presence helps reshape neural pathways.

4. **Practice Self-Compassion.** According to neuroscience research, compassion activates the same calming systems in the brain as those associated with secure attachment. Speaking kindly to yourself literally changes your physiology.

5. **Rewire Through Repetition.** Just as children learn through repeated, safe interactions, adults can develop self-regulation through consistent practices such as conscious movement, mindfulness, body-based therapies, or expressive writing.

As trauma expert Dr. Bruce Perry notes, "Regulation must come before reflection." We must feel safe before we can think clearly or make changes in our behavior.

Even without early coregulation, healing is possible. We can learn to become more secure and grounded with time, presence, and a supportive witness.

CHAPTER FOUR

Severe Times

*The new-come stepmother
hates the children born to a first wife.*

Euripides

When my father finally came home from Japan, I felt a flicker of hope, though it was laced with caution. I hadn't seen him in almost two years; by then, he was more of a distant figure than a father. But still, I wondered—would his return mean something new for us? Would we finally have the kind of relationship I imagined fathers and sons were supposed to have?

He arrived with a gift, a fly-tying kit from Japan. At first, it felt thoughtful, even exciting. I pictured us standing together at the edge of a stream, casting lines, and sharing something real. But that vision faded quickly. He had no intention of taking me fishing. Like so many of his gestures, the gift was more symbolic than sincere, an attempt at connection without the follow-through. I taught myself to tie flies, carefully twisting threads and feathers, hoping to braid a bond between us. But each finished fly only deepened the ache, a reminder of the time lost and the father I wished for but never had. Eventually, I threw the kit away and wept, not for the object, but for the absence it revealed.

Life with the Severes had at least been predictable. Jean was harsh, but her parents provided a bed, meals, and a routine.

My father's return shattered that fragile stability. His first announcement was that we were moving. He had been reassigned to Norton Air Force Base in San Bernardino, California. I hoped that would bring me closer to my grandparents and Aunt Billie in San Francisco, but San Bernardino wasn't close. Instead of feeling more connected, I felt even further removed from my family, a sense of belonging, or any sense of home.

Looking back, I wonder if my resemblance to my mother made it harder for him to see me. Maybe I was a reminder of the love he lost, of the pain he had never confronted. But at the time, I didn't understand any of that. I only knew that I felt invisible, like an afterthought in the life of a man I desperately wanted to notice me.

My father rented a modest two-bedroom house in a quiet suburban neighborhood off-base and enrolled me at the Elliot School for second grade. That was when a new kind of nightmare began.

Public school was nothing like the Waldorf school I had attended before. At Waldorf, the emphasis on creativity, rhythm, and gentle structure gave me a sense of safety. Elliot School was the opposite—crowded hallways, bells that shattered any sense of calm, cliques that formed walls I couldn't get through. Rules felt arbitrary, and the constant noise made it impossible to think. I felt like I had been swallowed whole, out of place, and desperate to escape.

My second-grade teacher, Miss Margret DeSinnett, was everything a teacher shouldn't be—loud, cold, and quick to punish. She had no patience for me. To her, I was nothing but a "smart-ass kid," and she made sure I knew it. Her booming voice and sharp discipline kept me on edge. I did my best to stay small, to go unnoticed, but it never worked.

One day, curiosity got the better of me. At the back of the room, a set of neatly arranged toy trains caught my eye, waiting to be explored. I slid out of my seat and moved toward them, drawn to anything that might offer a moment of escape.

I didn't get far.

"Young man, SIT DOWN NOW!"

Her voice cracked like a whip across the room. Before I could move, she towered over me, her face flushed with rage. She grabbed my arm and shoved me into a small wooden chair. Then, as if restraint was necessary, she retrieved a bundle of foul-smelling rags from the cloakroom and began tying my hands and feet to the chair. The stench of mildew and sweat made me want to throw up.

Laughter erupted around me. My classmates seemed to find it hilarious. Shame crawled up my spine. I was trapped, humiliated, and helpless.

But something inside me refused to stay still.

As she turned back to her desk, I made my move. With small, jerky hops, I inched my chair forward—just a few inches at a time. The classroom erupted in laughter, and my classmates began to cheer me on. It wasn't exactly solidarity, but in that moment, their laughter felt like a tiny crack in the wall of my shame—a brief reprieve from my humiliation.

Miss DeSinnett spun around. The laughter died instantly.

"That's enough!" she barked, her fury electrifying the air. "I'll speak to your parents about this, and you will be properly punished."

The words sent a jolt of dread through me. My father. The Severe Woman. The fallout that would come. I sat frozen, my cheeks burning, my chest tight. And then, before I could stop myself, I said something. I don't remember exactly what—something sharp, something defiant. Maybe "fat slob" or "stupid bitch." It didn't matter. I knew I had crossed a line when the words left my mouth.

Her face darkened. In one swift motion, she tore the rags from my wrists and ankles, yanked me up by my ear, and dragged me straight to the principal's office.

The stiff, cold, dominating principal reminded me of my father. He didn't ask what happened. He didn't care. He scolded me, his disapproval pressing down like a weight. Then came the worst part: the call home.

He called "my mother."

I corrected him. She wasn't my mother. But they didn't listen. Jean Severe arrived; her cold stare made my stomach churn. I knew what was coming.

The walk home was silent. That awful, punishing silence. Then, finally, she hissed the words I had come to dread:

"Wait till your father finds out about this."

She loved that phrase. She used it whenever I messed up or stepped out of line. But they never understood—I wasn't acting out for the sake of it. I wanted something. Attention. Love. Proof that I mattered. That I existed.

Instead, all I got was confirmation that I didn't belong—not at school, not at home, not anywhere.

That year, I made only one friend—Sammy, a lifeline in my otherwise bleak and lonely world. We bonded quickly, spending recess lagging pennies against the wall. He was one of the few who made me feel seen. Labeled "troublemakers" by teachers and peers, we wore it like a badge, a secret acknowledgment of our shared rebellion and misfit status. We talked about running away, traveling the world, and living life on our terms—dreams born from a mutual longing to escape the weight of our daily lives.

Sammy came from a rough neighborhood, and his home life was troubled. One day, he confided in me about his sister—how she was always crying. In a hushed, uneasy voice, he mentioned his father entering her room at night. I didn't fully understand what he meant back then, but his words stayed with me, echoing with a heaviness I couldn't name. Long after he was gone, they continued to haunt me.

Halfway through the year, Sammy stopped coming to school. At first, I thought he was sick or his family had moved. Then I heard the story: he had died after being bitten by a black widow spider hidden in his shoe. Even at that young age, I found it hard to believe. Sammy was always fearful, much like me. I couldn't shake the feeling that his death was tied to the same dark undercurrents he had hinted at in our conversations.

I was devastated. Sammy was the second friend I lost after Timmy Tarantino's death and disappearance. First my mother, then Timmy, and now Sammy. It reinforced my belief that anyone I cared about would disappear or die. The emptiness felt overwhelming, but I kept it to myself. Crying wasn't an option. My father's contempt for "crying sissy boys" was etched into my psyche. So I swallowed my sorrow, keeping it hidden to avoid showing weakness.

My father and stepmother seemed almost relieved. They dismissed Sammy as a "bad influence." Their coldness deepened my confusion. How could the one person who made me feel less alone be easily disregarded?

Losing Sammy became another brick in the wall of my growing isolation. It solidified my belief that forming connections was dangerous and that caring for others only led to pain. By the end of that year, I wasn't just lonely—I began to see the world as a place where love and friendship were a prelude to loss.

After Sammy died, I didn't want to go to school. I made no new friends and hated my home life. I started stealing quarters from the pregnant Kangaroo on my father's dresser. I don't know if he noticed, but I'd score several dollars a week to buy candy and junk. Then, I stole from stores on my way to and from school. I loved dill pickles, and one store had big barrels of them. I'd wrap one in a napkin and stick it in my pocket. Over time, I started taking little bottles of alcohol. The exhilaration of stealing and not getting caught became addictive. Once, I went into my stepmother's wallet and took a hundred-dollar bill. Somehow, I thought she wouldn't notice. She did. No amount of lying could get me out of that one. She even brought it up on her deathbed.

After attending Waldorf School in my first year, I found public school boring and useless. I didn't get along with my teachers or the other kids. I played hooky, but they sent the truant officer after me and called my parents—more restrictions, more punishment.

My childhood name was Mickey. "Mickey is a very capable child. He has tried to improve his work habits, but constant effort is still necessary. All written work is neat and well done, but not completed on time because he wastes time."—Mrs. Sorenson, my first-grade Waldorf teacher.

"Mickey has the ability to do the work. He has poor work habits and must be constantly disciplined." —Margaret DeSinnett, the scary teacher who tied me to my chair.

Disciplined? I was nothing but disciplined. "You need to do this. You can't do that. You must do this." Constant scolding, yelling, and correction. My father, a military officer, treated me like an uncooperative soldier. Every aspect of my life was controlled, scrutinized, and micromanaged. I didn't need more discipline—I needed love. What happened to playing outside, camping with your dad? My father never took me camping, never played catch, never spent time just being together. Everything was rules, discipline, and order.

My anger grew inside me, an ember turning into a blaze. Each command, each cold interaction fueled it. I needed to feel valued, seen, loved—but I was treated like a prisoner under constant watch.

One evening, I snapped. "Quit telling me what to do! I hate you!"

My father's face flushed red. "YOU WILL NOT SPEAK TO ME OR YOUR MOTHER LIKE THAT," he bellowed. "You need to learn respect and discipline!"

"Respect? How can I respect someone who doesn't see me and doesn't care about me? I'm not one of your soldiers!"

Silence.

My stepmother smirked, her eyes gleaming with satisfaction.

"You're out of control," my father said. "You will follow the rules, or there will be consequences. If you don't like it here, find someplace else to live."

The consequences were immediate. My anger had reached a boiling point, and I felt more alone than ever. I didn't want to live in that house, but I had nowhere to go. Sent to my room to "sit with my anger," I felt trapped, suffocated by relentless discipline and the absence of affection. My stepmother's favorite response— "What planet are you from?"—only made it worse. I felt alien. Unwanted.

I feared my anger. If I let it surface, I feared it would unleash destruction greater than anything the world had ever seen— more violent than the atomic bombs that ended World War II. In my mind, there were three bombs: Little Boy, Fat Man, and Little Mickey.

As a small, often-unliked child, I learned to navigate a world filled with bullies. When cornered, I used the intensity of my anger as a weapon. I would lock eyes with them, staring into their souls, silently repeating, "You killed my mother." My rage usually sent them running. But not always.

Butch Johnson, who lived across the street, was my friend—or so I thought. One day, that illusion shattered. On the school bus, an argument escalated. As we approached our stop, I felt a sharp jolt from behind. I barely caught myself before falling. I turned— Butch grinned maliciously. His smirk wasn't playful; it was cruel.

We stepped off the bus, and he struck again. He shoved me. My books and papers were scattered. Before I could react, he tackled me, fists raining down. He was twice my size—I had no chance. The kids cheered. Their laughter echoed like a cruel soundtrack to my humiliation.

The bus driver broke it up. Butch scrambled to his feet, gave me one last kick before retreating. I lay there, bruised, defeated.

I ran home, tears streaming, hoping for comfort. My father and the Severe Woman were there. "You need to go back out there and kick his ass," my father barked.

His words stung more than Butch's punches. I wanted love, not orders. I needed reassurance, not ridicule. That was the last time I cried in front of him.

Lying on my bed, bruised, I realized how trapped I was. In that house, that town, that life. I fantasized about running away. Moving constantly as an Air Force brat had been frustrating, but now, it felt like a blessing. The thought of leaving this place, these people, and the pain behind gave me a glimmer of hope.

The next day, I walked to school along the railroad tracks, head down, heart heavy. I longed for stability, for friendships that lasted. But deep down, I knew I would have to find that belonging myself. Until then, I carried an aching fear and deep pain, waiting for the next chapter, hoping it might finally bring relief.

I was told that very early in my life, I had been in an iron lung and suffered from numerous allergies while living with my grandparents, my mother, and Aunt Billie. I was allergic to cats, parrots, house dust, and various foods. My breathing problems worsened in Southern California, culminating in a severe case of asthma. Nights were particularly distressing—I often woke up gasping for air, overwhelmed by what would now be recognized as panic attacks.

I was marched to the doctor each week for allergy shots and further testing, accompanied by Jean Severe. Despite my protests, she never wavered in her duty. Unlike me, she followed orders without question, embodying a rigid sense of responsibility. I suspect she might have eaten her firstborn if she had ever had children.

REFLECTIONS

Those first two years in San Bernardino were among my loneliest and most disorienting. I felt utterly unmoored, disconnected from anything familiar. I ached for Aunt Billie and my grandparents in San Francisco, longing for the warmth and comfort they had given me. Living in the bar with my dad had felt like home, filled with laughter and people who treated me like family. Now, that life was a distant memory, replaced by a cold, sterile reality where I was neither wanted nor seen. My father was indifferent, and the Severe Woman made no effort to hide her contempt.

Every day blurred into the next—boredom, fear, and loneliness were my constant companions. The rare phone calls with my aunt or grandparents only deepened my grief, reminding me of what I had lost. My father and Jean spent most of their time at the officers' club, leaving me alone or with indifferent babysitters. I withdrew further into myself, consumed by fear, shame, and a growing sense of invisibility. I felt like an outcast—unwanted, unloved, and alone.

School offered no refuge. I struggled to connect with classmates or teachers, and no one noticed the storm raging inside me. I had no "caring witness"—no one to see or validate my pain. My father, shaped by generations of Danish "power-over" parenting, equated strength with silence. He told stories of his father yanking out loose teeth by tying a string to a door and slamming it shut. Whether true or just another lesson in resilience, the message was clear: pain was to be endured, not expressed. If I struggled, it meant I wasn't tough enough.

By the time I was seven, I had internalized a harsh identity: I was the problem. Labeled a liar, a thief, a troublemaker—angry, undisciplined, and out of control. My attachment was chaotic and disorganized, mirroring the instability of my environment. I didn't trust the world, its people, or myself. Every tantrum and every broken rule was a desperate attempt to be seen, even if it meant being seen as evil. At least then, I existed.

In the absence of secure attachment, I learned to rely only on myself. I mistook self-protection for strength and isolation for maturity. What I was living wasn't individuation, the unfolding of a true, connected self—it was individualism, shaped by fear and disconnection. I didn't know the difference yet.

Looking back, I see how deeply those years shaped me. Without a stable foundation or a person to reflect love or acceptance, my grief and fear became the core of my identity. My nervous system, wired for survival, kept me trapped between hypervigilance and numbness. Instead of trust and regulation, I learned to dissociate, suppress, and endure. It would take decades to unravel these patterns and discover that safety, connection, and healing were possible.

Through years of therapy, meditation, shamanic practice, and soul retrieval, I gradually began to reconnect with my father, mother, and ancestral line. My work with Thomas Hübl and other teachers helped me shape a four-part trauma integration process—one that brought coherence to my story, mended the fractures of disconnection, and restored a sense of belonging. Each time I guide someone through this process, my own bond with my lineage deepens, turning inherited pain into a pathway of healing, not only for myself but for those who came before me.

Then, suddenly, a bright light entered my life—a furry companion. It was love at first sight.

INDIVIDUATION AND INDIVIDUALISM

Individuation is not the same as individualism. It is the soul's journey toward wholeness—a psychological and spiritual unfolding that integrates the fragmented parts of the self. Carl Jung described it as "the process by which a person becomes who they are always meant to be." It's not about standing apart, but about becoming whole, aligned with something more profound and enduring than ego.

Individualism, by contrast, often glorifies separation. It's a cultural ideal that exalts independence and self-reliance, sometimes at the expense of connection, meaning, and responsibility to something larger than the self. In a hyper-individualistic world, we often mistake disconnection for freedom. But are we truly free, or simply reacting to inherited patterns and unintegrated trauma?

True freedom begins when we stop performing and start inhabiting presence. Individuation calls us back into the living stream of information—ancestral, collective, and personal—that flows through us. We are not isolated beings. In this moment, we are continuity—an unbroken line of life expressing itself through us.

Healing, then, is not just personal. It is a restoration of connection to our roots, one another, and the Earth. When we reclaim the story written in our bones, we move from fragmentation and scarcity to resonance and belonging. This work isn't about standing alone but remembering how to stand in a relationship.

CHAPTER FIVE

Bourbon, My First Dog

*Until one has loved an animal,
a part of one's soul remains unawakened.*

Anatole France

I received the greatest gift imaginable for my seventh birthday: a golden cocker spaniel. The moment I saw him, my world exploded from black and white into vivid technicolor. My father named him Bourbon, inspired by the deep amber hue of his favorite drink, but I didn't care what he was called. He was mine. After losing Sammy, I finally had a friend I could trust, a loyal companion to fill the aching void in my heart. It felt like the sun had broken through after a relentless, stormy winter, flooding my life with warmth and joy.

Some of my father's friends had suggested getting me a dog after Butch's beating and my father witnessing my tears. Whether Bourbon was their idea or my father's way of making amends, I never questioned it. He was gentle, affectionate, and easygoing—everything I wasn't. And yet, we fit together perfectly; a boy and his dog, inseparable. I loved him more than anyone, except maybe my Aunt Billie. We spent hours playing, running, and chasing each other, carving out a rare oasis of happiness in my otherwise chaotic world. For the first time in a long while, it felt like things were looking up.

That first night, he slept on the floor next to me. His soft, flaxen curls felt like silk beneath my fingers. I lay on my stomach, stroking his fur, drifting into sleep with my hand on his back. If nightmares came, I could reach out and feel his steady warmth, his heartbeat, and breathing reassured me that my new best friend was still there. He became my anchor, a light in my darkness.

The next few months were the happiest I had known since moving from the bar. I counted the hours at school until I could run home to play with Bourbon. We chased each other in endless loops, rolled together in the freshly mown grass, and shared secrets only he could hear. I taught him to sit and roll over, but mostly, we just played.

I made up stories, spinning wild adventures where he and I would run away together and see the world. I told him about Paris, London, Japan, China, Mexico, and Hawaii—places I dreamed of. I promised him that airplanes weren't scary—I'd flown before, and it was cool. I opened up about my stepmother's dreadful plastic-wrapped vegetables, which she just dropped into boiling water before serving, and about my father's cold, distant silence. I told him how much I hated Jean Severe—and how much I longed for my dad to spend time with me.

Bourbon became my whole world, my confidant. As long as he was by my side, I could endure anything. His presence steadied me, softened my rough edges. I stopped fighting my father and stepmother. I stayed out of trouble. He made me feel safe, if only for a little while.

But Bourbon's devotion to me had consequences. No matter how many times I pleaded with him, he insisted on following me to school, scaling the brick barbecue in our yard, and leaping over the fence to find me. His loyalty terrified me. "Bourbon," I whispered, crouching beside him, "If Dad finds out, he might take you away." But he didn't understand words; he only understood love and me, his faithful companion, a boy and his dog merged.

One morning, after I left for school, my father and stepmother decided they had had enough after the dog catcher picked him up. They tied him up in the backyard. I had no idea. I raced home as usual, cutting through the alley to reach our yard. But as I turned the corner, something caught my eye—something draped over the concrete fence. My heart seized, dread clawing at my throat. I ran toward what I already knew. It was Bourbon.

He had tried to follow me one last time, climbing onto the brick barbecue as always. But this time, the rope tethering him had stopped him short. He had jumped, trusting he could make it over. But he ran out of rope. His lifeless body dangled over the stone fence, suspended in midair, his golden fur catching the late afternoon light. His paws, which had once pressed eagerly into my chest when he greeted me, now hung limp, motionless. His head tilted unnaturally to one side, his amber eyes—once so full of devotion and joy—were vacant, staring out at nothing.

I stood there in the alley, unable to breathe. The world around me dissolved into a stark, silent void. My books slipped from my hands, landing in the dirt, but I didn't hear them fall. I felt the edges of my vision blur, as if reality was folding in on me, pulling me into some dark, suffocating abyss. My chest tightened, and my stomach churned, but I couldn't move. I couldn't look away. It felt like time had fractured—like I was floating outside my body, watching some terrible scene unfold that I was powerless to stop.

I don't remember how long I stood there or what happened next. All I know is that something inside me shut down completely. It was the same numbness I had felt after losing my mother, after Timmy, and Sammy—only now, it wasn't just people. The universe seemed determined to take everything I loved. A sickening understanding sank into my bones: no matter how much I loved or cared, everything was destined to be ripped away.

Bourbon's death was another cruel punctuation mark in a series of unbearable losses. I cried myself to sleep for weeks, months, and years. Around my father, I held the tears back, my whole body aching from the effort. I will never let anyone see me cry again.

Years later, before my stepmother Jean Severe died, she cut me out of my father's will. Her justification? "You didn't even cry when your dog died." Dumbfounded, I had no words. She didn't understand what it meant to be in shock, to have grief so overwhelming that it freezes the words in your throat.

After Bourbon, I stopped caring. Grief hollowed me out, and all I wanted was for the pain to end. Anger filled the empty spaces—blinding, uncontrollable rage. I stole more, skipped school, and snuck drinks from my father's bar. By nine, I was smoking, drinking, and getting into trouble regularly. I barely cared if I lived or died. Thoughts of death became familiar companions. I didn't want to continue living, and I continued my reckless behavior.

Home became unbearable. I lashed out, defied authority, and talked back to the Severe Woman, who relished reporting my every offense to my father. I refused to do homework, indifferent to their frustration. School felt pointless, and life felt pointless.

I had a model of an aircraft carrier with little airplanes on the deck. Bourbon had helped me build it, sitting by my side, watching, and leaning against me. I discovered this was how dogs say, "I love you." It was a model of the USS Forrestal, a super-carrier commissioned in 1955 named after the first United States Secretary of Defense, James Forrestal. The model was covered with little plastic fighter planes. I begged my father to buy it for me. I thought he would be proud of me when I built it, but he barely noticed when I finished it. He seemed more concerned about my homework and obeying my "mother."

One night, after yet another crime in my long list of childhood offenses, my father stormed into my room. I don't remember what I had done, but his fury was evident. He grounded me and turned to leave.

Something inside me snapped. I grabbed the two-foot-long aircraft carrier and smashed it over his head as he was leaving. The model shattered, and pieces of plastic and little fighter planes scattered across the floor.

My father didn't hit me. He didn't yell. He just looked at me—his expression unreadable, something dark and impenetrable settling between us. Then, without a word, he turned and walked away, closing the door behind him. I was left alone, surrounded by the wreckage of something that felt unretrievable, an infinite chasm between father and son.

I didn't know it yet, but they had already decided to get rid of me. They were planning to send me to military school.

REFLECTIONS

Losing Bourbon was one of the most devastating experiences of my trauma-filled life. His death left me hollow, as if I'd become a machine, moving mechanically through the motions of grief. For years, I couldn't recall the details of that day—too painful to face, too deeply buried. It wasn't until I began meditating and exploring my trauma that the emotions I had long suppressed began to surface.

As I allowed myself to feel again, the loss of Bourbon returned with startling clarity—raw and immediate, even more so than the earlier trauma of finding my mother hanging when I was just two and a half. That grief was tangled with guilt, confusion, and shame, and haunted me for decades. Bourbon's loss, by contrast, was pure sorrow. It crashed through me like a tidal wave—unfiltered, undeniable, and impossible to contain.

It took decades of inner work to begin understanding that pain. Through meditation and focused reflection, I unearthed memories I had hidden away—not just the horror of losing him but also the joy and love we had shared. Those memories became a lifeline. I understood that grief, derived from the Latin gravis, meaning "a heavy burden," was an unbearable weight I had carried alone for far too long.

My current dog, Buddha, has become an essential part of my healing process. Each night, he lies beside me, just as Bourbon once did. I feed him treats, scratch his belly, behind his ears, and feel the rhythm of his breath—his calm presence helping to soothe my nervous system and process the lingering effects of trauma. Buddha has even become part of my trauma integration circles. When someone is triggered, he's often the first to respond, offering a paw, a snuggle, or a quiet reminder that we are not alone.

One evening, as I tuned into Buddha's steady breathing, memories of Bourbon washed over me—not just the pain of that tragic day but also the joy of our time together. I remembered the laughter, the playfulness, and the unconditional love. Shifting from trauma to joy, I cried tears of gratitude. The sorrow didn't disappear, but it softened—interwoven now with warmth and memory. Grief and gratitude coexisted, each giving depth to the other.

With Buddha beside me, I can finally revisit those memories and fully feel what I once had to suppress. When I found Bourbon, there was no one to hold me or help me process the shock and devastation. But now, through revisiting that moment in mind, body, and heart, I've begun to release it. The joyful memories of Bourbon have become a resource—a reminder that love existed alongside loss, and they become mutually intertwined.

After many years of struggle, I'm learning to embrace love and pain. Bourbon was my first great canine love, and though I've had other dogs since, it wasn't until Buddha that I could fully open my heart again. He sleeps beside me each night, and I often reach out to feel his comforting presence. Above his bed hangs a worn, faded photo of Bourbon—a quiet tribute to two loyal companions who have walked beside me through suffering and healing. Together, we carry the past forward, dreaming of connection, love, and resilience.

The day I lost Bourbon was more than heartbreak—it was a moment of retraumatization. Finding him hanging on the fence hit me like a lightning bolt, reawakening the deep, unresolved trauma of my mother's suicide. Her death had lived in me as an implicit memory—nonverbal, right-brained, a silent wound with no clear story. But Bourbon's loss was painfully explicit. It didn't just bring its shock and sorrow; it shattered the fragile seal I'd placed over my earliest grief, unleashing the buried anguish I had suppressed.

In that moment, it was as if both traumas were happening simultaneously. The boundary between past and present dissolved, and I was no longer a growing boy—I was a helpless child once more, flooded with fear, sorrow, and a deep sense of powerlessness. My body responded as though no time had passed at all, reactivating the original wound as if it were happening now.

Bourbon's death heightened the hyper-vigilance I'd carried since childhood. It reinforced the protective walls I had built around my heart—walls that grew thicker, more complex, and harder to penetrate. My world narrowed. The grief didn't just take Bourbon from me; it deepened my isolation and cemented the trauma patterns that had shaped my life. And yet, even in that pain, there was a quiet truth: the depth of my sorrow revealed the depth of my love.

Grief, at its core, is a reflection of love. And now, with Buddha by my side, I've learned that healing doesn't mean forgetting. It means remembering with tenderness, allowing love to hold the sorrow, and trusting that the heart, broken open, can carry it all.

THE PSYCHOLOGICAL IMPACT OF LOSING A PET

Losing a pet can trigger profound grief, often comparable to losing a close human companion. Pets offer emotional support, routine, and unconditional love, and their absence can leave a deep psychological void.

Grief may show up as sadness, guilt, anger, numbness, or even relief—especially if the pet had been suffering.

These emotions are natural. According to psychologist Julie Axelrod, the loss of a pet is not only the loss of a companion but also a disruption to daily structure, purpose, and identity.

Research published in Anthrozoös shows that bereaved pet owners may experience symptoms similar to clinical depression or anxiety. Those with a history of childhood trauma may be particularly vulnerable to intensified grief reactions.

Coping and Healing

Grief is not something to "get over," but rather something to move through. Here are a few evidence-based ways to support yourself:

Acknowledge your grief. Suppressing emotions can prolong the healing process.

Seek connection. Support groups, friends, and therapists can validate your loss.

Honor your pet. Rituals and memorials can help process emotions and bring a sense of closure.

Care for your mental health. If grief lingers or worsens, professional support can make a significant difference.

As a therapist and veterinary social worker, Erin Schlicher notes, "Grieving a pet is real grief. It deserves space, compassion, and community."

In honoring your pet's memory, you're also celebrating the love and meaning they brought to your life, and that love never leaves.

CHAPTER SIX

Military School

*The rigorous structure and discipline of a military
school can create a sense of belonging and purpose,
but if not managed carefully, they can also potentially lead
to feelings of isolation and pressure, impacting emotional
stability and social function.*

National Institute of Health

By the time I was ten, trouble had become my shadow. After the Forrestal incident, I began stealing from stores, skipping school, and chasing the thrill of destruction, lighting cherry bombs in mailboxes just to watch them explode. My sharp tongue tested every adult's patience, but no one bore the brunt of my defiance more than my stepmother. The atmosphere at home grew increasingly volatile, thick with resentment and silence. Eventually, my parents concluded that I was too much for them to handle. Convinced I needed more structure and discipline than they could provide, they sent me to military school.

At first, the idea of leaving felt like an escape. Home had become suffocating—a minefield of judgment and emotional upheaval. Unspoken sorrow and rage seemed to fill every corner of the house. But as we drove toward the academy, relief gave way to anxiety. What kind of world was I being sent into? Would it be better or just another form of punishment?

The iron gates of Mt. Lowe Military Academy loomed like a verdict. Rows of wooden dormitories stood at attention beneath the looming San Gabriel Mountains. The grounds were once home to one of the most notorious speakeasies in the valley. It had been repurposed into a training ground for boys like me—exiled, discarded, or simply too much to handle.

My father made the arrangements, and my grandfather footed the bill. It felt less like an education and more like a prison sentence.

The first hours passed in a blur of shouted orders, new rules, and starchy uniforms. My shoes pinched, my belt felt like a restraint, and my cot's sheets were tucked so tightly they might as well have been a straitjacket. That night, under the flicker of hallway lights, I lay still, not homesick, but aware I had crossed into a world that was colder, more exacting, and deeply unfamiliar.

Military school was a cruel reflection of what I'd left behind: rigid rules, swift punishment, and no space for rebellion. Yet my anger didn't disappear. It merely went underground. Repressed but seething, it simmered beneath the surface, waiting for a crack in the façade.

This wasn't just discipline. It was indoctrination. The academy demanded obedience, reshaping my defiance into something small, contained, and silent. Fear was constant, but I had already learned how to numb it, to swallow it, to bury it deep beneath the shame of the boy who had once shattered a plastic aircraft carrier over his father's head.

That first night, staring at the blank ceiling, I felt the weight of this new reality settle over me—cold, rigid, inescapable. Survival, I told myself, was all that mattered now.

I entered the fifth grade in full uniform under the watchful eye of Major John Hayden Dargin, the academy's owner. He lived in a small, cinder-block cottage between the barracks and was always watching. We slept in vast green dormitories, separated only by flimsy plywood partitions. At night, the "captain", a 15-year-old cadet with a thirst for control, ruled the barracks through fear and intimidation. Disobedience meant punches, extra drills, or his favorite punishment: endless push-ups until your arms gave out.

Each morning, Reveille shattered the silence. We had 30 minutes to wash up, dress, make our beds, and stand in perfect formation. When the cadet commander barked, "Attennnn-shun!" we snapped to attention, breath held, hearts pounding. Major Dargin inspected every detail, creased collars, polished shoes, and clean fingernails. Failure meant instant demerits and physical punishment. Perfection wasn't rewarded. It was simply expected.

The air was thick with pressure. Dargin's footsteps sent jolts through the ranks. For most of us, boys from dysfunctional homes, or sent away by wealthy parents unwilling to deal with us, this was life now. We were misfits and deviants being molded by force into submission.. Rebellion was beaten down. Emotion was weakness. Back talk was forbidden. Consequences were swift.

And yet, within that rigidity, there was a strange relief. The structure, harsh as it was, created a sense of predictability. I knew what to expect, even if what I expected was punishment. So, I did what I had always done: I adapted. I hid. I complied outwardly while retreating inwardly. I made myself invisible when needed. I learned to survive.

Then came the fight.

It happened early in my time there. I don't remember what triggered it, just the blinding surge of fury and the sickening crack as my head hit against the mess hall's support columns. Pain and blood bloomed instantly. My front teeth were chipped. Both of us were dragged off to detention. The lesson was clear: defiance had a cost. And the damage stared back at me every time I looked in the mirror after that.

There were a few moments of respite, but one activity stood out: marksmanship. We took the bus to the Pasadena National Guard rifle range to practice shooting with bolt-action .22 caliber rifles. I liked it. I was good at it. Lt. Eastman kept score for the medals—Marksman, Sharpshooter, Expert—and I worked my way to the top. I imagined the targets were my father, Jean, and the kids who bullied me. Hitting the bullseye gave me a flicker of control, a taste of power. I became an Expert shot. Looking back, I'm grateful I couldn't access a weapon. At the wrong moment, that kind of darkness could've ended everything.

Sometimes, I think about the Hitler Youth and the League of German Girls, groups created to mold children into instruments of war. Mt. Lowe wasn't far off in spirit. It didn't succeed in indoctrinating me into the military-industrial complex, but it did teach me something important: I would never belong to it. That clarity may have saved me after being drafted during the Vietnam War.

We were granted leave every few months. My father was too busy, and the Severe Woman couldn't drive, so I took the bus alone from Altadena to San Bernardino and back.

I turned that solo journey into a business opportunity. At the bus stop, I'd swing by the local market, grab a bag, fill it with candy, and walk out without paying. Back at Mt. Lowe—our so-called "prison"—I stashed the loot in my footlocker and sold it to other cadets, who always had money to spend.

For a while, it worked. The thrill of outsmarting the system and the extra cash felt like small victories. Until the day I got caught. The store manager dragged me into his office. The police arrived. My father was called. They wanted to press charges.

My father, disgusted and embarrassed, cut a deal.

The punishment was swift and brutal. I repaid the store, lost all privileges, and spent weeks in detention—doing push-ups, cleaning bathrooms, and scrubbing floors. But the most brutal blow came from my father's eyes: not rage, but fathomless disappointment.

I wasn't sorry for what I did. I was only sorry I got caught. Genuine remorse and a sense of integrity would come much later. Back then, I just learned to be more careful.

In hindsight, I had the makings of a successful politician. Bending rules came naturally.

I attended Mt. Lowe through sixth grade. Then, just before I entered middle school, my father was transferred to Whiteman Air Force Base in Knob Noster, Missouri, a small town nestled between Sedalia and Warrensburg. It was a jarring shift from California's sunshine and sprawl to a small farm town with little more than a state park, a military base, and a main street with scattered stores and shops.

I'll never forget our first visit to the local IGA market. My stepmother, a sharp-tongued New Yorker, asked the clerk if they carried pumpernickel bread. He blinked and said, "Lady, nickel bread went out during the Depression." My parents retold that story for years at dinner parties, and it was always met with roaring laughter. I never found it funny.

Walking into Knob Noster Middle School at thirteen felt like stepping onto another planet. The hallway stretched like a runway. My sneakers squeaked against the polished linoleum, drawing attention I didn't want. With my military-issue haircut, shiny new braces, and stiff leather book satchel, I felt like a walking billboard that screamed: "Outsider."

The air was thick with the scent of stale sweat, mildew, and dust. My asthma flared immediately. Kids clustered in tight knots, laughing and joking in ways that seemed foreign to me. I kept my gaze locked on the floor, gut twisted in knots. No one spoke to me, but I felt I was being watched. Judged.

At thirteen, I was painfully awkward and shy. Everyone else seemed to understand the rules, how to talk, where to sit, and what to wear. I didn't. My braces throbbed constantly, my lips cracked over the wires, and even though I hadn't made a single friend yet, I dreaded the names I knew were coming: brace face, metal mouth. I felt like a carnival freak, on display, yet invisible. Desperate to disappear into the woodwork.

I struggled to find my locker, fumbling with the lock, afraid to ask for help. I could feel the sideways glances from older kids, probably smirking at my ineptitude. I just wanted to vanish into that metal box and disappear.

The braces lasted only three months. One night, I sat alone in my room, the humiliation and pain too much to bear, and reached for a pair of pliers. I yanked, twisted, and snapped wires, mangling the braces beyond repair. My mouth bled. I didn't care. I just wanted them gone.

When my father found out, his rage boiled over. His face turned crimson, and he ranted about money and responsibility, his voice sharp with betrayal. I stood silent, hands stuffed in my pockets, unable to meet his eyes. I was detached. Numb. Eventually, he drove me back to the orthodontist to have the remnants removed. His fury hung in the air the whole way. But I felt nothing. At least they were gone.

In biology class, we were assigned a project to display for the class. I decided to assemble a frog skeleton for show and tell. I stole a preserved frog from the lab, one soaked in formaldehyde. I'd heard boiling a frog could strip away the skin and flesh, leaving behind clean bones. Then, I would simply reassemble the skeletal structure, just as I would when building model ships and planes. I didn't know this technique only worked with live frogs, not ones pickled in poison.

I brought the dead frog home when no one was there, set a pot of water to boil, dropped it in, and forgot all about it as I ran off to play in the woods.

When I returned, fire trucks were parked in front of the house. There was the Severe woman, arms folded, hip cocked, wearing that permanent look of disgust, like someone had farted in church. When she saw me, she said those familiar words: "Wait till your father hears about this."

The water had boiled away, and the frog was reduced to a blackened crisp. Worse still, the chemical brew released toxic formaldehyde gas, filling the entire house with a nauseating stench that lingered for months. I was grounded, again, my default setting, and sent to my room, which felt safer than enduring their outrage.

My parents were regulars at the officers' club. They attended cocktail parties and dinners and always drank. They'd leave me home alone often.

One night, I was asleep when I woke to the sound of violent retching. I crept down the hallway, peered into the bathroom, and saw The Severe Woman—Miss High-and-Mighty—half-naked, face down in a pool of vomit. She'd passed out cold from drinking, and the stench was overwhelming.

I wiped her face with a towel, dragged her to bed, and covered her up. I'm still not sure why. Maybe it was instinct. Perhaps it was some faint flicker of compassion. My father wasn't home—probably still at the club or off with someone else's wife.

I never said a word. But I always wondered what she thought when she woke up in bed the following day.

One summer day, I hit my limit. I packed sandwiches, jumped on my bike, and ran away. I didn't know where I was going; I just had to get away.

I rode my bike for hours, aimless and alone, letting the steady rhythm of the wheels soothe my restless thoughts. As night fell, I drifted toward a glowing drive-in theater, its massive screen flickering against the darkening sky. A Brigitte Bardot film was playing. I slipped through the fence, laid my bike down, and stretched out on the cool grass to watch.

Her sensuous beauty stirred something primal in me, an ache I didn't yet have words for. It mingled with memories of Mary's gentle touch and the hidden stack of Playboys I'd discovered in my father's dresser, as if he didn't expect me to find them. Maybe he thought they'd toughen me up, make me more of a man.

But all I felt was a confusing swirl of longing, curiosity, and loneliness. That night, under the stars and the spell of the silver screen, I brushed up against the mysterious edges of desire.

After the movie, it was dark. I was 40 miles from home, cold, lost, and scared. I panicked. I didn't want to return, but didn't know what else to do. I climbed on my bike and started pedaling back towards home.

Then, like a scene from a movie, a car pulled up beside me. A window rolled down.

"Michael?"

It was the base Chaplain—of all people—returning from a family vacation. He was one of the men my father had once enlisted to "fix" me. I told him, through tears, that I was running away but didn't know where to go.

He gently loaded my bike in the trunk and drove me home. But the house was empty. My parents were still out drinking. Of course.

The Chaplain eventually talked to them, but it didn't matter. Nothing changed. I remained an embarrassing burden, the boy who scandalized the base: their son, the screw-up, the troublemaker.

For the next two years, I stayed in Knob Noster through eighth grade. But the trouble didn't stop. It only evolved.

I began sneaking out with my father's Cadillac late at night, cruising while they slept it off. I never got caught. Then, one night, I dragged my friend, Tony, into the fun. We decided to take his parents' shiny Chrysler New Yorker for a spin. But he panicked, slammed it into reverse, and crashed into the garage door with a deafening boom.

The thrill vanished in an instant.

He wasn't allowed to hang out with me after that. I was grounded, confined to my room, where meals were delivered like prison rations. Fine by me. I didn't have to endure my father's constant barking: "Stop fidgeting. Elbows off the table. Chew your food. Don't eat so fast."

He threatened military school again.

One weekend, my seventh-grade teacher, Mrs. Jones, invited me to her family farm to help me memorize the Preamble to the Constitution. I expected punishment, but I found warmth instead.

She was soft-spoken and motherly, with three kids and a kitchen that smelled and looked like real food. Dinners were loud, fun, and full of love. It reminded me of being with my grandparents and Aunt Billie at the dinner table.

I helped with the farm chores, and they let me drive the tractor. I laughed a lot that weekend. For once, I felt like a kid. And she made learning feel like a game, not a punishment.

When Sunday came, and I had to go home, it felt like being dragged back to prison. But for a brief, beautiful moment, I had seen what family life could be.

On Halloween, a buddy and I broke into a military supply building and stole bundles of shiny aluminum strips. They looked like festive Christmas tinsel, perfect for decorating the base housing area, and cars, or so we thought.

We had no idea we were stealing military chaff, a type of military countermeasure used by aircraft to jam enemy radar systems during combat.

We gleefully scattered the strips everywhere, on cars, houses, and buildings, and watched them flutter in the wind like silver snow.

By the following day, we'd unknowingly knocked out critical radar and communications systems across the base.

A base that housed atomic weapons.

Oops.

My father later blamed me for never making full colonel. Maybe he was right. Leaving condoms on the general's patio to humiliate his bombshell, beautiful daughter probably didn't help either.

And then there was the golf course incident.

I worked there as a caddy. One night, friends and I broke into the clubhouse, stole beers, and decided to race tractors on the fairway. I drove mine straight into the lake. The engine sputtered, water gushed, and I stood soaked and humiliated.

We outran the Air Police that night, but not for long. The following day, they showed up at our door. My father was livid, almost to the point of tears. He sent me to my room.

I was fired from the golf course, where I worked as a caddy and cleaned and polished golf shoes. Once again, I was grounded, shamed, and silenced, as if the punishment might erase the deeper ache underneath.

These wild stunts weren't just rebellion. They were my twisted attempts to be seen. To matter. But they only deepened the divide between my father and me.

You can see why he finally sent me away to another military boarding school to complete my high school education.

Kemper Military School was located on a sprawling 46-acre campus in Boonville, Missouri. Founded in 1844, its Latin motto, Nunquam Non-Paratus (Never Not Prepared), rang hollow for me. I was anything but prepared.

From day one, I hated it. The stiff uniforms, barking orders, and endless drills all felt like a punishment rather than a path to maturity. I had always scraped by in school, hiding behind feigned innocence, rebellion, and half-effort. Every report card echoed the same tired refrain: "Good potential, but lacks discipline." I suppose that's how I ended up at Kemper in the first place.

The one saving grace was Mr. Quackenbush, our English teacher. Mr. Q., as we called him, was a wiry man with spectacularly bad breath and a surprisingly gentle heart. Unlike the others, he didn't yell or shame us into submission. He began our first class by asking us to write a paper on any topic we chose, just to get a feel for our writing voices.

I couldn't resist the chance to stir the pot. I turned in a half-crumpled essay titled "Why All English Teachers Should Be Deported Back to England to Learn Proper English." I misspelled words on purpose, scrawled in my worst handwriting, and tore the corner to make it extra insulting. I was sure I'd get an F or a chewing-out.

But when he handed it back, there was no grade, red ink, or corrections.

Just a note in his looping cursive: "Very creative!"

That moment cracked something open in me.

Over time, Mr. Q did more than just teach me—he opened doors I didn't even know existed. He got me reading, writing, and eventually, to my surprise, even curious about poetry. His steady belief in me was nothing short of radical for a kid who felt perpetually misunderstood, defended, and invisible. I honestly don't think I'd be writing this book today if it weren't for him.

Reading had always been a struggle. My mind wouldn't stay still, nor would the words—they floated, blurred, and slipped away. I thought it meant I was stupid, so I worked hard to hide it. But the effort left me exhausted and ashamed.

The Severe Woman once tried to read to me while I was in the tub. I splashed around like any kid, and her stiff, starched hair got soaked. That was all it took. She never offered again. It didn't take much for her to quit on me. I wasn't her kid, and she never let me forget it.

Whenever someone said I looked like her, she'd quickly correct them and tell them she wasn't my real mother. Yes, that was painfully clear, but the message I heard was that I didn't belong.

Somehow, despite Mr. Q's attempts, I made it through Kemper without reading an entire book. And when graduation finally came, I couldn't get out of there fast enough.

But there was one small, surprising moment of pride. My father showed up to the ceremony in his full-dress Air Force blues. Seeing him standing tall in that uniform stirred something unexpected—respect, maybe even love—feelings I rarely allowed myself to feel toward him. Mostly, I felt this deep longing to feel seen.

California was calling. High school was over. Freedom. Girls. A new life.

I was ready to express my newly acquired freedom…

REFLECTIONS

For most of my life, I tried to hide my neurodiversity, what I used to call "the hole in my brain." In the 1950s, no one had the language or awareness to recognize what was happening. I wasn't lazy or undisciplined. I was struggling with an internal battle within my mind.

Early trauma had rewired my nervous system. Constant hypervigilance, poor memory, and difficulty with sequencing were just a few of the symptoms. On top of that was undiagnosed ADHD. I lived in survival mode. My restlessness, racing thoughts, and inability to sit still weren't personal failings. They were adaptations, signs of a nervous system working hard to keep me safe.

But I didn't know that at the time.

So I did what many kids do—I compensated, acted out, or acted like I had it all under control.

Years later, while living in Canada, I bought a barbecue grill. I carefully laid out the parts and the instructions. By step three, I was utterly lost. I felt the familiar panic rising—the same shame I'd known as a boy. My friend Elijah offered to help. This time, I didn't pretend. I let him.

In minutes, he assembled what I couldn't, without even looking at the instructions.

I realized I had spent my life pretending to be competent in a world built for brains that worked differently than mine. When I finally heard the term "neurodivergent," something clicked. It gave a name to what I'd lived, and permission to stop pretending.

I began to recognize how deeply my old story had shaped my identity: I'm the lost, unwanted, motherless boy who is always in trouble. I was always misplacing things—my keys, my wallet, my mind—and each loss would send me spiraling into shame, panic, criticism, and self-doubt.

After much reflection and inner work, I recognize that when that familiar wave rises, I can catch it. I pause and gently remind myself, "You're doing your lost child thing again." I breathe. I return to the present. And each time, I reclaim a little more of myself.

Our experiences and family history shape the lens through which we perceive the world, forming our sense of reality. But that reality isn't fixed. It can be questioned, unraveled, and rewritten. Even after an inhospitable childhood, we can craft a more empowering narrative that helps us navigate life with greater clarity, resilience, and possibility.

One of the most powerful tools I've discovered is keeping a journal. Asking myself questions like:

Is this true? What is the age of this belief?

What am I protecting?

What emotions and sensations are present?

What am I hiding? Who in my family has similar beliefs?

These questions open space between who I am being and who I'm becoming. They allow for something new to emerge.

As Abraham Maslow once said, "The ability to be human is rooted in our capacity for self-transcendence."

Healing doesn't mean forgetting or erasing the past. It means integrating it—carrying our wounds forward, not as burdens, but as threads woven into the fabric of who we are becoming. Our trauma does not define us; we are the storytellers, the meaning-makers. And with each step, we get to choose how the next chapter begins.

For me, that next chapter began with a restless urgency I didn't yet understand—a nervous system shaped by early rupture and wired for movement, escape, and adventure. What I later came to recognize as undiagnosed ADHD was, in those days, simply a fire in my chest and a longing in my bones. I craved freedom, spontaneity, connection, and aliveness. I wasn't just running—I was searching. And that search would carry me far from everything I knew, onto the open road, into cities and countries I had only imagined, and deep into the mystery of who I was becoming.

ADHD THROUGH A SOMATIC LENS

ADHD is not a disorder of attention—it's a disorder of regulation. What looks like distractibility, impulsivity, or hyperactivity is often a nervous system shaped by early stress, relational rupture, or trauma. These patterns aren't flaws—they're intelligent adaptations to overwhelming environments.

> *The tuning out—the absentmindedness—is not a disease; it's a coping mechanism. It's not an inherited disorder, but a response to the environment.*
>
> Dr. Gabor Maté

Somatically, ADHD often reflects a disconnection from the body—a survival strategy rooted in early developmental wounding. The child learns to stay alert, scan for danger, or disconnect altogether. Over time, these strategies solidify into habits that interfere with focus, memory, and presence.

Healing doesn't come from fixing or suppressing symptoms. It begins with safety, attunement, and presence. Practices like trauma-informed movement, co-regulation, breathwork, and relational repair help restore a sense of wholeness. We don't "get rid of" ADHD—we integrate the parts of us that had to adapt, welcoming them back into connection and wholeness.

CHAPTER SEVEN

On The Road

So shut up, live, travel, adventure, bless, and don't be sorry.

Jack Kerouac

I graduated from Kemper Military Academy in 1962, ready to party, and was California dreaming! I wanted to drive my 1936 Chevrolet, my first car, West, but my dad wouldn't allow it. Instead, he offered to drive me and buy a car for me when we arrived. That may have been the longest time I'd spent with him since our days living in the bar.

I enjoyed the drive. Even with his usual undercurrent of criticism, something about the open road softened the edges. He even let me drive sometimes, a rare treat that made me feel trusted, if only briefly. I soaked in the rhythm of the tires on pavement, the open sky ahead, and the strange sense of possibility that came with every mile. Heading West felt like stepping into a new life. Despite our complicated history, sharing that space with my father felt like a tentative bridge between us. For those brief stretches of highway, the road was more than asphalt; it was a moment of connection.

Once I arrived in California, I enrolled at the Menlo School of Business in Menlo Park, another all-boys school, but this time softened by the nearby presence of California girls, which made the experience far more bearable. There was something different in the air, something lighter. California felt like a clean slate. For the first time, the future didn't feel like a sentence I had to serve; it felt like a promise, a doorway to something new, wide open with possibility.

I had a good friend from Kemper, Mike Wiley, whose mom and stepdad lived in Atherton, CA. I spent a lot of time with Mike and his mom, Dorothea Sturgeon, who became like the mother I never had. Warm, caring, and creative, Dorothea always made me feel welcome and special. A beautiful silver-haired woman who had been named Miss Kansas City in her youth, Dorothea was very attentive and loving, a stark contrast to the strict and distant environment in which I grew up.

One afternoon, Mike and I took off into the mountains in his new car and happened upon a music festival in Strawberry. As we wandered through the crowd, a girl approached Mike and said, "Your friend looks like Stoney Burke." Without missing a beat, he leaned in and whispered, "Don't tell anyone, but it is him he's keeping a low profile."

Stoney Burke was a TV cowboy known for his signature denim jacket, much like the one I wore at the time. The more I denied it, the more convinced people became. It quickly turned into a hilarious game. From that day on, Mike and his mom started calling me Stoney, and the nickname stuck.

At school, everyone knew me as Stoney. Most assumed the name came from being perpetually stoned, not an unreasonable guess. But really, it was a happy accident, a playful twist of fate that became part of my college identity. Later, I legally changed my last name from Ullstrom to Stone. It wasn't just the nickname; it was practical. Ullstrom was a difficult name to remember, especially in real estate, where name recognition is key. Stone was simple. Memorable. Mine.

Of course, my father didn't see it that way. Encouraged by the Severe Woman, he saw it as a betrayal of family pride. It was about carving out my identity, something straightforward and uncomplicated.

About six months into the school year, my father came to visit. I took him to a bar across the street that accepted my fake ID. I had a crush on one of the waitresses there—a kind, flirty woman who reminded me of my childhood babysitter, Mary. In the haze of youthful fantasy, I imagined we might become lovers.

But within ten minutes of walking in, she was on my dad's lap, giggling at his stories about being a fighter pilot. My heart sank. The woman I had been dreaming about had turned her attention to the man who had always seemed out of reach to me—my father, my reluctant hero. When she slipped him a piece of paper, likely her number, I knew I'd lost her. And not just her, something more profound. I felt humiliated. Replaced. Invisible, again.

Years later, fate gave me a strange kind of revenge in Florida. My dad, Jean Severe, and I were out for dinner at the Officers' Club when a stunning young woman invited us to her home for cocktails. She oozed confidence and sexuality and was clearly drawn to my father, but she flirted with me too, playing some kind of coy game.

The Severe Woman pretended not to notice. Her disapproval hung thick in the air, but for once, I wasn't the one shrinking under it. Watching her squirm was oddly satisfying. Later that night, I borrowed the car and returned to the woman's house. She answered the door with a surprised smile and let me in, whispering that her kids were asleep.

We made love quietly, lost in the warmth of shared desire and whispered conversations. As dawn approached, she gently nudged me to go before her children woke up. I left her house grinning, the early morning air crisp on my face. I didn't say a word to my father. But in my mind, I thought, "Turnabout's fair play."

Still, even as I savored the moment, a shadow awareness crept in. I had become what I once resented, someone who used women to soothe the ache of feeling empty and unlovable. Beneath the surface thrill was a more profound truth: misogyny had seeped into me, too. That realization lingered longer than the sense of victory from my past humility.

I didn't do particularly well at Menlo. My attention was consumed by cars, girls, parties, drumming, and drugs. By the end of my freshman year, the draft board came calling. Not eager to be shipped to Vietnam, I decided to take the summer off and head to Yosemite.

With my camping gear and food strapped high on my little Honda 50, I wobbled through back roads, avoiding freeways because the bike couldn't handle them. A three-hour drive became an eight-hour saga. But the vision of Yosemite kept me going.

I arrived in the middle of the night and quietly slipped into the valley, setting up camp under the stars. The velvety silence was soft and soothing, broken only by waterfalls, the wind rustling in the trees, and the fresh mountain air filling my lungs. The exhaustion faded as I drifted to sleep, and a rare peace settled in.

I wanted to be a writer, despite the fact that school had left my reading and writing skills underdeveloped. Still, I carried notebooks and scribbled terrible poetry in them. I wore a little black beret for flair and spent over two months camping in Yosemite. I got to know the staff, skirted rules, and made friends.

Sitting around a campfire with some new friends one evening, I listened as they swapped stories of recent European adventures. Their tales lit a spark in me. I'd been reading On the Road by Jack Kerouac, and something in me stirred, a deep, restless hunger to break free, to explore the world beyond my limited horizon. Forget the Army. Forget Vietnam. I didn't want orders or uniforms. I wanted freedom.

The next day, I called a girlfriend in Palo Alto and asked her to pick me up. She showed up, and we spent a couple of wild days hiking and partying in Yosemite, soaking in the moment. Then, I loaded my little motorbike into the back of her car, said goodbye to the Valley, and headed back to the Bay Area. But the idea of hitting the road for real had already taken hold of me.

I worked at a music store during college and built a pretty sweet record collection. When the travel bug bit, I sold it all for about $500. That cash felt like a golden ticket. I called my half-brother Peter, who was living in Berkeley, and asked if he wanted to go on an adventure. He was in. I hitchhiked up there and crashed at his place for the night.

The following day, we hit the road with nothing but our thumbs and a vague idea of going East. As Kerouac wrote, "There was nowhere to go but everywhere, so just keep on rolling under the stars." We drifted into Utah, where we met Floyd, a young, charismatic, black man with an infectious smile and magnetic energy. We hit it off immediately, and he joined our little crew.

In Salt Lake City, we had the wild idea to choreograph a hitchhiking dance—spins, waves, exaggerated gestures. We thought it was hilarious. The locals didn't. A Black man and two scruffy white guys dancing on the roadside wasn't exactly a welcome sight in conservative Utah. The stares were icy, the glares even colder, and no car stopped. After a long day of rejection, we scrapped the routine and stuck out our thumbs the old-fashioned way.

Eventually, someone gave us a ride, but only as far as Floyd's hometown. We said our goodbyes and pushed on. In Colorado, Peter and I decided to try something we'd only read about, riding the rails.

We snuck into the rail yard, expecting trouble, but found kindness instead. One of the workers pointed us toward a train headed East. We climbed into an open gondola car and waited, hearts pounding.

After an hour, a suitcase suddenly came flying into the car. A second later, two pudgy hands gripped the edge, followed by a bug-eyed, round-faced man who hauled himself in like he'd done it a hundred times. Without a word, he flopped down, pulled his suitcase over as a pillow, and fell asleep.

About 45 minutes later, he sat up, gave us a stern look that said, Don't touch my stuff, and disappeared over the edge of the railcar. He returned with a piece of cardboard, laid it down like a seasoned pro, repositioned his suitcase, and went back to sleep. He was no rookie, and we respected that. We gave him space.

As the train pulled away and gathered speed, Peter and I stood at the front of the car with our new hobo friend, wind in our faces, waving to kids in backyards as we passed. It was filthy and loud and oddly magical.

At one point, our silent companion pulled out a worn tobacco pouch and, with quiet precision, pinched a wad of shag and stacked it on his thumb. The wind seemed to conspire with him, scattering it gracefully across the paper. With a practiced twist, a lick, and a match flick, he lit up—calm as a Zen master. All this as we were going about forty miles an hour. He said nothing. Just stood there, exhaling smoke and mystery.

Eventually, we rumbled into Lincoln, Nebraska, caked in rail yard grime. I remembered Marie, an ex-girlfriend from when my father was stationed at the nearby Lincoln Air Force base. I found her family's name in the phone book and called her from a payphone. She answered. Her parents were out of town, and she invited us over.

When she pulled up, her face said everything—disbelief, a hint of horror, and something softer underneath, like affection trying to remember its way back. We were filthy, covered in sweat, grease, and road dust. The smell of grime clung to us like a second skin.

Still, she opened her arms. Not a full embrace—more of an awkward A-frame hug—but it was enough.

Back at her place, she treated us like kings—hot showers to wash off the rail yard grime, fresh clothes, and a home-cooked meal. She and I slipped easily back into the rhythm of an old affection, our bodies remembering what our minds had set aside. For a little while, the road disappeared. I felt clean, fed, held, and human again.

Peter had always been a little jealous of the women I attracted. He used to joke about it, but it ran deeper than that, some kind of competitive thing. There was tension, unspoken but real.

We both agreed it was easier to hitchhike solo, so we parted ways. I stayed one more day with Marie, savoring the comfort and warmth. Then I hit the road again. I made it to New York in under two days, catching a night ride with five labor union activists headed to a Socialist conference in the city. We rode through the dark of night, talking politics, dreams, and disillusionment.

I was supposed to meet Peter at my friend Ann's place in New York, and from there, we'd fly to Europe together. But he never showed up. After waiting a week, I gave up and bought a one-way ticket to London for $183, with a layover in Iceland.

I didn't hear from him until I was already in Europe. When I called Ann, she told me Peter had arrived the day after I left, sporting a black eye and a bad attitude. He'd hitchhiked on a potato truck. Europe would have to wait. The road had taken us in different directions.

During the layover in Reykjavik, something unexpected and delightful happened. I met two young schoolteachers on the plane, and we decided to explore the city together. I fell in love with it almost instantly. Reykjavik felt strangely familiar, as if something ancient in me recognized the land.

Later, I understood—I was walking the ground my Viking ancestors once did. In the late 9th century, around 874 CE, Norse settlers arrived in Iceland, seeking new land for farming and fishing. They carved out a life from the volcanic rock and harsh winds, drawn by the island's raw beauty and abundant resources. These early settlers, primarily Norwegians, became the foundation of Iceland's population and my lineage. Even today, about 60% of Icelanders trace their roots to those Viking pioneers.

Before they came, Irish monks had briefly lived on the island, but they left rather than share it with the arriving "heathens." The blood of those heathens ran in me. No wonder the land felt like home.

From Iceland, I flew to London. I hit the streets after settling into a hostel and locking up my bag. I ended up at a bar, had a few drinks, and later realized I'd been shortchanged—given only half the proper return from a hundred-pound note. I went back to complain. The place was closed, but a woman answered the door. When I demanded my change, she refused. I threatened to call the police, and suddenly, a brute of a man appeared, knocked her aside, and charged after me, wielding a table leg. I tore through the streets of London, running for my life.

I thought I'd lost him until a Jaguar roared up onto the sidewalk, chasing me. I broke some personal speed records that night. Eventually, I spotted a police car and flagged it down. Gasping for air, I explained what had happened. They eyed the peace symbol around my neck and mocked me, another "troublemaking peacenik. They refused to help, so I stumbled back to the hostel and collapsed. That was my first night in London.

The next day, someone I met told me there was a person who wanted to meet me. That someone turned out to be Michael Ramsey, the Archbishop of Canterbury. A kind, gentle man with a sharp mind and deep empathy, he invited me to stay at Lambeth Palace. The place was grand—lush gardens, quiet courtyards, and a sacred stillness. People called him "Your Grace," but he felt more like a wise, warm grandfather. He genuinely listened to my thoughts on Vietnam, my story, and my questions. His opposition to the war mirrored my own. The few days I spent there felt healing, like being seen by someone who didn't want anything from me. For a moment, I felt what it was like to be fathered.

After London, I headed to Amsterdam, and it was love at first sight. The jazz scene was electric. Many big-name musicians started and ended their European tours there. I quickly made friends. Shortly after my arrival at a party, I mentioned wanting to find a place to live. Everyone laughed: "You'll never find one! There's a seven-year waiting list." However, a week later, I met Jan, a filmmaker working for IBM, who was moving to Los Angeles to attend film school. I helped him and his girlfriend find a place in LA, and even arranged an au pair job for her. In return, Jan gifted me his quirky, spacious two-bedroom apartment in a condemned building.

He'd MacGyvered the place—hacked the electricity over the rooftops, rigged the plumbing, and installed hot water on demand. The building leaned, so he hung the bed frame from the ceiling to keep it level. During lovemaking, it swayed like a hammock. You couldn't pour a cup of coffee to the top, or it would spill, but I didn't care. I was home—and best of all, no rent.

The original Provos, a gang of radical, mischievous anarchists who challenged authority with humor and absurdity, lived downstairs. They "liberated" bicycles, painting them white and leaving them around the city for anyone to use, turning rebellion into public service. We threw wild parties upstairs, where art, poetry, and politics collided. That's where I met incredible characters, including Ted Joans, a surrealist poet, jazz trumpeter, painter, and former New Yorker who had once moved to Timbuktu to raise camels. He was a founding spirit of the Happenings movement, where art, music, and mayhem blurred the line between performance and revolution.

In 1964, I attended my first Happening, held in a massive warehouse. As hash smoke filled the air, the curtain lifted on a mint-condition '59 Cadillac Coupe de Ville. Then, in a surreal twist, a dozen naked people appeared, caressing the car, a satirical take on American consumerism and excess. On opposite ends of the stage, two French saxophonists battled it out. Ted took the mic and read a haunting poem about JFK's assassination and government corruption. It was wild, poetic, and electric. The revolution had begun.

Through Ted, I met James Baldwin. We shared a long lunch talking about war, racism, oppression, love, and courage. Like Ted, he saw me. I was young, but they made room for me. That was my first real initiation into conversations about race, colonialism, and the deeper shadows of American history.

At some point, I met a young woman I called Tiger. I can't remember her real name. We became lovers and decided to head south when the bitter Dutch winter set in. I quit my dishwasher and coffee barista job at Gerzon, a women's department store on the Kalverstraat, and we hitchhiked through Germany. Tiger, fluent in German, refused to speak it, still carrying the weight of inherited war trauma. After many adventures, we ended up in Ibiza, then Formentera, the smallest of the Balearic Islands in the Mediterranean.

On our first night, we slept on the beach. In the morning, I woke up blind, my eyelids swollen shut from mosquito bites. We looked like zombies. Eventually, we found a place in San Francisco, the island's main village. We met a tribe of fellow travelers, draft resisters, and spiritual seekers. It felt like home, but Tiger soon fell ill. A visit to the clinic revealed she was pregnant, not with my child, but from her prior relationship. She returned to the Netherlands for socialized medical care and family support. It was a necessary goodbye. Years later, I tracked her down. She was married with three kids. I smiled, knowing she'd become the nurturing mother I always saw in her.

I stayed in Formentera for about nine months, partying and cooking for a Swiss psychiatrist. Then I decided to hitch to Paris for something new when my job ended. Near Zaragoza, Spain, a police officer spotted me thumbing for a ride. I braced for jail. Instead, he took me to a local bar and introduced me to the patrons, who fed me wine and hors d'oeuvres. He said, "Stay here, I'll be back." I still wasn't convinced that he wasn't going to take me to jail.

An hour later, he returned and brought me to his home. I met his wife and children, and they served a feast of chicken, ham, and all the fixings. Later, we attended the town's Christmas Eve dance. I danced with his beautiful daughter and felt like the town's honored guest. At 3 a.m., we returned to their home. One of the kids gave up their bed for me.

The following day, Mama hugged me and handed me a picnic basket for the road. Her husband stopped traffic at the edge of town and found me a ride into France. That evening, I opened the basket and wept. Beneath the food was a 100-peseta bill. Their generosity changed me. I vowed my home would always be open to travelers needing a place to stay, and for years, I honored that promise, welcoming and meeting travelers, seekers, and strangers from around the world.

In France, a sharply dressed man picked me up in his shiny new Peugeot. He spoke only French for an hour until he finally laughed and revealed he was an American expat selling life insurance to military families in Orleans. He took me in and helped me get a job at the NCO Club. It was risky since I was a draft dodger, but I passed myself off as a military dependent, which, of course, I was.

One night, I saw the club manager loading whisky into his car. He caught me watching and started digging into my background. Not long after, I received a letter from my

California draft board informing me I had been drafted almost two years earlier. "Report immediately," it read, ending with the cruelly ironic "Best wishes."

It was time to disappear again. I planned to go to Israel and live on a kibbutz where I had a friend. But Don, my host and new big brother, sat me down. "You don't want to be a man without a country," he said. Put your time in—two years. Then you're done." I decided he was right.

After two life-changing years in Europe, I returned to California. I stopped in New York to visit Anne, then hitchhiked home. I was determined, more than ever, to resist the war. I had already lain on train tracks in Berkeley to stop troop transports. I'd marched, been arrested, and stood in the streets. Now, I would resist from the inside and see where that would take me.

REFLECTIONS

Looking back on the time I cuckolded my father with one of his lady friends, I feel a deep wave of shame and sorrow. I hadn't realized it then, but I was reenacting his patterns, relating to women not as equals, but as sexual conquests, objects of desire, and status. I had inherited his wounded masculinity and acted it out. The remorse was genuine, but it would take years before I could break the cycle and start thinking and choosing differently.

The shame didn't come all at once—it took years to surface fully. On the surface, I was just a young man following desire. But underneath was a deeper fracture: I longed for maternal love and care, yet I tried to find it through seduction and performance. I wanted a partner who would both nurture me and make me look good—someone to fill the hole an absent mother leaves, while also serving as a sexual prize. The contradiction was always beneath the surface, but I didn't have the emotional tools to name it, let alone unravel it. I was chasing wholeness through serial relationships, while sidestepping the vulnerability that real intimacy demands.

My constant travel—the adventures, the hitchhiking, the wild parties and jazz-fueled nights—became a kind of anesthesia. As long as I kept moving, I didn't have to feel the more profound layers: the fear, the self-doubt, and the frozen grief lodged in my nervous system. I was disconnected from my body, living primarily in my head, and when that got too noisy, I numbed it with weed, wine, and women. The wandering gave me a sense of freedom, but was often a flight from the ache inside.

Restlessness became my rhythm.

I now see how many extraordinary people crossed my path and extended unexpected kindness, far more than I could recognize at the time. The Spanish policeman's family, the Archbishop of Canterbury, Don Stiles in France, the poet Ted Joans—each of them saw something in me I couldn't yet see in myself: a flicker of light, a trace of goodness, a quiet potential. Again and again, people offered care and recognition, but I didn't know how to receive it. The pattern repeated, I was seen, and pulled away, convinced I didn't deserve it or couldn't trust it. Still, their presence left an imprint. Even fleetingly, they reminded me I mattered, that I wasn't invisible.

Beneath the movement and mischief, I was starving for something I couldn't yet name. I wasn't just running away—I was also searching. A vague yearning pulsed beneath the surface, nudging me toward something more real, more whole. I devoured the writings of Hermann Hesse, Jack Kerouac, and Thomas Merton, not just as entertainment but as guideposts. Each carried a thread of the question I couldn't shake: What is my life for?

There was a stirring inside me, faint and persistent, like a whisper I couldn't quite catch. A sense that there had to be more than sex, drugs, rebellion, and the next wild adventure. Something in me was calling for depth. A calling of the soul. For healing. But I wasn't ready to surrender to it—not yet.

Though it may have looked like freedom from the outside, I was caught in a loop—repeating familiar dynamics, seeking resolution through reenactment. I haven't yet seen that true healing doesn't come from revisiting the same wounds in disguise, but from breaking the cycle with awareness, compassion, and the courage to choose presence over reaction.

Healing begins the moment we pause to notice our patterns—not as flaws to fix, but as messengers from within. Each reaction, each trigger, is a thread pulling us gently back to an unmet need, a buried wound, or a forgotten part of ourselves longing to be seen, heard, and embraced.

This awareness is the turning point. When we choose to meet these moments with curiosity instead of judgment, with compassion instead of criticism, we reclaim the power we once gave away. What felt like fate transforms into freedom. What felt like repetition becomes revelation.

And in that choice, a choice to stay present, to stay open, we step into something entirely new: a way of being that is rooted in wholeness, guided by love, and alive with possibility.

The next chapter isn't about self-improvement. It's about self-remembrance. Not fixing what's broken, but reuniting with what was always whole. This is the invitation to walk forward with tenderness, to trust the unfolding, and to know that the journey ahead holds more than healing.

It holds your becoming.

TOWARD WHOLENESS: MEETING TRAUMA WITH PRESENCE

> Trauma doesn't always announce itself with drama—it often hides in how we move through life: in our thoughts, habits, relationships, and reactions. These patterns can feel so normal that we stop noticing them, but healing begins when we do.

To heal is not to fix what's broken, but to honor the wisdom of our responses. What we call symptoms are often intelligent adaptations to overwhelming experiences. With compassion, we begin to integrate what was once fragmented and remember our innate wholeness.

We might notice a sense of disconnection from our bodies, emotions, others, and the natural world. Numbness or loneliness may follow, even in a crowded room. Reconnection begins with simple awareness: I am here. We remember we belong through breath, touch, movement, and presence.

A lingering feeling of "not enough"—of time, love, worth, or safety—can drive us to overwork, compare, or consume. Gratitude, even in small doses, invites the nervous system into sufficiency. It's not bypass; it's reclaiming our capacity to savor what is.

Trauma distorts time. It pushes us to rush, to escape discomfort, and traps us in a state of urgency. Healing invites slowness. In stillness, the nervous system settles. Life deepens—and so do we.

Control often masks fear. We grip tightly to people, plans, or outcomes, trying to feel safe. But safety arises when we loosen our hold and surrender—not in defeat, but in trust. Letting life move through us is a profound act of courage.

Perhaps most of all, trauma pulls us out of the present. We distract, dissociate, or numb rather than feel what once overwhelmed us. Presence is the medicine.

When we can stay with breath, sensation, or another human being, healing unfolds. We say, "I'm here. I can be with this."

Wholeness is not perfection—it's integration. Each symptom is a threshold. When met with awareness and care, it becomes a path back to ourselves.

Let this be an invitation—not to fix, but to remember. To soften. To return.

We often repeat emotional roles—such as caretaker, victim, or rescuer—in relationships without realizing why. These roles are taken to adapt, survive, and soften the pain of not being seen, felt, hurt, or held.

Importantly, repetition compulsion is not the same as OCD. While both involve repetition, OCD behaviors are driven by anxiety and attempts to control it; repetition compulsion is driven by the unresolved emotional charge of the past seeking expression or completion.

A Path to Freedom:

Bringing compassion and awareness to these cycles is the first step toward freedom. When we recognize the unconscious pull behind our actions—not with judgment, but with curiosity—we create the possibility of choosing something new. In this light, repetition is not failure, but an invitation: to return to the wounded places, this time with presence, support, and the capacity to transcend and transform.

CHAPTER EIGHT

Healing Journey Begins

*To heal is to touch with love that which
was previously touched by fear.*

Stephen Levine

My military career often felt like living inside the book Catch-22, a world where logic twisted in on itself and the absurd became routine. I take a peculiar pride in having entered and exited the Army as a private, a testament to a path less traveled. But that's a story for another book. The best I can say is I survived and I learned.

In 1968, I was honorably discharged from Fort Lewis, Washington. I had planned to return to school, but registration had closed when I got out. I stood at a crossroads, restless and hungry for movement and meaning. So, I packed up and headed to South Lake Tahoe for the winter, determined to learn to ski and figure out what was next for me. The crisp air and fresh snow felt like a reset button—a way to shed the rigidity of military life and step into something freer, wilder, more alive.

Winter in Tahoe was pure magic: long days on the slopes, rowdy après-ski nights, and a tribe of ski bums trading stories and laughter at the local bar. Barbara was the queen of the scene—her dad had helped build Heavenly Valley and other ski resorts—but her friend Maidye captivated me. She was cool, gorgeous, distant, and untouchable. Which, of course, to me, made her irresistible.

One night, Barbara asked me to give Maidye a ride home. I jumped at the chance. She slid into my new Volkswagen van without much fanfare, and we drove in silence through the pine-lined roads to her lakefront rental. No small talk. No smile. When we pulled up, she opened the door, jumped out, and vanished without as much as a thank you. Annoyed, I threw the van into reverse—wham! I backed right into a tree. She glanced over her shoulder, expressionless, then disappeared into the dark. That was it. I was hooked.

A few days later, I asked her to dinner. To my surprise, she said yes. When I arrived at her place, she told me to wait while she finished getting ready. I flopped onto her bed to relax and felt something hard under the pillow. I reached under and pulled out a silver pistol with a mother-of-pearl handle—engraved, heavy, and shockingly beautiful. It felt both intimate and loaded, like a warning and an invitation all at once. I didn't know what it meant, but I knew I was in.

By the end of the ski season, we were serious. We were married on a deck at the Virginia City Hotel, overlooking the wide-open desert that Maidye loved. We thought we'd pulled it off quietly, but her parents found out within hours. Bitty, her mother, was furious—she'd imagined a doctor or a lawyer for her daughter, not a "long-haired veteran war resisting candle making real estate selling schmuck." I didn't bother telling my father until much later.

'And the cat's in the cradle and the silver spoon
Little boy blue and the man in the moon...'
'When you coming home, son?' 'I don't know when'
But we'll get together then, Dad
You know we'll have a good time then...

Harry Chapin

After ski season, we moved to San Jose. I enrolled at San Jose State to study photography, got my real estate license, and started selling homes. But it was candle-making that truly lit me up. I'd taken a class through the Midpeninsula Free University at the San Gregorio beach and became obsessed with sculpting candles with driftwood, sand, and gems. Soon, they were in demand. Our Victorian dining room was transformed into a candle studio and shop.

Maidye fascinated me. A professional ski instructor and barrel racing champion, she had a near-mystical connection with horses. She understood them in a way most people never could—reading their body language, sensing their moods, and communicating in a silent dialogue of trust and instinct.

She was brilliant—one of the sharpest minds I've ever encountered, but she could be cold and aloof with people. While I was more social, she had little patience for small talk or surface-level niceties. She didn't argue or explain if she didn't like someone; she just turned away. Several times, she walked away, just leaving someone standing on our doorstep, staring through the window. I admired her blunt honesty. She was unapologetically herself.

At parties, she'd often sit in a corner and read a book while the rest of us mingled. I recognized that part of her—an outsider energy I carried, too—but I masked mine with charm and flattery.

Then Bitty, her mother, came to visit.

What was supposed to be a short stay stretched into months. A close friend of Margaret Mitchell (wife of Nixon's Attorney General, John Mitchell) and a major Republican donor, Bitty spent hours on the phone with Margaret, saying things like, "You tell Dick this…" She despised me. I was simply unworthy of her daughter.

After one too many nights enduring Bitty's contempt, I snapped. I made love to Maidye, packed a bag, climbed out the window, and left for Europe. I couldn't stand another minute in that house.

Don and his wife, Giesela, had recently visited from France. My candle-making impressed them, and they floated the idea of teaming up overseas. It sounded like a lifeline, a way out, time for a new adventure.

Once again, I ran, giving in to that old reflex to flee when things got too hard, heavy, or close.

I landed in Freiburg, Germany, nestled in the heart of the Black Forest. Giesela and I opened a candle shop there. We called it Hexenkunst, German for "witchcraft." It wasn't just a catchy name. It touched something deeper, something ancient and mysterious. To me, candles were never just ornaments. They were ritual, intention, energy, poured and shaped into light.

The shop drew people like a hearth in winter. Travelers, misfits, and wandering souls drifted in. Some crashed on the floor for a night. Others stayed to help pour wax or sell candles in exchange for a few Deutsche Marks and a warm place to land.

Germany hadn't been my favorite country when I traveled through years earlier, but the candle shop took off despite that. Most Germans were used to rigid, molded candles and traditional candlesticks—practical and predictable. I offered something entirely different: hand-poured, richly layered creations bursting with color and texture. Each candle felt more like a sculpture than something you'd simply burn. The originality stood out, and before long, word began to spread.

Sourcing materials, though, was a challenge. In California, I could pick up wax, wicks, dyes, and essential oils at will. In Germany, I had to get creative. I struck a deal with BASF to produce wax to my specifications. I fashioned molds from PVC pipes and metal trays. It was a kind of alchemy—improvising with whatever I could find, turning the raw elements into beauty.

Through Don, I gained access to U.S. military bases, which turned out to be a goldmine. Hungry for something familiar and handmade, American soldiers snatched up my candles, especially around the holidays.

But the vibe started to shift. The German police didn't like the energy around my shop—too many hippies, too much counterculture. I was drawing attention, but not the kind I wanted. Eventually, they stamped my passport and gave me 60 days to leave the country. I could've fought it, but I didn't want to. My time there had served its purpose. I felt the pull of California like a current calling me home.

By the time I was 27, it felt like I had already lived several lifetimes—loss, war, addiction, constant upheaval, and a marriage that never quite held together. In 1972, I returned to California and landed in Marin County, staying with my half-brother Peter in a stunning glass, oak, and teak home in downtown Mill Valley.

The place was a dream, a hidden Eden tucked behind the bustle of our little village. Roses climbed two-story trellises, cherry trees bloomed along the patio, and the view of Mt. Tamalpais was majestic. Evenings were spent by the fire or in the hot tub, watching the fog roll down the mountain like a dream you didn't want to wake from.

The day after I returned, the phone rang. It was Earl Shuttleworth from Fox and Carskadon Real Estate. I'd interviewed with him nearly two years earlier, just before I left for Europe. Now, out of the blue, he was offering me a job. The synchronicity was undeniable. I met with him, said yes, and easily slid back into selling real estate.

There was a woman named Alicia in our office. At first, she rubbed me the wrong way—too intense, too much. But something shifted when she got involved in est, a self-development training led by Werner Erhard. I couldn't deny the change in her energy—there was a lightness, confidence, and grounded presence. She invited me to an introductory meeting. I went. Something clicked.

I signed up on the spot.

Before the training, we were asked to write down what we hoped to gain from it. I went all in—over a hundred goals scribbled across the page. They told us, "The training begins the moment you register." And they were right. Things started to line up fast. My Uncle Pete helped me get a car. Within weeks, I sold a house, landed a listing, and had money coming in again.

A few months later, Earl offered me a chance to join a new real estate firm they were launching. I didn't hesitate. Around the same time, Peter moved out, and I took over the lease on the Mill Valley house—eventually buying it for $42,000. It felt like the universe was saying, You're ready.

Then came the est Training itself.

It was October 1972, and I arrived at the Jack Tar Hotel in San Francisco, joining about 150 other seekers. The ballroom was tacky—plastic chandeliers, hard straight back chairs, and fluorescent lights. Werner stepped onto the stage and didn't waste a breath:

"YOU ARE ALL ASSHOLES, AND YOU DON'T KNOW YOUR ASS FROM A HOLE IN THE GROUND."

Everyone froze. But it worked. He shattered any illusions of comfort right away. His style was raw and confrontational, but it cut straight to the heart of our unconscious. If you could stay open, he'd dismantle your story—and show you the freedom underneath.

He said, "The purpose of the est Training is to transform your ability to experience living so that the situations you've been trying to change or putting up with clear up, just in the process of life itself." That landed like a bolt of lightning. I realized how often I tried to fix the world around me instead of feeling and trying to understand the chaos, tension, and fear in my body.

After that first weekend, I walked through San Francisco as if seeing the world for the first time—everything seemed sharper, more vivid, more alive. It felt like the past, present, and future had collapsed into a single, undeniable reality. I saw how much of my life I had spent trapped in the past, believing life was happening to me. But now, I understood—it was happening through me. I was becoming a conduit for life.

That realization changed everything. Instead of being weighed down by old narratives, I asked a new question: What if life was happening for me? What if every experience, even the painful ones, was an invitation to grow? The est Training emphasized that true freedom comes not from escaping the past but from fully facing it—seeing our recurring patterns for what they are and meeting them head-on. By bringing them into awareness without judgment, we could finally stop reliving the same struggles and start truly living.

One of est's most powerful teachings was the distinction between what's happening and how it occurs to us—how we interpret events through our internal lens. Much of what we experience isn't based on objective reality, but on the stories we tell ourselves—stories shaped by past wounds, assumptions, and conditioned beliefs. We don't just see what is; we see through a filter we rarely recognize. Realizing this was like waking from a dream. It allowed me to question those old narratives and, more importantly, rewrite them. In doing so, I began to see possibilities that had never occurred to me before.

Another key teaching was integrity, not as a moral concept, but as alignment with our authentic selves. est taught that integrity is the foundation of power and effectiveness—when we are true to our inner knowing, transformation happens naturally. It also meant "honoring our word as ourselves." Precision in language required absolute commitment to doing what you said—no stories, explanations, or excuses.

> *Responsibility begins with the willingness to be cause in the matter of one's life. Ultimately, it is a context from which one chooses to live.*
>
> Werner Erhard

The distinction of Context brought another breakthrough—an unseen framework constantly shaping our perceptions, potential, and possibilities. I realized that how I viewed my life wasn't fixed, but filtered through my beliefs and perceptions. A simple shift in context—from "What I do doesn't matter" to "I make a difference"—had the power to change my thoughts and my entire way of being in the world.

This understanding was incredibly transformative in breaking free from limiting beliefs like "I'm not enough" or "I'm unlovable," patterns deeply rooted in past trauma. These weren't objective truths; they were narratives I had unknowingly carried for years.

Seeing them as mere interpretations rather than reality opened the door to profound change. I no longer had to be bound by old wounds. I could choose a new way of seeing myself and the world.

After completing the training, something stirred—I still had feelings for Maidye. We hadn't seen each other in nearly two years, though we'd exchanged a few letters while I was in Germany. I reached out, and she agreed to meet with me. I brought her to a Werner presentation, hoping she'd catch the spark I had. But afterward, when I asked her with hopeful anticipation. Her response was, "It was an interesting sociological experience."

And at that moment, I knew.

We were no longer walking the same path. Our marriage had been a beautiful detour, but it had run its course. We finalized a quiet, uncontested divorce. There was sadness, but also a strange peace. I had crossed into new territory—deeper, more authentic, and finally, my own.

REFLECTIONS

Maidye had a way of walking away—effortlessly—from people, places, and anything that no longer served her. At the time, I admired it. I mistook it for strength, even freedom.

But now I see something else.

Our relationship became a mirror, reflecting the unhealed wounds and unfinished business inside me. I was drawn to her fierce independence—maybe because I'd spent a lifetime chasing what I imagined she possessed: strength, freedom, safety, recognition, and a sense of worth I hadn't yet found in myself.

Our separation didn't feel like an ending. It was more like the quiet recognition of an old pattern. This time, I didn't cling or collapse. I simply let go. No drama, no spiraling pain—just a subtle shift, a quiet awareness settling into my body. In that stillness, something softened. I began to see how my longing for connection had been shaped by the silent ache of childhood—the tender, invisible efforts of a little boy who just wanted to be seen, held, and loved.

That ache had always been there, even when I couldn't name it. Looking back, I understand now that my acting out as a child wasn't rebellion for its own sake—it was communication. Each outburst, each rule I broke, was a flare sent into the night sky, a desperate signal for my father's attention. And even when it didn't work, I kept trying. Because being a "problem" at least made me visible.

But no matter what I did, I couldn't reach him. I couldn't make him see me. And yet, I idolized him. I longed for his approval. Deep inside, I believed he'd love me if I could become more like him.

But I never was.

Over time, I came to understand that it was never really about me. My father never recovered from losing my mother. Whenever he looked at me, I suspect he was reminded of her and everything he couldn't hold on to. Maybe he loved me in the only way he knew how. Perhaps he'd never truly felt loved himself.

The older I get, the more compassion I feel for him. I see now that he never truly had a childhood—life stole his innocence too soon, hardening him into someone who didn't know how to soften. He couldn't give what he'd never received. Understanding this lifted a weight I'd carried for decades: the belief that I was unlovable, unworthy, unseen. I can now recognize that as a story I told myself to make sense of what I couldn't comprehend as a child.

For years, I saw myself through the lens of my wounds. But life has a quiet wisdom—it sends teachers when we're ready to learn. One of mine was Werner Erhard. Through the est Training, I began to peel away the victim identity that had clung to me like a second skin. I came to see that life wasn't happening to me—it was happening through me. That realization opened a doorway I never knew existed.

Healing isn't about forgetting the past; it's about meeting it with new eyes. It's the alchemy of turning fear into understanding, anger into compassion, and pain into wisdom. It's reclaiming the parts of ourselves we once exiled just to survive. When we stop guarding against the ghosts of our past and bring awareness to our fractured places, we begin to inhabit our lives more fully.

And just when I thought I had reached the edge of transformation, more teachers appeared—each carrying a lesson I hadn't yet known I needed.

WHAT IS HEALING?

Healing is not a destination but a sacred unfolding—a return to the truth of who we are beneath the wounds, adaptations, and survival strategies that once kept us safe. It's the process of reclaiming the lost and fragmented parts of ourselves, restoring a felt sense of wholeness, safety, and aliveness.

It's not about fixing what's broken. We're not broken—we are human beings shaped by experiences that overwhelm our capacity to cope. Trauma interrupts the connection within our bodies, thoughts, feelings, and relationships. Healing restores those connections. It brings coherence to the nervous system, clarity to the mind, and openness to the heart.

Healing is inherently relational. We do not heal alone. We need spaces of safety and resonance, where our pain can be witnessed with compassion and our long-silenced truths can be spoken. It happens in the sacred field between presence and permission.

We're not asked to relive the past but to revisit it with greater support and capacity. The body—often misunderstood—is not the enemy but the guide. It carries both the imprint of trauma and the wisdom of healing. Through breath, movement, and attuned care, we begin to renegotiate what once felt unbearable. We learn to feel without being overwhelmed, to stay present in the face of discomfort, and to respond rather than react.

The path isn't linear—it spirals. Some days we touch joy, others we meet grief. Both are part of the process. Healing may look like slowing down, setting boundaries, letting tears rise, or finally receiving the love we once braced against. In these moments, we begin to shift from surviving to truly living.

Integrating what was once fragmented expands our capacity to love, connect, and feel a sense of belonging. Personal healing ripples out into the collective, making us safer for others and living as reminders of what's possible.

Ultimately, healing is love in action—love for the child who endured, love for the adult who keeps showing up, and love for the mystery of becoming whole. Healing is how we return to ourselves again and again.

CHAPTER NINE

Teachers & Awakenings

Education is not the filling of a pail but the lighting of a fire.

William Butler Yeats

I've always searched for something, though I wasn't entirely sure what. Unlike many, I never followed a singular career path. Instead, I moved from one profession to another, each holding my interest for a time before restlessness set in, a familiar pattern for those with ADHD.

My grandfather, hoping to guide me toward stability, arranged an interview at the Bank of America. I remember stepping into the high-rise in San Francisco, the elevator carrying me to the 52nd floor for a meeting with a senior VP, a close friend of my grandfather's. He spent most of our time praising my grandfather's virtues before extolling the benefits of a stable career at B of A.

But something became crystal clear as I sat in that towering office, looking out at a world I'd rather be in than observing from behind glass walls. The thought of being tethered to a 9-to-5 existence, confined to a sterile high-rise, felt suffocating. I left the meeting with a deep appreciation for my grandfather, but an even more profound certainty that I belonged elsewhere.

By my mid-20s, I had declared myself terminally unemployable. My path would be unconventional and unpredictable, one that I would define.

I explored many paths—photography, candle making, writing, even selling real estate—before setting off across the U.S. and Europe, taking on a range of odd jobs that taught me more about people than any classroom could. Eventually, I landed at IMSAI Computers, where I led the sales and marketing department for the world's first personal computer. That unlikely chapter launched me into the world of transformational education, first through est and Landmark, and later into a 30-year career in organizational development. My flagship course, "Presence, Power, and Performance," became both a financial success and a soulful calling. I thrived in the challenge, relished the freedom to choose my clients, and found deep joy in working on my terms.

Over the past decade, I have focused on trauma education and integration, guiding others through deep healing processes and programs. This feels like the culmination of my lifelong search, a path that weaves everything I've learned about transformation, purpose, and the human journey. In the 1960s and 1970s, I was captivated by writers such as Hermann Hesse, Ram Dass, Carlos Castaneda, Pema Chödrön, Jiddu Krishnamurti, and Jack Kerouac. Their words spoke to my longing for adventure and awakening, stirring a hunger for transcendence and the dream of breaking free from suffering into spiritual union and abiding peace.

Over time, I've realized that awakening isn't about reaching some ultimate enlightenment—it's not a finish line. It's a living, breathing process of healing, integration, and remembering. Each insight, each breakthrough peels back a layer, not just for me, but for the collective—a ripple that touches my family, culture, ancestors, and the broader web of life. True awakening is not solitary. It's relational. It occurs in connection with teachers, among themselves, and the sacred. It's a constant unfolding into deeper awareness, and often, it's messy. Growth asks us to face what we've long suppressed—wounds inherited from our ancestors, the shadows of our culture, and the fear-based patterns that shaped our lives. And yet, in this courageous unraveling, something beautiful emerges: a sense of belonging, purpose, and a shared evolution. This journey is not just mine—it's ours.

TEACHERS

WERNER ERHARD

After Werner Erhard started me on the healing path, I began deconstructing my image of myself as a victim of life. I realized that no matter how broken I thought I was, I could still live a happy, healthy life and contribute to the world. What follows is a look back at some of the most influential people in my life and evolution.

> *Happiness is a function of accepting what is.*
> *Love is a function of communication. Health is a*
> *function of participation. Self-expression is a function of*
> *responsibility.*
>
> Werner Erhard

Following the est Training, I became an avid student and teacher of the est and Landmark Education programs for many decades. I led their weekly seminars, the Advanced Course, the Communications program, and was a Wisdom Course leader. I loved teaching these programs. However, as I evolved, two things were missing for me: a spiritual context and little or no emphasis on the body or emotions, which ultimately became very important in my development.

Werner opened doors to a world of visionaries—artists, scientists, spiritual leaders, and changemakers—sparking deep growth and possibility. Even amid personal struggles, addictions, and the chaos of the '70s, I was surrounded by bold ideas, meaningful connections, and a sense of purpose. From salons and potluck dinners to gatherings like the World Future Society, that era was alive with creativity and hope. I knew then that I wanted my life to make a difference.

GABRIELLE ROTH

My work is giving space, learning of its way, and being in its service at the same time. We each have a responsibility to express ourselves. And in this expression is the key to our healing.

Gabrielle Roth

Werner was always connected with amazing people and thought leaders. One of those people was Gabrielle Roth, the "urban shaman," founder of the 5Rhythm® moving meditation practice and maps of consciousness. Her work focused on helping people become more aware by encouraging them to connect with their bodies and feel their emotions, an area where I was previously numb.

Werner hosted a party in 1974. It was a dance, though I didn't realize it at the time. I arrived late at the Jack Tarr Hotel in San Francisco. Everyone else had already gone in. Strange, ethereal music drifted through the doors, drawing me closer.

As I stepped into the ballroom, I was met by long vertical strips of multicolored silk, layered and swaying gently. I brushed through them, spinning into a shimmering world—and suddenly,

I was in a room filled with undulating bodies, moving to rhythms I had never heard before.

In that moment, something shifted. I felt like I had arrived. I was home.

That night marked the beginning of my lifelong connection with Gabrielle Roth and her teachings. Her dance opened something profound in me that had long been waiting.

Gabrielle passed away in October 2012, but I still feel her presence in my body, blood, and bones. After dancing with her in person and in spirit for over 50 years, her rhythm still moves through me.

The 5Rhythms® is a moving meditation practice that synthesizes elements from various indigenous and global traditions, including shamanistic, ecstatic, mystical, and Eastern philosophies. Additionally, it incorporates principles from Gestalt therapy, the human potential movement, and transpersonal psychology.

Unlike traditional dance forms, the 5Rhythms® practice does not involve following specific steps or learning choreography; there's no "right" or "wrong" way. The only prerequisites are having a body that breathes, a heart that beats, and a mind that's open to exploration.

Gabrielle Roth taught that "Waves move in patterns. Patterns move in rhythms. A human being is just that: energy, waves, patterns, rhythms—nothing more, nothing less."

She offered more than poetic insight—it was a map back to our true nature. When we begin to see ourselves not as fixed identities or stories, but as ever-shifting energy in motion, we open the door to transcendence. Embracing this phenomenon—

this fundamental truth of being—allows us to move beyond the suffering of our overactive, analyzing minds.

We drop into the body's intelligence instead of being trapped in restless thought loops or old narratives. We begin to move with the rhythm of life itself. In this space, healing happens not through force or analysis, but through surrender, breath, and movement. We remember that we are not broken—we are in motion.

After 15 years of dancing the 5Rhythms®, I completed the two-year teacher training and began teaching in Nevada City, Sacramento, and Reno. The practice taught me how to hold space for healing, creativity, and connection—and it became a lens through which I saw everything. I began mapping Flowing, Staccato, Chaos, Lyrical, and Stillness onto my organizational work, helping others launch businesses and navigate change. The rhythms revealed a universal pattern: grounding, action, disruption, flow, and integration—a cycle present in all creation, whether building a business, making love, or painting a canvas. It's a simple, elegant map for the human journey.

EKNATH EASWAREN MEDITATION

Live only for yourself, and you will never grow;
live for the welfare of all those around you, and you will
grow to your full stature.

Eknath Easwaren

EKNATH EASWAREN

In the early '70s, I attended a meditation retreat at Ramagiri Ashram in Marin County, CA, hosted by Indian-born spiritual teacher, author, translator, and interpreter of Indian religious texts, Eknath Easwaran. This was my first foray into meditation, and I found it highly challenging for my hyperactive, multitasking, disembodied mind. But Easwaren was gentle and encouraging. The experience from that weekend over 50 years ago still inspires me today. He taught me the prayer of St. Francis, which I would repeat in my meditation practice to calm and focus my mind. To this day, I still repeat this prayer when my mind succumbs to its incessant chatter.

PRAYER OF ST. FRANCIS

Lord, make me an instrument of your peace:
where there is hatred, let me sow love;
where there is injury, pardon;
where there is doubt, faith;
where there is despair, hope;
where there is darkness, light;
where there is sadness, joy.

O divine Master, grant that I may not so much
seek to be consoled as to console,
to be understood as to understand,
to be loved as to love.

For it is in giving that we receive,
in pardoning that we are pardoned,
and in dying that we are born to eternal life.

Amen.

Through years of stop-and-start practice, meditation and mindfulness helped me reconnect with my body and emotions. Meditating for an hour a day has become essential to my well-being. I've come to see that shutting down emotionally was not a flaw, but my nervous system's intelligent way of protecting me from the unbearable pain of childhood.

Rather than resenting this disconnection, I now honor it as a necessary act of growth and survival in a world that once felt too dangerous to feel fully.

Shadowwork has revealed a profound impulse for connection and healing that lies beneath our pain and sense of separation. The rage, anger, and fear I carried felt too overwhelming to face, so it seemed safer to remain numb than unleash the wild energy inside me—my inner Kali force.

Growing up on Strategic Air Defense bases only amplified my anxiety. I was unsettled watching pilots drink at the officers' club, knowing they'd fly planes armed with atomic bombs the next day. At school, we practiced hiding under desks in case of a nuclear attack, while at home, our linen closet became a makeshift food storage area.

Despite these precautions, I couldn't reconcile them with the reality of Hiroshima and Nagasaki. My fear shaped an early sense of the world as a place that was unsafe and unpredictable.

ROLFING

Strength that has effort in it is not what you need; you need the strength that is the result of ease.

Ida Rolf

ROLFING

Shortly after meeting Gabrielle, I discovered Rolfing, a deep inner body manipulation to relieve muscular and psychological tension and restore balance. My Rolfer, Dub Lee, had worked directly with Dr. Ida Rolf, the founder of the method. Though I didn't know much about it, many of us "esters" were trying it, so I gave it a shot. It was horribly painful, like ripping the tissues from the bone. After three sessions, he said, "Michael, you're the first person I've worked on who doesn't realize he has a body!" I made it to seven or eight sessions before quitting, but he was right—my body was numb..

BUCKMINSTER FULLER:
A WORLD THAT WORKS FOR EVERYONE

Dare to be naïve. You never change things by fighting the existing reality. To change something, build a new model that makes the existing model obsolete.

Buckminster fuller

A few years after connecting with Gabrielle, Werner met Dr. Buckminster Fuller, a visionary mathematician, designer, inventor, and global citizen. Together, they presented a series of talks titled *"Creating a World that Works for Everyone, with No One and Nothing Left Out."* In their dialogue, Bucky shared an analogy from his Navy days: trying to turn a large ship with only the rudder would tear it off, but using smaller trim tabs to turn the rudder could easily turn the direction of the big ships. He likened us to trim tabs in society, where small changes can spark significant transformation in the world.

> *Never doubt that a small group of thoughtful, committed individuals can change the world. In fact, it's the only thing that ever has.*
>
> Margaret Mead

Bucky Fuller's visionary thinking helped inspire Werner Erhard and John Denver to launch The Hunger Project—one of the world's most effective NGOs, dedicated to transforming the systemic roots of hunger through grassroots empowerment. At the heart of its mission are the Vision, Commitment, and Action (VCA) workshops, which guide participants from "I can't" to "I can" to "We can," empowering individuals and communities to envision and create a future of their design.

I was so moved by the possibility of making a global impact that I became an active supporter, hosting home seminars, sharing the mission, and diving headfirst into this work. I became a devoted fan of Bucky, whose presence embodied the wise and loving grandfather archetype. The last time I saw him, in 1983, he gently pinched my cheek and said, "Keep up the good work, Michael." It felt like a blessing from all the grandfathers of the world.

LYNNE TWIST

> *Our greatest wealth is in our ability to share and connect with others.*
>
> Lynne Twist

I led weekly est seminars, which later became Landmark Education, sharing the teachings with over a hundred people each week. It was a powerful training ground, and my life worked best when I immersed myself in this work. We often announced events and opportunities to create change in the community, but the highlight for me was always Lynne Twist. As the lead fundraiser for The Hunger Project, she lit up every room she entered—every word she spoke was pure inspiration.

> *When you let go of trying to get more of what you don't really need, it frees up oceans of energy to make a difference with what you have.*
>
> Lynne Twist

Lynne Lynne traveled the world with The Hunger Project, igniting hearts and galvanizing communities to take bold action toward ending world hunger. She inspired countless individuals and organizations to embrace compassionate leadership and create meaningful change. Her path brought her alongside some of the world's most revered changemakers, including Mother Teresa in Calcutta, the Dalai Lama, and Archbishop Desmond Tutu in South Africa. She seemed to move effortlessly among those shaping the future of humanity. Lynne embodied the spirit of global service, carrying a vision that sparked a sense of purpose wherever she went.

After years of tireless dedication, Lynne fell ill and took a break from the Hunger Project. Then she received a call which she later described as coming directly from the Amazon rainforest and Mother Earth Herself. In 1995, she and her husband, Bill, traveled to Ecuador with author John Perkins, responding to an invitation from the Achuar people.

The Achuar, an Indigenous People with a Rich Dream Culture, place profound importance on the wisdom of their dreams. In their collective dreaming, they saw that their land, traditions, and very way of life were under grave threat from the increasing climate disruption of our ever-expanding industrial society. Seeking allies beyond the forest, they extended a courageous invitation to help "change the dream of the modern world"—to awaken from the trance of overconsumption and shift toward a life-honoring culture rooted in balance, reciprocity, and reverence for the Earth.

I was honored to travel with Lynne and Bill to the Amazon several times. I became a leader of the "Awakening the Dreamer" Symposium, a powerful program dedicated to cultivating an environmentally sustainable, spiritually fulfilling, and socially just human presence on Earth. The journey invited participants to examine our current reality, uncover the unconscious assumptions fueling our global crises, awaken to new possibilities, and commit to meaningful action. Leading this work transformed me. It shifted my focus from getting what I needed to discovering what I had to give and awakened me to my place in a global movement for change.

IMSAI COMPUTERS

Through my work with Werner, I met Bill Millard, founder of IMSAI Computers, who created the first personal microcomputer based on the Intel 8080 chip. He hired me as head of sales and marketing. When IBM and Apple entered the market with superior machines, we adapted rather than competed. We converted our distributor network into franchises, laying the foundation for Computerland.

Bill was an influential mentor. From him, I gained a deep understanding of organizational systems and became fascinated with applying est/Landmark principles, like integrity, transparency, interconnectedness, and empowerment, to business. Though I was eventually fired, that experience sparked a three-decade journey into consulting, coaching, leadership development, team building, and launching start-ups.

PETER BLOCK

The essential challenge is to transform the isolation and self-interest within our communities into connectedness and caring for the whole.

Peter Block

After a brutal stretch of events in the mid-1970s, I returned to school and completed my Bachelor of Science in Psychology and Communications at Sacramento State, then earned a Master's in Organizational Development at Pepperdine. One of my advisors was Peter Block, the renowned author and organizational development innovator. I liked Peter so much I told him—half-jokingly—that if he didn't hire me, I'd camp on his lawn in Mystic, Connecticut, and ruin the neighborhood. He hired me, and I began teaching consulting skills with his company, Designed Learning. That marked the start of my journey into Organizational Development.

With hands-on experience in management and consulting, I discovered a deep passion for teaching Peter's work and helping heal fragmented organizational systems. I traveled to various companies, thriving on the dynamic nature of the work and growing more confident in navigating complex structures.

Eventually, I launched my own signature course, "Presence, Power, and Performance," which focuses on leadership, coaching, and communication. I found great fulfillment guiding individuals to tap into their potential and step into authentic leadership.

Peter also brought poet David Whyte into corporate settings. While working with Microsoft, they asked if I could collaborate with David. He joined me and completely stole the show. Of the twelve senior executives in the room, only one or two were still with the company two years later.

DAVID WHYTE

We learn, grow, and become compassionate and generous as much through exile as homecoming, as much through loss as gain, as much through giving things away as in receiving what we believe to be our due.

David Whyte

After our workshop, Microsoft initiated a work-life balance program because many employees had become burned out while working there. It was inspiring to see how David utilized poetry for healing, awareness, connection, inspiration, and conflict resolution in organizational settings. It became a big part of my teaching. One executive in a group I worked with at Prudential said, "You sound more like David Whyte than he does." That brought a good laugh to our group. Indeed, I learned a lot about sharing transformational poetry from David. I also sponsored him, producing several workshops for him in our Northern California area. I learned a lot about freedom and belonging from David.

You must learn one thing. The world was made to be free in. Give up all the other worlds except the one in which you belong.

David Whyte

David and I became friends, and I decided to go on one of his Ireland tours, where I had the good fortune of meeting John O'Donohue, the poet, priest, Druid, Jesuit, philosopher, and one of the most loving people I have ever met. John and I hit it off, and I also brought him to Nevada City several times to visit and do a "blast," which is what he called his sermons or teachings.

JOHN O'DONOHUE

One of the most beautiful gifts in the world is the gift of encouragement. When someone encourages you, that person helps you over a threshold you might otherwise never have crossed on your own.

John O'Donohue

There was always so much laughter and joy around John in Ireland and the States. I became hooked on Ireland and went on another tour with David and John. One night, we were in a pub in Ballyvaughan, County Clare, in the West of Ireland, having a bit of Guinness with John's brother PJ, when I innocently said, "I don't know why I keep coming back to Ireland. My ancestors are from Denmark, and I've never been there." Whereupon PJ piped up and said, "Of course, you love it here, sonny; yur fucking ancestors raped and pillaged their way through our country." I spit up my beer laughing, and we all howled. But it lingered with me, and I realized the horrible truth of the transgressions of my Viking ancestors.

One night when John was visiting, we'd already downed plenty of beer and wine at Friar Tuck's and got home past midnight. I was ready to crash, but John came upstairs with a bottle of Jameson's and said, "Sit down; time to talk." I couldn't refuse. We poured drinks, traded stories, and laughed until 2 a.m. John was a brilliant storyteller—larger than life, always encouraging of my work. His sudden death from heart failure at 53 was a heartbreaking loss. But his big heart lives on in his books, poetry, and my heart.

The following day, I woke with the worst hangover and pounding headache of my life. Meanwhile, John bounced out of bed, cheerful and ready for the day's "blast." Thankfully, my team had everything covered, as I was unable to function. John, as usual, was on fire—every word he spoke captivated the room.

During our lunch break, my tenant Arthur, neighbor Sue, and I strolled to a local restaurant. John took a separate table for some quiet time, giving us the perfect window to hatch a little surprise. Sue drove a horse and carriage in downtown Nevada City and arranged for her partner to swing by in full ceremonial dress.

When John stepped outside and spotted the carriage waiting, he burst into laughter. We all piled in, John and Sue lounging in the back, Arthur and I facing them up front, and rolled down Broad Street like a royal parade. A gaggle of kids ran alongside us as John waved theatrically, channeling Queen Elizabeth with his radiant, bearded grin.

Then Sue quipped, "John, you should be the Pope." He paused a moment, scratched his beard, grinned, and replied, "You know, you're right, and when I'm selected, I'm going to have Tina Turner sing 'What's Love Got to Do With It.'" We roared with laughter, tumbling out of the carriage and into the Veterans Hall, where the next round of magic was about to begin.

SANDRA INGERMAN

Whenever we experience trauma, a part of our vital essence separates from us in order to survive the experience by escaping the full impact of the pain.

Sandra Ingerman

Another profound influence in my life was my shamanic teacher, Sandra Ingerman. After years of reading about shamanic traditions and traveling to Peru and the Ecuadorian Amazon to work with Indigenous healers and plant medicines, I felt a deep calling to explore how trauma impacts the soul—how it dims our essence, silences our purpose, and fractures our connection to the divine within.

Sandra, "Sandy," as I came to know her, brought these teachings to life with clarity, humility, and a remarkable sense of grace. I'm deeply grateful for the years I spent learning from her. One teaching that especially resonated was the concept of "Soul Loss"—the understanding that trauma can cause parts of our soul to fragment, and that healing requires their intentional and loving retrieval.

I immersed myself in soul retrieval practices, joining many ceremonies and gaining profound insight. And yet, I noticed something: while the ceremonies often brought moments of deep healing, many people, once back in the rhythm of daily life, returned to familiar, self-defeating patterns. It became clear that healing the soul wasn't just about powerful moments but about integration and shadow healing.

Later, Sandy encouraged me to teach Embodied Shamanism through the Shift Network, a global community of evolutionary change-makers. As a faculty member, I wove shamanic wisdom, depth psychology, movement, and shadow work into an integrative path of healing and transformation.

This work naturally evolved into hosting the annual Shamanic Wisdom Summit, where I had the privilege of guiding rich, heartfelt conversations with shamanic practitioners worldwide for eight years. Together, we shared ancestral teachings with a global audience—until it was time for me to pass the torch and let the circle grow without me.

MY RADIO SHOW

In the early 2000s, someone from our dance community encouraged me to join KVMR, our local radio station, to share my music. I took their broadcaster training and began filling in on morning shows—spinning tracks and inviting inspiring guests to share their work. This evolved into a talk show called Conversations, later renamed WE Earth Radio when I moved the show to a Canadian station.

The show became a platform for exploring environmental education, wellness, and conscious evolution—a shift from ego-consciousness to eco-consciousness. It also became an author's showcase, a place "to heal the wounds that separate, alienate, and marginalize us." Hosting the show allowed me to meet some of the leading thinkers of our time. Whatever topic intrigued me, I'd invite the authors, read their books, and dive deep into conversation. I made no money, but the wealth of insight I gained was priceless.

I even paid to attend climate change conferences worldwide, fueled by a deep desire to learn and share what I discovered. Many of those powerful, heartfelt conversations are now archived on the WE Earth Radio podcast, which is available on Spotify, Apple, and other major platforms.

Below are just a few of the incredible and inspiring guests I've had the honor of interviewing. I remain deeply grateful for this unexpected journey that began with a spark from our beloved local radio station.

Our featured guests have included: Van Jones, Lynne Twist, Joanna Macy, David Whyte, Michael Mead, Joan Halifax, John O'Donohue, Vandana Shiva, Duane Elgin, David Korten, Barbara Marx Hubbard, Peter Russell, Brian Swimme, Rupert

Sheldrake, Andrew Harvey, Paul Hawken, Michael Pollan, Jean Houston, Ram Dass, Elisabet Sahtouris, Mark Nepo, Angeles Arrien, Sandra Ingerman, Hank Wesselman, Alberto Villoldo, Paul Ehrlich, Brother David Steindl-Rast, Bill McKibben, Riane Eisler, Raffi, Marianne Williamson,, Gregg Braden, Tara Brach, Gabrielle Roth, Bruce Lipton, Miranda Macpherson, Dan Siegel, Lynne McTaggart, Ervin Laszlo, Jack Kornfield, Adyashanti, Peter Senge, Otto Scharmer, Terry Real, Thomas Hübl, and many more…

THOMAS HÜBL

Unresolved systemic, multi-generational traumas delay the development of the human family, harm the natural world, and inhibit the higher evolution of our species.

Thomas Hübl

One of One of my most inspiring guests on WE Earth Radio was spiritual teacher Thomas Hübl, who has since become my primary teacher. His presence and wisdom immediately captivated me. Our first interview, centered around his book on Collective Trauma Healing, left me stunned by the depth of his insight. It had been a long time since I encountered a teacher who challenged me, pushing me to my edge and beyond. The last one had been Gabrielle.

Thomas's teachings brought me full circle, back to my roots in psychology, illuminating a deeper meaning and purpose within my own trauma. His words gave voice to what had long felt unnamed inside me. What once was a burden I needed to overcome transformed into profound intelligence, an opening to deep personal, collective, and ancestral healing. My relationship with trauma shifted from resistance to reverence.

With Thomas, I had finally found my home, where all the threads of my life wove together with purpose. Every challenge I'd faced, every insight I'd gained, seemed to lead to this moment. The first words I ever heard him say were, "We are living in a sea of trauma." Something in me lit up. Suddenly, I could see trauma not as a personal flaw or isolated struggle but as a deep, unspoken force shaping much of our world's individual, collective, and planetary challenges. In that moment, I understood that to heal humanity, we must begin by healing trauma in all its many forms and manifestations.

This journey led me to deepen my exploration through workshops and trainings with remarkable teachers like Gabor Maté, Peter Levine, Arielle Schwartz, Bessel van der Kolk, Dick Schwartz, Dan Siegel, Steven Porges, and many others at the forefront of trauma integration and healing. While much of this work was driven by a desire to tend to my wounds, Thomas helped me see that personal, collective, and ancestral healing are not separate paths but are deeply intertwined.

Looking back, it's clear I've always been on a path, even when I didn't know it. The people I met, the teachings I followed, the struggles I endured—it all feels, in hindsight, divinely choreographed. However, it wasn't until I encountered Thomas and his community that everything truly fell into place. The healing, expansion, and awakening I've experienced through this work have been transformational—personally, spiritually, and intergenerationally. This book exists because of that meeting. And I hope these words might light a path for others, too, toward wholeness, connection, and the deep, shared healing our world is longing for.

REFLECTIONS

*The only way we can build a better world
is to build it in this world. We need to use every moment to
co create the world we wish to live in instead of wishing for
it to happen tomorrow.*

Thomas Hübl

I used to feel ambushed by life. But over time, through the guidance of inspiring teachers and meaningful relationships, that sense of separation began to soften. I came to see that how I live truly matters, that my choices, presence, and way of being ripple outward. Setbacks still came, but many became catalysts for growth, urging me to reflect, learn, and evolve.

We can't grow in isolation. We need others, teachers, friends, witnesses, to talk with, reflect alongside, and be real. I bow deeply to those who have walked with me.

Connection is essential for our development. From birth to death, it shapes who we become. Yet without safety, we withhold ourselves. Our conversations stay on the surface, and we slip into isolation. We all long for connection, but real connection also scares us. Each time we're hurt or triggered and no one helps us process the pain, that experience can become frozen in our bodies, stored as numbness, tension, or dissociation. It piles into our trauma backpack, feeding the shadow parts we try to hide from others and even ourselves.

My teacher, Thomas Hubl, has a lovely practice of "feeling myself, feeling you, feeling me and the space between us." It begins with our practice of presencing, witnessing, and embracing our trauma responses. When we are in touch with our felt sense of the body, emotions, and mental activity, we begin to include others and sense them. Can you feel them feeling you? When we are truly connected, our bodies speak to bodies, emotions speak to emotions, and minds speak to minds. The more we engage in this embodied practice, the deeper we can feel each other, and the more we can feel our natural and innate capacity for connection.

Again, Awakening is a process, not a destination. It's imperative to let go of trying to be somewhere we are not and continue to deepen our capacity to cultivate presence, connection, and mutuality. This is perhaps the most essential quality for healing ourselves and our world.

FOUR-PART TRAUMA HEALING AND INTEGRATION PROCESS

Process healing begins with intention. We remain lost in old patterns if we don't set a clear course. To move beyond the pain of my past, I intended to release my anger, hatred, and blame toward Jean Severe. I slowed down, became still, and grounded myself in the present moment—this was the first step toward transformation.

Presencing – I anchored myself in the now moment, breathing deeply, feeling my feet on the ground, and noticing my emotions and sensations without resistance. This created a foundation of grounded safety and openness.

Witnessing – I invited an image of Jean Severe into my awareness. My body tensed, my breath shortened, and anger surfaced. Instead of pushing it away, I observed it. Then, I envisioned her as a child, and something shifted—compassion crept in. Seeing her innocence softened my perception and loosened the grip of my resentment.

Embracing – As I sat with these emotions, I recognized her pain intertwined with mine. Her coldness wasn't about me; it was her own unhealed wounds speaking. This realization opened space for curiosity rather than judgment. My body relaxed, and for the first time, I felt something unexpected—peace.

Integration – This shift didn't erase my pain overnight, but it transformed its hold on me. I began to see her actions as a reflection of her suffering, not a reflection on my worth. Over time, this understanding reshaped my relationship with my past, breaking cycles I had unconsciously repeated in my own life.

This process helped me begin to forgive Jean Severe. It illuminated how my nervous system kept recreating familiar wounds in my relationships.

Healing isn't about forgetting—it's about seeing with new eyes, making space for compassion, and allowing integration to unfold naturally through deepening awareness.

Through this work, I found freedom and greater inner spaciousness, not just from my stepmother's shadow but also from the repetitive patterns that had defined my life.

CHAPTER TEN

Death Wasn't All That Bad

It is worthwhile dying to find out what life is.

T. S. Eliot

In the early '70s, I made a living buying and selling real estate in Marin County. My stunning teak and glass bungalow in Mill Valley quickly became a hub of activity. It was a place filled with energy—lively parties, creative projects, and travelers passing through. On Sundays, I hosted potluck salons where I invited people to share ideas and engage in thought-provoking conversations, often inspired by my experiences with est. These gatherings were vibrant, and the discussions ranged from personal growth to deeper philosophical inquiries.

After purchasing the house, I created a serene Japanese garden with a hot tub perfectly positioned to face the majestic view of Mt. Tamalpais. This became my sanctuary, a place to relax and take in the beauty of nature after the buzz of my social events.

One spring, the Berkeley Massage School rented my sun-drenched Mill Valley home for a workshop. We set up massage tables beneath the cherry trees, just as they burst into bloom. As we took turns tending to each other's bodies, a breeze carried soft petals down like whispers from the sky. They mingled with oil and skin, gently pressed into flesh by warm, gliding hands. The air was thick with scent, sensation, and something electric—an invitation to surrender. It was a time of sensuality and awakening, of erotic exploration woven into the cultural fabric of the Bay Area's blossoming revolution. In that delicate rain of blossoms and touch, body, heart, and soul met in deep, unforgettable communion.

However, during a financially challenging period, I decided to sell the beautiful glass garden property to the manager of the Doobie Brothers, more than doubling the purchase price after less than two years. At the time, I thought I had made out. Today, that property is valued at $8 to $10 million. Looking back, I realize how much of a treasure I possessed back then, both in its monetary value and the beauty and memories it gave me. It was my first real home.

Soon afterward, I found another lovely home in the canyon in Mill Valley and purchased it with my friend Earl Shuttleworth, who had started the new real estate company where I worked. It was also a beautifully landscaped home that had belonged to a National Geographic photographer and his wife, who had retired and moved out of the area. The most exciting part was its fully equipped and functional dark room. I was excited about returning to photography, a passion I had earlier in my life.

Earl was a fastidious gay man, and we had some significant differences in our lifestyles. For Earl, everything had its place; for me, things were, well, let's say, more random. Our social circles were quite disparate, but for the most part, we got along pretty well. I had some pain in my wisdom teeth, so I went to a dentist in San Francisco, which some of my friends from est recommended. After consulting with the dentist, I decided to pull all four teeth out simultaneously and get it over with, not realizing what a severe procedure and a significant shock to the body I would have to endure.

It proved to be a very painful and prolonged extraction. I'm not sure how I made it home from San Francisco. I'm sure I wasn't driving. I suspect a friend brought me back to Mill Valley. I took painkillers and went to bed upon arriving home. I woke up gagging on blood and stumbled to the bathroom, and that was the last thing I remembered. Earl came home later that evening and found me unconscious in a pool of blood on the bathroom floor. He called an ambulance to take me to the hospital.

The next thing I remember was that I was lying on a gurney surrounded by people in white coats who were frantically scurrying about with concerned looks on their faces. I heard them say I had no vital signs. Then I realized I was hovering above, looking down at myself as if from a convex mirror or a fisheye lens. I felt very calm and peaceful, and you might even say ecstatic. It was curious looking down on my body lying on the gurney. I thought about my mother and wondered how death was for her. It all seemed sort of a matter of fact, this whole business of dying. I felt no fear, just an overwhelming feeling of peacefulness and curiosity.

Then, the strangest image came to me—so vivid, so unlike anything I'd known. I saw a hand and arm reaching down toward me, translucent and made entirely of light. It wasn't just a vision; it felt real, alive. I felt an overwhelming urge to reach up, to take hold of it. But just as I began to lift my hand, a thought came—clear and certain: No, I have things to do in this life. I pulled my hand back. In that instant, I came to—awake again on the rolling deathbed. For days, I drifted in and out of consciousness as the doctors replenished my blood and slowly brought me back. But something had changed. I had touched the edge of something vast and mysterious—and returned.

From the way my family treated my mother's death, I learned that death was something to fear—a mark of shame or failure, especially when tied to mental illness or suicide. But during that profound experience, I saw death differently—not as an end, but as a passage, a sacred return to the ancestral stream. Since then, my understanding of ancestors has deepened. Their bodies may be gone, but their lives—their struggles, resilience, wisdom—live on in us, encoded in the cellular memory of our flesh.

When I began studying shamanism and working with family constellations, my ancestors emerged as the allies I never knew I had. Our bodies, like a living Library of Alexandria, hold everything: the famines, wars, displacements, and also the strength, resourcefulness, and insight that carried them forward. All of it lives in us. Through their survival, we came to be. Life wants to live—and it wants to live through us. We are the living proof of this evolutionary unfolding.

Death is the only wise advisor that we have.

Carlos Castenada

REFLECTIONS

Looking back, I see that this brush with death was a turning point, though I couldn't have known it then. Confronting death and feeling an unexpected sweetness in its presence awakened something deep within me. It was a spiritual opening. As Castaneda wrote, "When you need an answer, look over your left shoulder and ask your death." Death became not a threat, but a wise teacher—a compass in times of crisis and confusion. In befriending it, I learned to live more fully in the present, to cherish the gift of life, and to honor the sacred unfolding of my soul's journey.

Accepting death's inevitability cracked open the my spiritual path. It called me beyond the physical into the mysteries that lie beneath the surface of daily life. It loosened my ego's grip and made space for a more profound reverence—for all experiences, for the preciousness of being alive. Knowing our time is finite sharpens our appreciation. It invites us to live more fully, honor what was passed down through our ancestors, and consciously shape what we pass on to future generations.

The near-death realization, "I have things to do in this life"—combined with my work with Werner Erhard, Lynne Twist, Buckminster Fuller, and the Hunger Project shaped my understanding of purpose. What does it mean to live a committed life? The Hunger Project was about more than ending hunger. It was about a fundamental shift in consciousness. It helped me see hunger not as inevitable but as something we could end by transforming the systems of inequality that sustain it. I didn't fully grasp the power of that mindset shift at the time, but it planted a seed that would grow. I began thinking less about my struggles and more about our shared humanity. That shift alone is was healing.

The Hunger Project is built on a bold and deeply human foundation: All people are born free and equal in dignity and rights—including the right to food, health, and education. Its work empowers women—those most directly connected to the food supply—mobilizing local communities and nurturing leadership from within. To date, it has trained over a million people worldwide. My involvement showed me that committed, purposeful action rooted in dignity doesn't just change the world—it transforms the person taking the action. At the time, I was still living with trauma symptoms, reactive patterns, tension, numbness, and an addiction to busyness. But something deeper was moving. I couldn't name it then, but I was evolving—from a survivor into a global citizen. I was beginning to sense that my life mattered and that I was intimately woven into a much larger whole. In embracing death, I began to embrace life and discover a deeper gratitude for life.

For most of my life, I wrestled with a sense of lack. No matter how much I accomplished, it never felt like enough. There was always a low-level anxiety—would I make it? Would there be enough? These fears were rooted in childhood, passed down generationally, and reinforced by a culture steeped in scarcity. But they weren't just mine. They were part of a collective mindset.

Everything began to shift after my brush with death. I experienced profound peace in that liminal space—a connection to something beyond myself. Returning to life, my old fears began to loosen. The obsession with survival began to give way to a longing for my life to be a meaningful contribution.

The deep desire to be seen, valued, respected, and connected transformed into a larger vision for my life. I resonated with the visionaries I'd studied—Fuller, Erhard, Roth, Twist, and others—who spoke of a world that works for all. This wasn't abstract. It felt like a calling. A new question emerged: What if, instead of focusing on securing personal survival, we built systems centered around the well-being of all?

I began to see that my relationship with money—marked by fear, control, and striving—was part of a larger collective story rooted in the trauma response of separation and self-protection. I saw how our current economic model feeds on fear, reinforcing inequality, individualism, separation, and disconnection. But what if we changed the story?

What if we saw money not as a symbol of power or security but as a tool for healing, service, and connection? What if sufficiency—enough for all—was the new measure of success?

This wasn't just philosophy; it became practical. I gradually began participating in a broader healing process by shifting my mindset from one of scarcity to one of sufficiency. Personal transformation became a ripple in the collective field. I realized that by doing our inner work, we would begin to shift the collective consciousness of the culture.

This transition—from fear to purpose, from isolation to interconnection—is what the world needs most. Our economic systems are failing not because of a lack of resources but because they are built on fear. True transformation begins when we dare to imagine—and work toward—a world where no one and nothing is left out.

THE MYSTICAL PERCEPTION OF DEATH

You may die a hundred deaths without a break in the mental turmoil. Or, you may keep your body and die only in the mind. The death of the mind is the birth of wisdom.

Nisargadatta Maharaj

Death is not the end—it is a threshold, a soft veil parting to reveal a deeper truth. From the soul's perspective, it is not a failure or punishment, but a sacred passage, a return to source. We die a thousand little deaths in this life—of identity, of certainty, of control. Each one whispers the same invitation: Let go. Evolve.

The mystics speak of ego death—the crumbling of the false self, making room for something vaster, wiser, more true. It is not destruction, but transformation. Like the snake shedding its skin, like the caterpillar dissolving into imageless goo, we dissolve to become something new.

Near-death experiences echo this truth. Those who return often speak of timelessness, light, union, and love that defies words. It's as if they tasted the edge of the Infinite—and it changed them.

To embrace death is to embrace impermanence. Everything born will pass. And yet, nothing is ever truly lost. The soul remembers. Life reshapes. The cycle continues.

What if we let go of our fear of death—and instead, let it teach us how to live? To love more deeply. To hold things lightly. To walk with reverence, knowing this moment is sacred because it will pass.

When we welcome death as a teacher, we begin to truly live.

REFLECTION: SITTING WITH DEATH

Find a quiet place. Sit or lie down comfortably.
Close your eyes. Let your breath soften.

Bring your awareness to your heart. Imagine it as a doorway.

Now, gently invite the presence of death—not as fear, but as a wise teacher, a quiet companion. Ask:

What are you here to show me?

What am I holding too tightly?

What is ready to be released?

Let the questions hang like stars. Listen with your body.

Feel what arises—grief, peace, resistance, relief.

Now breathe into the truth of impermanence.

Everything changes. Everything passes.
And still—something endures.

Inhale presence.

Exhale surrender.

When you're ready, open your eyes.

Carry the wisdom with you, gently, into your day.

CHAPTER ELEVEN

Sonia Romance & Reality

Being deeply loved by someone gives you strength, while loving someone deeply gives you courage.

Lao Tzu

I would sell and buy another home every few years to make money. The rhythm mirrored my own restless heart. One day, standing in the living room of my Mariposa Street home in San Anselmo, a moment stopped me. Out the window, I saw her—petite, radiant, magnetic. She was laughing with a neighbor, her presence lighting up the street like morning sun breaking through fog.

I called my roommate Calvin, "Hey, Cal, check this out." I couldn't take my eyes off her. He sighed, pulled away from his magazine, and joined me.

"Wow," he said.

"I'm going to marry that girl," I said, half-joking, but feeling an irresistible pull, a deep heart longing.

"You don't even know her name," he scoffed.

"I don't need to. I just know."

And I did.

Later, I learned her name was Sonia. She lived in San Francisco and worked for my dear friend, Kress. When I asked Kress to introduce us, she hesitated. "No, Michael," she said, "she's in a relationship." I pressed gently. "I just want to meet her," I said. Eventually, she relented—but warned me she would be with her partner.

Kress invited us all to dinner. Sonia came alone. During the meal, she announced that she and her partner, David, were breaking up. Within two weeks, we were dating. A month later, we were living together. I was head over heels. Within a year, I proposed. She said yes.

For three golden years, we were inseparable—wildly in love, spiritually awake, physically alive. We dove into Landmark Education, read books aloud to each other, traveled, hiked, skied, and danced through life like two kids discovering joy for the first time.

Once, my new car broke down on a joyride in West Marin. I called AAA and had it towed back to the dealer. We hitched a ride to a tiny town called Marshall and ended up at a tavern where we danced, laughed, and charmed the waitress into finding us a lift home. Two strangers offered rides—one in a Ferrari, one in a Cadillac. I took the Ferrari. Sonia, wisely, chose the Caddy. Our drivers turned out to be neighbors in San Anselmo. That night ended in laughter and new friendship over drinks in our home—one of those spontaneous, perfect days that etches itself into memory.

We returned to Marshall often. I once joked that Tomales Bay was where all the tamales were grown. Sonia, raised in Montreal, believed me. Later, she repeated the story to friends. When she realized I'd been teasing, she laughed and playfully boxed my ears. Her humor was quick, gentle, and forgiving.

One of my fondest memories occurred during a Landmark program on "Impeccability and Presence." We'd been scrubbing the floor of our old Victorian kitchen with toothbrushes when we decided to do a "Be With"—a silent practice of sitting face to face, gazing into each other's eyes. As we settled into the familiar process, something extraordinary happened. I suddenly felt myself dissolve, transcending the moment—I looked through her eyes into my own, and she, through mine, into hers. The sensation was so powerful that we both jumped off our cushions, startled. It was a shared moment of pure connection and transcendence that deepened our intimacy in a way nothing else had. I've never experienced anything like it again, though I often share the "Be With" practice in my workshops, hoping others might glimpse the same magic.

On another trip, we drove to Aspen in the new little red BMW I had bought for Sonia's birthday. We packed our bags and set off for a week of skiing with friends. The drive from California to Aspen felt like an adventure in itself. The crisp mountain air, the anticipation of the trip, and the joy of being together created a magical atmosphere. We had only two tapes in the car: John Denver and Olivia Newton-John. We played them on repeat, belting out songs like 'Let Me Be There' and 'Take Me Home, Country Roads' at the top of our lungs, our voices blending with the hum of the road.

But Aspen also raised a shadow. We met a charming man who invited us to his lavish apartment one night. One drink led to another, along with a joint, and he proposed a threesome. It was the 1970s. We said yes. But as I watched another man touch Sonia, something old and buried tore open in me—abandonment, betrayal, the ghosts of my childhood. I never told her. We moved on, but the wound lingered quietly, shaping things unseen.

Still, most of those years were joyfully, intensely alive. We dreamed together, laughed easily, and found magic in the mundane. I had just become Director of Sales and Marketing for IMSAI Computers, a pioneer in personal computing. It was an electrifying time, full of innovation and possibility—and through it all, Sonia was by my side, grounding me in love and reminding me what truly mattered.

She was more than a partner. She was a mirror, a muse, and a moment in time that felt timeless, eternal.

While I was chasing the early waves of the tech revolution, Sonia was running a friend's dress company—a perfect canvas for her creativity and leadership. She was all heart and style, gracefully managing everything from design to sales. People were drawn to her. She was vibrant, dedicated, and had an effortless way of making others feel seen.

Though we were both immersed in our careers, we never stopped showing up for each other. After long days, we shared dinners, stories, struggles, and quiet moments. Ours felt like a true partnership—built on mutual admiration, respect, and a love that felt steady and deep.

It felt like we had everything—passion, purpose, and a bright future full of promise. Then, we got pregnant.

For Sonia, it stirred something long buried. At sixteen, she had secretly given birth and placed her daughter up for adoption, hiding it from her parents. She never met that child. The loss lived quietly in her bones. This new pregnancy unearthed old grief, grief that had never truly been given space to heal.

For me, it awoke childhood fears I thought I'd outgrown—fear of abandonment, of not being enough, of loving and losing.

My history was a trail of vanishing: my mother, my dog, and my father, in his way. I was thrilled to become a father, but underneath, I was terrified that it might drive a wedge between us, that somehow, I might lose Sonia too.

At the same time, my career at IMSAI began to unravel. I was let go—officially for not keeping precise records, though the truth ran deeper. Years later, I'd learn I was neurodivergent—ADHD, specifically. Back then, I didn't have a name for it. I knew that numbers and detail work baffled me, and that shame lived in every missed report or forgotten task. I compensated with charm, intuition, hard work, and vision, but it wasn't enough in a company built on precision.

It was over when my new assistant exposed my struggles to the founder, my mentor. I was fired days before IMSAI transitioned into Computerland, missing out on stock options, bonuses, and a seat at the table of a revolution I helped build. The loss hit like a punch in the gut.

I sat in my car outside the building, paralyzed. Tears streamed down my face as shame wrapped around me like a fog. All I could think about was Sonia—pregnant, glowing, vulnerable. How could I tell her? How could I be enough now?

We still had a small income from a side business selling vitamins and health products, and I clung to that sliver of hope. I threw myself into a new venture—opening a health-conscious café at a racquetball club in Marin, called Off the Wall at Wall Bangers. The idea had promise. Early feedback was encouraging. The opening night buzzed with energy. Beer, smoothies, chatter—it felt like a fresh start.

But racquetball players don't want meals after they've played hard. They want something light, fast, and hydrating. Despite my best efforts to adapt, business dwindled. My dream of a vibrant, post-workout eatery faded into a trickle of loyal friends and empty tables.

Stress piled on. The baby was coming. The bills didn't stop. My confidence crumbled under the weight of uncertainty. I was trying hard to prove myself, be strong, and succeed—but the harder I pushed, the more I feared I would be abandoned again. The fear from my early childhood losses was overwhelming. My younger wounded self was taking over.

The neurodivergence I didn't yet understand made everything more complicated—details slipped through my fingers, and the creativity and deep connection that were once my strengths felt muted beneath layers of shame and fear anxiety. I was lost in a dark, lonely period, crushed by the relentless weight of failure. Each day felt heavier than the last, and no matter how hard I tried to reframe my challenges or imagine turning them into strengths, the fear, shame, and self-doubt were all-consuming. I couldn't see a way out.

I wanted to be there for Sonia, to show up as the partner she needed and deserved—but I was drowning. She was carrying her grief, silently unraveling under the weight of a past she rarely spoke of. The changes in her body, the hormones, the memory of the daughter she had given up for adoption—often left her curled on the floor in tears. On the outside, she looked composed and strong, but I could feel the fear radiating from her. And I was terrified, too. We both needed comfort, presence, reassurance—things neither of us could fully give the other at that time. The silence between us grew heavy, thick with everything unsaid. We still occupied the same space, but emotionally, it felt like we were stranded on separate islands, each reaching out but unable to touch.

Then, on July 4th, 1977, our beautiful daughter, Sasha, was born.

I was flooded with joy—and terror. I wanted to meet this moment with strength and grace, to rise as a father and partner, but I felt unsteady, cracked open by all that had come before. And I was drinking heavily to kill the pain.

We had planned a home birth, envisioning something sacred and calm. But when complications arose, our dream dissolved into hospital lights and beeping machines. The labor was long and grueling. Sonia was in pain, her body and spirit pushed to the edge. I sat beside her, helpless, trying to offer comfort while quietly unraveling.

Inside, I was breaking down—ashamed, hollowed out, and barely holding on. The weight of recent failures clung to me. I couldn't stop the loop of self-doubt: I'd lost my job, the business was faltering, and now, I wasn't even sure I could be the husband or the father I longed to be.

When Sasha finally arrived, I held her against my chest, her tiny fingers curling instinctively around mine. She was perfect. Her presence was anchoring, a small but steady heartbeat against the chaos that threatened to pull me under. In that first moment, I was flooded with wonder, with awe, with love so fierce it felt like it could tear me open. But beneath it all was an aching grief, a silent mourning for everything that had already slipped away.

The intimacy Sonia and I once shared had become a faint echo, worn by time and strained by everything we couldn't say. The connection that once lit us up now flickered in the background, dimmed by exhaustion, unspoken resentments, and the quiet loneliness that had crept into our bed. We weren't just lovers anymore. We were parents. And the weight of that transformation settled into my bones like winter.

I wanted to rise to the occasion—to be the father she could trust, the partner she could lean on, the man I imagined myself becoming. But the truth was, I was unraveling. The joy of Sasha's arrival was pure and total—but it braided itself around a sorrow I couldn't name, not for her, but for the dream that had once brought us together. A dream that now felt like it was cracking under the pressure of reality.

Still, I held our daughter close. Her breath was soft and rhythmic against my chest. And something stirred—a fragile flutter of hope, or perhaps the faintest whisper of resolve. A sense that maybe, just maybe, I could still find my way back to myself.

But I was caught in the space between who I longed to be and who I feared I had already become.

The restaurant limped along, a daily reminder of the pressure mounting on every front. Sonia drifted deeper into her own silence, her pain folding in on itself like paper. We moved through the days like ghosts—haunted, polite, exhausted.

And I waited. For a sign. A break. A moment of clarity. Something to tell me how to hold together all that was slipping through my fingers.

But nothing came. I couldn't imagine what was to come.

REFLECTIONS

Looking back, Looking back, the patterns are painfully clear. My father's absence after my mother's death left a hollow space where safety should have been. My mother's mental illness and suicide when I was just two and a half carved a wound so deep it shaped the very architecture of my being. Love, loss, abandonment, fear, and shame became my native tongue.

That early trauma didn't just hurt me—it defined me. It set the tone for how I would relate, attach, and come undone. As time passed and more losses followed, friends gone, loved ones dead, grief wrapped itself around me like a second skin. I was too numb to notice it at the time, but I kept finding myself in relationships that echoed those early wounds. I wasn't healing. I was reliving. Haunted by what I hadn't yet integrated, I vanished into my pain. My adult self faded. The frightened boy was frozen in time, feeling unseen and unfelt, aching to be held.

When Sonia began to pull away, something ancient tore inside me. Her mistrust didn't just hurt, it shattered. I wasn't just losing connection with my partner; I was standing again at the feet of my mother's hanging body, abandoned, terrified, alone. I couldn't face that. I told myself I was protecting her from my darkness, but the truth was, I was protecting myself from feeling too much, from falling apart.

Shame gripped me. Fear hollowed me out. I disappeared—not only physically, but emotionally, relationally, and spiritually. I stayed in the room, but I wasn't there. I'd inherited that pattern from my father: disappear when it gets too hard. Escape into work, busyness, and anything but the stillness where grief lived. And I did.

Sonia was steady, grounded—like a Cadillac built to endure. I was more like a Ferrari: fast, reactive, impossible to maintain. She embodied the safety and consistency I'd always craved but never believed I deserved. So I raced ahead—not for the thrill, but out of terror. Slowing down meant feeling. And feeling meant facing a lifetime of sorrow I'd kept locked away.

When the betrayal at work happened, it didn't just take my job but my sense of worth. The floor beneath me gave way. I lost my footing in every direction. At home, the gap between Sonia and me widened into silence. She tried to reach for me, but I was too ashamed to meet her. I felt like a failure, not just as a provider, but as a man, a partner, a father.

One night, in the stillness of our living room, she said quietly, "I feel like you're not here with me." Her voice was calm, but it cut through me. And she was right, I wasn't there. Not with her. Not even with myself. I looked down, swallowed by shame. I didn't know how to respond, so I said nothing. Silence was a familiar shield.

But something cracked open at that moment.

I saw the loop. I saw how my fear of abandonment was recreating the very thing I dreaded. I was repeating the pattern, again and again, handing down my pain like an heirloom. And for the first time, I didn't run.

I stopped.

Not because things were better—they weren't. Sonia and I were still circling each other from a distance, wounded and wary. But something in me shifted. I made a quiet decision to stay. To sit with the ache. To stop pretending I wasn't bleeding. It didn't fix anything overnight, but it was a start. A flicker of something real. Not for Sonia. Not even for Sasha. For me. For the boy who never got to feel safe. For the man I still hoped to become.

I wanted to feel it all—the sorrow, the rage, the longing—but I was numb. Frozen in a body that had learned too well how to shut down. Still, some part of me knew: if I were ever going to live fully, I'd have to stop running from the pain. I would need to begin feeling my emotions.

What I didn't know—what I couldn't possibly have imagined—was what was coming.

The kind of rupture that cracks time in two.

The kind of grief you don't walk away from the same.

But that's another chapter.

THE GIFTS OF EMOTIONS: A JOURNEY INTO EMBODIED AWARENESS

I would love to live like a river flows,
Carried by the surprise of its own unfolding.

John O'Donohue

Emotions are the language of our inner world, the threads that weave our experiences into a cohesive whole. They are how we connect to ourselves, others, and life itself.

Without them, we lose touch with our humanity. Avoiding emotions doesn't make them go away—it only buries them, where they fester, influencing our actions and reactions in ways we don't understand. Unintegrated emotions will eventually lead to health issues. Feeling our emotions, as painful as they can be, is the gateway to healing. It allows us to release what we've held onto, make sense of our experiences, and open ourselves to the possibility of growth, connection, and transformation.

Emotions are the raw, primal language of the body—energy in motion, vibrant and alive. On the other hand, feelings are their mental counterparts, shaped by memories, learned behaviors, and past experiences. Together, they create the rich tapestry of our human experience.

While often used interchangeably, emotions and feelings are distinct. Emotions are immediate, visceral responses to events—a quickening heartbeat, a flush of heat, or a sinking sensation in the gut. Feelings arise as the mind interprets these bodily signals, weaving them into stories and perceptions that color our reality.

Both emotions and feelings are essential to our well-being, but healing and integration must begin with the body—the vessel where emotions live, flow, and sometimes get stuck. We can process and release these energies by tuning into the body's wisdom, creating space for clarity, balance, and wholeness.

Emotions are neither good nor bad; they are elemental forces of life energy essential for our health and growth. They connect us to ourselves, to others, and to the world. They are how we relate and communicate, often bypassing words altogether.

Emotions speak directly to other people's emotions, not the mind. When fully embodied, emotions allow us to meet life with presence and congruence.

However, many people, like me, are disconnected from their emotions, either dissociated or overwhelmed, leaving them unable to feel their own emotions or empathize with the feelings of others.

Emotional maturity involves grounding these energies in the body, allowing them to flow without becoming stuck or overwhelming. In doing so, we gain access to their gifts, transforming our relationships with ourselves and others.

Fear: The Gift of Awareness

Fear is an essential guardian, heightening our awareness and focus in the face of danger, real or imagined. Rooted in the kidneys, fear awakens instincts, clarity, and readiness. But in its unprocessed form, fear can paralyze us, locking us in cycles of anxiety about loss or change. When adequately embraced, fear transforms into excitement and dynamic engagement with life. It asks us, What action needs to be taken right now?

Anger: The Boundary Protector

Anger arises to defend our integrity when our boundaries are violated. Held in the liver, it fuels conviction, honor, and healthy self-esteem. Authentic anger is precise and justified, guiding us to restore balance and protect what matters. Bottled-up outrage, however, becomes destructive while ungrounded anger overwhelms us. When expressed authentically, anger often transitions into compassion, helping us understand others while remaining true to ourselves. It asks us, What must be protected or restored?

Sadness: The Power of Release

Sadness helps us let go of attachments and expectations that no longer serve us. Held in the lungs, it connects us to our vulnerability and clears space for new beginnings. Avoiding sadness results in superficial happiness, while embracing it leads to authenticity and renewal. It asks us, What must be released or rejuvenated?

Joy: The Energy of Expansion

Joy is the natural outcome of emotions flowing freely. Held in the heart, it is vibrant, light, and spontaneous—a whole-body experience of connection and gratitude. True joy comes when we allow fear, sadness, and anger to move through us without suppression. Joy invites us to live fully in the present, celebrating the radiant beauty of life.

Compassion: The Fruit of Emotional Integration

Compassion is born from experiencing and integrating fear, anger, sadness, and joy. It allows us to feel another's emotions while staying grounded, responding with what is genuinely needed. Compassion isn't about pity but about presence—it supports others in accessing their authentic emotions and offers what serves their growth. Compassion embodies the flow of all emotions, rooted in the stillness from which they arise.

The Body: The Container for Emotions

Our bodies are the vessels through which emotions flow. When emotions are grounded in the body, they move like a river, dynamic and alive. Fear contracts, anger ignites, sadness releases, joy expands, and compassion integrates. By cultivating embodied awareness, we create space to meet emotions with clarity and grace, transforming stress and overwhelm into a sense of spaciousness and connection.

Living in Emotional Congruence

Emotions are the fabric of our relatedness, the undercurrent of all human connection. To fully experience and share this gift, we must feel them in our bodies, allow them to flow, and let them guide us toward greater authenticity and wholeness. When we embrace the gifts of our emotions, we unlock the wisdom and vitality needed to navigate life's challenges with resilience and love.

CHAPTER TWELVE

Sonia - The Unimaginal

That the unconscious is trying to resurrect the past, is not a matter of habit or blind compulsion but of a compelling need to heal old childhood wounds.

Harville Hendrix

The first weeks after Sasha's birth were a whirlwind—sleepless nights blurred with emotional highs and crushing lows. Becoming a father should have felt like a new beginning, but instead, it unearthed fears and insecurities I had buried for years. Holding my daughter in my arms was both joyful and terrifying. Beneath the surface, an unrelenting anxiety gnawed at me: I wasn't enough. I feared I couldn't provide for my family or hold everything together. It felt like the carefully patched cracks in my life were splitting open, exposing wounds I could no longer ignore.

Our he first weeks after Sasha's birth were a whirlwind—sleepless nights blurred with emotional highs and crushing lows. Becoming a father should have felt like a new beginning, but instead, it unearthed fears and insecurities I had buried for years. Holding my daughter in my arms was both joyful and terrifying. Beneath the surface, an unrelenting anxiety gnawed at me: I wasn't enough. I feared I couldn't provide for my family or hold everything together. It felt like the carefully patched cracks in my life were splitting open, exposing wounds I could no longer ignore.

Our relationship began to fray under the weight of it all. The restaurant I had poured my heart, soul, and borrowed money into was floundering. No matter how hard I worked, I couldn't turn it around. Financial strain loomed over us like an unrelenting storm, compounding the pressure I already felt. Meanwhile, Sonia had been drowning in the depths of prenatal and postnatal depression and anxiety. She cried often, her pain palpable, yet I didn't know how to be there for her. I was too caught up in my emotional firestorm, numbing myself to the shame, fear, and overwhelming sense of being lost.

Sonia's struggles ran deep. Her insecurities about her body were a constant undercurrent. Having grown up watching her mother and sister struggle with obesity, she carried a visceral fear of following in their footsteps. Once, she half-joked, "If I ever look like that, just shoot me." Her words were laced with humor, but they revealed a profound vulnerability. She was battling demons I couldn't fully grasp, and my inability to comfort her only widened the gulf between us.

The tension between us grew heavier by the day. My spiral of fear and self-doubt left me haunted by the possibility of losing Sonia, my best friend and anchor, while simultaneously facing the looming specter of financial ruin. The shame of failing as a provider cut deeply, dredging up old wounds from my childhood, familiar feelings of abandonment, inadequacy, and a desperate need to prove my worth.

Sasha's birth brought joy and stirred a tidal wave of past traumas at the same time. Memories of loss, fear, and instability came flooding back with a vengeance, leaving me scared, depressed, and unbearably lonely. The weight of my unresolved pain and the uncertainty of the future collided, trapping me in a cycle of shame and self-loathing.

How could I climb out of this dark place? How could I support Sonia and Sasha when I could barely hold myself together? These questions haunted me, their answers elusive. The dreams we had built, the family I cherished, and my fragile sense of self all seemed on the verge of collapse. What would it take to rebuild, to find a way forward, when all I could see was the wreckage of what once was?

One day, Sonia and I were having yet another heated argument. Frustrated and overwhelmed, I went into the kitchen to make tea, hoping the simple act would calm me down. But as I stood there, staring at the tea kettle, my mind churned with anger and unresolved emotions. Time felt like it was dragging, each second stretching my patience thinner. Finally, something inside me snapped. I grabbed the tea kettle off the stove and started slamming it onto the gas burner repeatedly, the sound of metal on metal ringing in my ears.

The next thing I knew, I started throwing plates, sweeping everything off the counters in a chaotic frenzy. The crash of breaking dishes fueled my rage as I lost myself in a storm of barely understood emotions. When Sonia appeared in the doorway, her eyes wide with shock, I reached the height of my rampage, tipping over the refrigerator and attempting, in vain, to push it out the kitchen window. It was too heavy, even for my adrenalized body. I collapsed on the floor, panting and spent, surrounded by the wreckage I had created.

For a moment, we just stared at each other in silence. Then, unexpectedly, we both burst out laughing. The situation's absurdity broke through the tension, and for a brief, beautiful moment, we remembered why we loved each other. It felt like a glimpse of hope, a reminder of our connection beneath all the pain and chaos.

But that moment didn't last. My drinking and getting stoned only fueled my downward spiral, driving an even deeper wedge between Sonia and me. That outburst wasn't just about the argument; it expressed an eruption of pent-up emotions I'd carried since childhood. It was as though the lonely, rejected boy inside me had finally broken through, desperate to be seen and heard. For a fleeting moment, I let it all out, the frustration, the fear, the hurt I hadn't known how to process for so many years.

But the cost was high. The damage extended far beyond the kitchen, echoing through the heart of our relationship. It wasn't just the broken dishes or the mess I had created. It was also the growing sense of instability, mistrust, and emotional distance between us. Each outburst added another crack to the fragile foundation we had built together, which was already weakened by unspoken fears, unresolved pain, and the weight of our pasts.

Sonia became more withdrawn, her warmth giving way to guardedness. I could see the hurt in her eyes, but I didn't know how to bridge the gap I had created. The love we once shared began to feel less like a source of connection and more like a tenuous thread, fraying with each argument, each broken promise, and each moment I chose numbing over vulnerability.

What hurt the most was the awareness that, deep down, I truly wanted to love her better, to be the partner she deserved. I longed to show up fully for her, to honor the connection we had built. But I was trapped in my inner storm, unable to confront the cycles of anger and despair that kept resurfacing in my life.

The damage went far beyond the arguments or the moments of distance between us. It wasn't just the cracks in our communication but the erosion of the trust and intimacy we had carefully nurtured over time. That trust, once solid and secure, had been worn away by my inability to face my inner demons. Each unaddressed wound, each unspoken truth, chipped away at the foundation of what we had built, leaving us in a place of hurt and disconnection.

In a moment of poor judgment, I made the mistake of hiring Suzanne. She had been a part of my life long before Sonia, an infatuation I had tucked away when I first met Sonia. I was totally in love with Sonia. Suzanne was single and stunning. Her emerald green eyes seemed to hold a magnetic pull that I couldn't ignore. I was struggling in my marriage, feeling abandoned and emasculated, desperate for validation. Suzanne's attention was intoxicating, a balm to my wounded ego. It felt like a lifeline when I was at my lowest. I think she was drawn to me because I was unavailable—her interest was a contrast to the vulnerability I was desperately trying to suppress.

One evening, the lines blurred further after a few drinks and a joint. I was too far gone, too tangled in my own self-loathing and desire for validation. We crossed a line I could never undo. We slept together. It wasn't just a betrayal of Sonia, it was a betrayal of everything I wanted to stand for, everything I wanted to be but couldn't manage to uphold. I knew it was wrong then, but I couldn't see the consequences and grasp how deep the wound would go.

When I finally told Sonia, her fury was palpable. Her anger wasn't just directed at me; it was a culmination of everything she had endured in my spiral of self-destruction. The betrayal of our marriage, the betrayal of her trust, was the final straw. She had given me so much of herself, and I had torn it apart with my reckless actions. She moved in with our friend Kress, and we co-parented Sasha, but the emotional distance between Sonia and me continued to grow. The bond we had once shared was shattered, and I was left alone, drowning in my guilt and longing to feel her love again. I was lost, paralyzed by my actions.

Amid the chaos of my life, I spiraled even further. One night, under the haze of acid and pot, my judgment was clouded entirely. I missed a turn on a winding road and drove my Volvo off a cliff. The car flipped end over end, tumbling violently through the air in a one-and-a-half dive before crashing into the field below. I found myself hanging upside down, the seatbelt cutting into me as I dangled, disoriented. Blood rushed to my head, making everything spin and adding to the surreal chaos of the moment.

When I finally managed to unbuckle the seatbelt, I fell hard onto the grass beneath the open sunroof, my body still shaking from the crash. I crawled out of the wreckage, but the world around me spun. My vision blurred as I saw the flashing lights of police cars on the road above. Desperate, I crawled back into the wrecked car, retrieving the drugs I had stashed in the glove box. Crawling through the bushes, I hid them, trying to stay low and hoping they wouldn't see me. Once I had hidden the evidence, I finally waved my arms, hoping someone would notice me.

The fire department responded quickly. An officer rappelled down a rope to haul me up the hill. I was so stoned that everything felt detached, like I was watching it all unfold from a distance. My mind was hazy, and nothing seemed real. Somehow, I passed the drunk test, though I couldn't fathom how. Maybe the officers felt pity for me or didn't want to deal with me, but they let me go. I knew them from my work at the local newspaper as a reporter. My office was right behind the police station; I had written positive articles about them before. The entire experience felt like a blur, too surreal to process.

The next day, I woke up with only minor scratches, but my body was covered in painful, rising sores from the poison ivy I had crawled through. The physical pain was almost irrelevant, overshadowed by the crushing emotional devastation that weighed on me. My life felt like it was unraveling slowly, and I felt powerless to stop it.

At that point, Sonia had had enough. She couldn't watch me self-destruct any longer. I'm sure she feared for Sasha's safety because of my reckless behavior. Between my infidelity and my increasingly dangerous actions, she couldn't stay. She packed up, taking Sasha, now two and a half years old, the same age as when I lost my mother, and returned to Canada.

I was left alone, devastated. The weight of my actions was crushing, and I had no choice but to confront the reality of what I had done—not just to Sonia and Sasha but to myself and the life we had been building together. It was the lowest point of my life. The guilt wrapped itself around me, a relentless companion, dragging me deeper into darkness. ., further away from the man I wanted to be.

After a few months of sobering up and missing them, I visited Canada to see Sonia and Sasha. We talked, and she agreed to return so we could raise our daughter together. Profoundly depressed and still drinking, I had shamefully closed the restaurant and started bankruptcy proceedings. Then, Sonia was offered a job with Levi's, which meant moving to the Carmel area, a three-hour drive from Marin County. I was lost. We planned to co-parent as much as possible, but the distance made it difficult.

I considered relocating to Carmel or Monterey, hoping we would figure out how to get back together again. I still had bouts of depression and drank too much, but I started another business doing energy consulting and selling solar products, and felt things were starting to look up.

And then I got the call.

I was on my way to Carmel to take care of Sasha and give Sonia a 10-day break to go on a vacation. I had started to get my life back together and was primarily sober. I had stopped at a client's workplace in Palo Alto, where my assistant had left a message that I needed to call the Monterey sheriff's office. They told me there was an accident, but wouldn't tell me what happened. I raced at high speed to Carmel and went directly to the sheriff's office. I thought that Sonia, who wasn't the best driver in the world, might have been in a car accident, and something had happened to Sasha. I never imagined what I would hear when I arrived.

On October 15th, 1981, my wife was found brutally murdered in her new home while our daughter, Sasha, was in preschool. Sonia had been sexually assaulted and strangled to death with her pantyhose. At that time, Sasha was four and a half years old. The police told her that her mother had been killed and that they were holding her in custody. I was furious that they would tell her without me there. I wanted to go to her right away. I knew she needed me. But, at that time, they considered me a suspect, and her grandmother, in her grief, wanted to take Sasha. I loved Sonia's mother and understood her grief. But she told the police that I might be a child molester, and eight days went by before I was able to prove my innocence and get her back. Those were the longest eight days of my life.

I became frantic and in another "white-out"; to make it worse, I tried to drown my pain and loss with alcohol. The detective I talked to met me in a bar and told me later that I was pretty drunk. It was all just too overwhelming for me. That week became a blur, and I remained numb. I went to the funeral home and sat with Sonia's body for hours. I couldn't even cry. I couldn't even feel the grief. I thought about how it must have been for my father when my mother committed suicide. He remained numb his whole life. I was turning out just like my father: drunk, broke, and numb.

The molestation story began the year before, when I was caring for Sasha. She complained about a painful rash, and I didn't know what to do. Concerned, I asked a trusted female friend for advice. She suggested applying a bit of Vaseline to soothe the irritation—something gentle and practical. I followed her advice, never imagining it would lead to suspicion.

Later, Sonia spoke to her mother about it. Her mom, whom I had always found kind but painfully uninformed—someone who got most of her information from supermarket tabloids—planted a terrifying seed of doubt: "What if he's a pedophile?"

That word alone split the ground beneath me.

Sonia took Sasha to our family doctor in Mill Valley for an examination. I was left reeling—afraid, ashamed, and confused—caught between my innocent intention and the horrifying possibility that I might now be seen as a threat to my own daughter. The mere suggestion was unbearable. It didn't just call my actions into question—it called my very being into question.

And I knew then: once that kind of shadow is cast, it doesn't easily go away.

After examining Sasha and speaking with her directly, Dr. Estes was clear and unwavering: there was no evidence of abuse. Still, the damage had been done. The false accusation, once spoken, took root in the minds of extended family, acquaintances, and even strangers on the periphery of our lives. Despite the doctor's professional reassurance, suspicion lingered like a shadow I couldn't shake.

The police followed up, spoke with Dr. Estes, and confirmed I had done nothing wrong. But the system had already taken hold. Child Protective Services was holding Sasha, and I felt powerless, trapped in a nightmare I couldn't wake from.

Then, my beloved Uncle Pete stepped in. He called the social worker in charge and spoke with calm authority. "Do you think Sonia was a good mother?" he asked. "Of course," she replied. "Then do you really believe a good mother would knowingly leave her daughter with someone dangerous for ten days?"

There was a long pause. And then, finally, they released Sasha back into my care.

The relief was immense, but the wound was already there. I had been marked by suspicion, and something in me, something tender and trusting, had been shaken loose.

I was allowed to pick up my daughter from the people caring for her. That's when I could finally cry, if only a few teardrops. She was as happy to see me as I was to see her. We hugged and cried together. The family she stayed with was very nice. The man was a musician and had written a song for Sasha about her loss.

When I arrived at the funeral parlor to see Sonia for the first time since her murder, the air in the funeral parlor felt thick and suffocating, saturated with the sharp, acrid scent of chemicals mingled with the undeniable undertone of death.

As I walked in, my body moved on autopilot, each step feeling heavier than the last. I approached her, lying so still, her bruises and wounds meticulously concealed under layers of makeup. They had tried to make her look peaceful, but it felt unnatural, wrong—she was supposed to be full of life, not lifeless in front of me.

I sat there, frozen. My chest throbbed with a heaviness I couldn't name—an ache that wanted to cry, to scream, to break open—but couldn't. It was as if my body had gone offline, numbed by emotions too vast, too unbearable to feel. A cold fog settled over me, muting everything. I was there, but not really. Distant. Hollow.

Why wasn't I there to protect her?

Guilt came crashing in, wave after relentless wave. My mind spun in helpless circles, grasping for reasons, for anything that could make sense of the senseless. But there was nothing. Only silence and the sickening echo of shame.

A crushing weight began to settle in my chest—a familiar, suffocating voice whispering that somehow, this was my fault. Just like before. Just like when I was a child, believing my mother's death was because I'd left the electric train on. "You're going to burn the house down and kill us all," my grandmother had said.

That old belief, that I was the cause of the catastrophe, had returned—merciless and uninvited.

The smell of the embalming chemicals, sterile yet sickening, heightened my sense of unreality. I felt faint, like I was floating above the scene, watching it unfold from afar. It reminded me of the time I died. I wanted to die again, for good. But I was now a single father. I couldn't do what my father had done to me. Time lost meaning; I was frozen in a surreal nightmare. Sonia—the love of my life—was gone.

Sitting in that room for hours, surrounded by death's undeniable presence, I couldn't stop my mind from reviewing our time together. I thought of all the wonderful moments we had shared, the connection that had once burned so brightly between us. But those memories were shadowed by regrets—missed opportunities, things I wished I had handled better, and communication I had so often fumbled about. I replayed my hope that, despite our separation, we might somehow reconcile, rebuild what had been broken, and find our way back to each other. That hope had kept me going. Now, it had disappeared.

At the time, I didn't fully realize it, but I was still chronically disembodied and emotionally paralyzed—a survival mechanism I'd developed years earlier in the wake of other traumas. That numbness had shielded me from pain, but it had also kept me disconnected from my feelings, from Sonia, and ultimately from myself.

The funeral in Carmel was brutal. I felt like everyone was staring at us. My embedded guilt, shame, and fear from my past and the feeling of needing to defend myself came up as Sasha and I took our place in the church pews. We had an open casket, and when Sasha saw her mother lying there, she said, "She looks like wood, Daddy." I said, "Yes, her spirit has left her body, but she will always be with us." I think that might have further triggered her young mind because, at the end of the service, she started hitting me and crying with everyone looking on. I didn't know what to do, so I picked her up and held her. It felt like every eye in the church was staring suspiciously at me. That old feeling of needing to protect and defend myself came welling up.

We returned to Marin and found a six-month rental in San Anselmo. I started going to therapy, trying to figure out what to do next. My therapist suggested I take Sasha somewhere where people didn't speak English. It seemed strange, but I managed to get us tickets to Puerto Vallarta, Mexico, and off we went. We spent six weeks there, going to the beach and walking around the town. It became a beautiful bonding time and a perfect break for temporary healing.

As I mentioned earlier, when I first visited the sheriff in Monterey, they informed me that I was a suspect. But after checking on my whereabouts on the day and time of the murder, they concluded that I no longer remained under suspicion. However, Sonia's family and many other people we knew—and didn't know—were still convinced that I had committed the murder.

In July 1982, they arrested Sonia's 25-year-old neighbor, Michael Glazebrook, a swarthy, muscle-bound tradesman who had recently moved across the street from Sonia. The sheriff's department team was confident they had the right man, and he became the only real suspect in the case.

In a few minutes, the suspect changed his story numerous times while talking with the arresting officer, Detective Lins Dorman. He explained that the gash on his cheek, going all the way down his jaw and neck, occurred from a piece of fiberglass that broke while working on his boat, but with no blood or fiberglass on his workbench. Then he told them he got cut in a fight with some black students at the nearby college. He said he didn't know Sonia; then he said, yes, he often came into the house and that they were having an affair, but he didn't kill her. A girlfriend told the police that he had told her he had been in the house. He failed a lie detector test, and his blood type was a match with the blood found on Sonia's broken fingernail, ruling out 70% of the population. There wasn't any DNA testing in those days.

The trial started in November 1983, and while the detectives felt they had a strong case, things went from bad to worse in the courtroom. The judge threw out all the evidence collected by Detective Dorman because they arrested Glazebrook on a traffic violation and questioned him about a murder case. The mug shot of the suspect with the gash on his face had disappeared. They said the camera had malfunctioned.

The girlfriend, who informed the detectives that Glazebrook told her he had been in Sonia's home, got on the stand and said that she lied and only said that because the "cops were pressuring her" and she was mad at Glazebrook. His parents lied on the stand and said that he didn't have a scratch on his face the morning of the murder.

The jury handed down nine guilty verdicts and three not guilty verdicts. The judge declared a mistrial. They released Glazebrook and sent him back to the streets. The detectives were overwhelmed with frustration and concern. They knew that a violent rapist and murderer had been free in their community, and there was nothing they could do about it. Who knows what other brutal crimes he may have committed or might commit next?

In many people's minds, I was still the killer. I struggled with depression, anxiety, and fear of what people thought of me. I even questioned myself for a while and thought, did I do it, and just block it out like I had blocked out so much trauma in my life? I even had dreams that I drove around with Sonia in the trunk, and one night, I dreamed that I killed her and hid her body in a wall somewhere, which I closed off with bricks and mortar, and that the police were on my trail and I was soon to be arrested and spend my life in prison. In short, I was losing my mind and trying to keep it together to take care of my daughter.

I was lost again. If I didn't have my daughter to care for, I would likely have drunk myself to death or overdosed on drugs. But, like my father before me, I became a functional alcoholic, able to keep it together, and started a new career doing organizational consulting.

Sitting there, I was confronted with a stark truth: grief doesn't disappear when ignored. It waits patiently, relentlessly, until it's felt. My inability to cry or truly mourn wasn't resilience; it was a wall. What once protected me had become a cage, keeping the pain locked inside. That unprocessed grief, rooted in a childhood of silent sorrow, had calcified over the years. And now, it was no longer just about the past—it was standing between me and any real healing.

REFLECTIONS

My relationship My relationship with Sonia was initially rooted in a profound intimacy and connection. We often practiced the "Be With" exercise, a simple yet powerful invitation to presence. It beautifully embodied what Dan Siegel calls intra-connectedness: a state of being deeply attuned to oneself while simultaneously attuning to another. Unlike inter-connection, which implies a link between two separate selves, intra-connection arises from within—a shared field of awareness that transcends individuality.

In those moments, the boundary between self and other began to dissolve. There was no subject or object, no giver or receiver—just a spacious, silent presence flowing between us and through us. It was more than emotional closeness; it was a transcendent experience, a merging into something greater than either of us. The sacred "we" emerged and felt timeless, whole, and intensely alive. We weren't just together; we were being together in a way that felt like coming home.

Thich Nhat Hanh referred to this connection as inter-being: a merging with the sacred other where all separation dissolves. In that space with Sonia, I felt wholly seen and joined. I have never experienced anything like it before or since, but I hold the memory with reverence and hope to feel it again one day.

Despite the pain of our breakup, both the hurt I caused and the suffering I endured, Sonia remains the great love of my life. I still speak to her in quiet moments, mostly in prayerful conversation about our daughter. Her presence continues to live within me. The loss of her, especially in the violent and unresolved way it happened, is a grief I still carry.

For many years, self-forgiveness felt impossible. Grief clouded my days, and guilt seemed to eclipse the joy we once shared. Slowly, I began to focus on the beauty of what we had. Once wrapped in pain, those memories started to soften and bring warmth. Over time, I came to understand that while our relationship had its challenges, her death was not my fault.

The guilt I carried was deeply rooted—an old survival pattern formed in childhood when I had to make sense of my mother's abuse, her suicide, and my father's absence. Blame became a way to feel in control, even if it meant turning that blame inward.

For decades, I held my grief tightly in my mind and heart, unable to let it fully move through me. Only in recent years have I found the courage to feel it in my body—to let the tears come, to allow the ache to breathe.

That process has been both painful and healing. It reminded me that love and loss are never separate; they are two expressions of the same depth of feeling.

After Sonia's murder, my daughter and I moved to Nevada City, hoping to escape the gossip, suspicion, and quiet judgments from people we once called us friends. But we couldn't outrun the pain. It came with us—grief, fear, and the heavy silence of being misunderstood.

I threw myself into work—teaching, coaching, consulting—and devoted myself to caring for my daughter. I was determined not to abandon her as my father had abandoned me. Still, like him, I had to work to provide. That balance—being present while needing to provide—was a constant tension.

In this new town, I felt profoundly alone. I didn't want to remarry, but I yearned for a loving, compassionate partner—

someone to help carry the weight of it all. More than anything, I wished Sonia were still beside me, as if this were just a terrible dream I might wake from. But she was gone.

Still, I searched for love, even as I remained buried beneath layers of unresolved pain. I couldn't truly connect with the women I dated, because I hadn't yet made that connection with my pain.

My relationships during that time mirrored the unspoken battles within me. I kept attracting women who, like me, carried unhealed trauma and unacknowledged pain. Their criticisms echoed my own self-doubt, confirming the belief that I was never quite enough.

The more I tried to be a good father, a reliable provider, a man worthy of love, the more disconnected I became from others, and from myself. Each relationship seemed to pull back a layer, exposing the grief, guilt, and fear I had long buried.

That period was a crucible—a relentless initiation into the parts of myself I had tried to outrun. Looking back, I see how each connection, no matter how painful, offered me a mirror. And in that reflection, I began to glimpse the shape of the sorrow I hadn't yet dared to face.

The time I spent with Sonia's body in the funeral parlor had quietly planted a seed. I didn't know it then, but something in me had shifted. A deeper awareness was beginning to take root.

Only by turning toward the unbearable weight of my grief—by allowing it to be felt, rather than avoided—could I begin to move through it. And in that movement, slowly, something else stirred: the possibility of life after devastation.

The next chapter reflects on those relationships, the truths they uncovered, and how each one, however heartbreaking, led me closer to the healing I so desperately needed. This wasn't just a journey of survival. It was the beginning of transformation.

GRIEF AS A DOORWAY TO LOVE AND ALIVENESS

Grief and love are sisters, woven together from the beginning… There is no love that does not contain loss, and no loss that is not a reminder of the love we carry for what we once held close..

Francis Weller

Grief is not a sign that something has gone wrong. It is a sign that something mattered deeply. In a world that often urges us to move on, to stay strong, or to keep it all together, grief is an invitation to slow down and feel—to remember our capacity for love, tenderness, and connection.

To grieve is to affirm that we dared to love, that we opened our hearts to life and allowed ourselves to care. It is not a weakness, but a profound strength—a testament to our humanity. Yet grief in our culture is often silenced, privatized, or pathologized. We're told to get over it, to distract ourselves, or to carry it alone. But grief was never meant to be endured in isolation. It is meant to be shared, expressed, and witnessed. It is part of the sacred work of being human.

Grief is praise, because it is the natural way love honors what it misses.

Martin Prechtel

When we allow ourselves to fully feel our grief, without rushing, bypassing, or minimizing, it transforms us. It carves rivers of compassion through the landscape of our hearts. It deepens our presence. It softens our judgments. It brings us closer to others. It brings us closer to what is essential.

Grief reminds us that we belong to each other, to the earth, to the great turning of life and death. It humbles us, awakens us, and ultimately connects us more deeply to our aliveness.

We don't heal from grief by forgetting. We heal by remembering, together. By letting it move through us, shape us, and ultimately open us to even greater love.

Grief is not the end of love. It is love, in its deepest form.

CHAPTER THIRTEEN

Marriage & Relationships

The romantic vision promises 'shadowless' relationships, but it is precisely by wrestling with the relationship's shadow, with disillusionment, that deep intimacy is sustained.

Terrence Real

In earlier chapters, I shared stories of Maidye and Sonia—my first two wives—who profoundly shaped me. These relationships taught me about love and loss, but they also exposed my inability to escape the emotional patterns I carried from childhood.

Like my father, I drifted through flings and one-night stands, yearning for intimacy but sabotaged by fear and old wounds. Beneath every connection lived the shadow of abandonment. I chased love while dragging behind me a tangled web of grief, guilt, shame, fear, and longing for a mother I barely knew and a father who was never really there.

I wanted a deep connection, but my fear of vulnerability made it hard to let anyone in. I dreamed of a partner who could embody the maternal warmth I missed growing up, but I chose women who mirrored my unhealed pain. Relationships became a cycle of codependency—hopeful beginnings unraveling into loneliness and disconnection.

After Sonia's death, I moved to Nevada City with my daughter, hoping for a fresh start. She had just turned five, and I was determined to be the kind of father mine never was—present, loving, and available. But I still had to travel for work, so I arranged for an Austrian au pair to join us.

That's how Brigitta came into our lives—radiating light, laughter, and warmth. She was everything I had hoped for in a caregiver and much more. That summer, we lived in an unfinished cabin on our new property, waiting for the tenant we had inherited to move out of our new home. The land felt like something out of a surreal painting, surrounded by forest, a creek, and a cascading waterfall. It was a time of deep healing. We spent our days swimming, picnicking, and slowly reclaiming a sense of joy, and Brigitta's presence played a big part in that. She brought lightness back into our world.

One day, a biker friend offered her a ride on his Harley. Off she went—blonde hair flying, red lips smiling, throwing a goodbye kiss as they roared off. When they didn't return for two days, I was furious. But when she rode up on the back of his bike, calm as ever, and said in her heavy Austrian accent, "Good help is hard to find these days," I couldn't help but laugh. Something softened between us after that. We grew closer and became lovers. For a time, it felt right.

However, as her visa neared its end, Brigitta yearned for marriage and children. I wasn't ready. She returned to Austria, where she eventually married and had a family. We lost touch, but I always felt that chapter ended as it should, with deep gratitude and fond memories.

After she left, the loneliness returned. I began drinking more heavily. Though I tried to stay strong for my daughter, I felt adrift, grieving Sonia, questioning myself as a father, and searching for comfort and some sort of stability.

FRANCIS

I met FI met Francis at Friar Tuck's bar. She had a daughter the same age as mine, and we soon began spending time together. At first, it was casual companionship, shared drinks, and fleeting comfort. But the cracks emerged quickly. Francis started pushing for more. I wasn't ready for marriage, but my daughter, longing for a mother, urged me toward it. Out of a sense of responsibility, I offered to support Francis and her daughter financially, on the condition that we maintain an open relationship. She agreed, or so I believed. We got married under what I thought was a mutual understanding.

But things unraveled quickly. Francis began telling people I was abusive and had cheated on her, even confiding this to a close colleague at Landmark. When I started seeing someone else in Reno, she retaliated with anger and accusations. Suddenly, my private life was bleeding into my professional world. She denied the open arrangement we had agreed to. I maintained that we had one. It didn't matter. The damage was done.

Our relationship spiraled into chaos. Arguments escalated—loud, drunken confrontations, followed by cold silences and blame that cut to the bone. Francis became physically aggressive. And yet, to those outside looking in, I was the villain. In the era of Me Too, the truth is not always straightforward. Pain distorts perception, and not every story fits neatly into the expected narrative.

One day, during another explosive fight, she was screaming and hitting me in the chest. I felt pushed to the edge—afraid of what I might do if I didn't find a way to stop the escalation. In a desperate moment, I opened a drawer and pulled out an unloaded revolver. I pointed it at the ceiling—not at her—and shouted, "Get the fuck out of my house." She did. But before the door closed behind her, she called the police.

That night, I went to jail. She returned to the house, took whatever she could carry, and handed the revolver to the authorities as "evidence." It was a gift from a dear friend. I never saw it again.

After my release, I filed for divorce. Though we'd been married less than five years, she walked away with a significant settlement, including half of my graduate school tuition, which had been paid for by the company I worked for. Only later did my daughter confide that Francis had been abusive to her all along, physically, emotionally, and with chilling threats to stay silent about her actions.

Since then, Francis has spiraled further, run-ins with the law, substance abuse, violence, elder abuse, and even attempted embezzlement. Looking back, it's hard not to wonder how I missed the signs. But I was lost too, searching for love, healing, and a home life I'd never known.

MILA

My teaching, My teaching, training, and consulting company was thriving. I traveled extensively across North America and Europe, landing several major clients for my Presence, Power, and Performance workshop. With money finally flowing in, I reinvested in my education, enrolling in a two-year post-graduate program through IGOR in Munich and the Cleveland Gestalt Institute. The International Systems in Organizational Development (ISOD) program aligned perfectly with my goal of deepening my skills and working internationally, particularly in Europe.

Every other month, we studied and practiced in a different country, conducting live interventions with organizations in Italy, Israel, Spain, Sweden, the Netherlands, and the UK. Like my master's program, it was off-campus and experiential. I loved the mix of personal awareness and organizational work, and it eventually led to a consulting role with the European Union's finance division, where 14 languages were spoken throughout the office.

The Netherlands became my European home base. Since my first visit to Amsterdam in the early '60s, I have felt a familiar sense of belonging there. Despite the biting winters, the city's vibrant culture, art, and music drew me in. I once rented a houseboat on a quiet canal, sinking into the rhythm of life there.

I met Mila at a party on a friend's boat one night. She was electric, stunning, and sharp. She held two master's degrees—one in Human Resources (HR) and the other in Organizational Development (OD). She worked as a nude model to fund her studies and was recently crowned Europe's Penthouse Playmate of the Year. She was only a few years older than my daughter, but something in me said, "This could work."

Our connection was immediate—part lust, part eerie familiarity. I hadn't yet seen how our unresolved traumas were magnetized to each other. Mila seemed to seek a benefactor, someone to help launch her career. I stepped into the role of protector; she, the ambitious dreamer. It was intoxicating, intense, and unstable from the start.

We spent a year shuttling between California and Alkmaar, Holland. Eventually, I invited her to live with me. "This is your home," I told her. "Change anything you like." It was a heartfelt gesture, but it opened the door to a chaotic chapter.

When I returned from a consulting job a few weeks later, I found she had held a garage sale, selling things deeply personal to me. "Look at all the money I made!" she beamed. She could be disarmingly charming, and I let it go. I envisioned us working together, but watching her lecture corporate executives—more with seductive flair than seasoned insight—was painful. She assisted in some training and showed genuine enthusiasm. I hoped time would temper her and we could build something real.

Just before Christmas, I was teaching a workshop in Texas for Humana Inc. Mila was back in Holland. She called that night and said her father in Spain wanted to know how I planned to support her. She wanted a financial contract before she would return to California. I was crushed. Her ultimatum triggered my deepest abandonment fears. I should have ended it, but I clung to the fantasy instead. She still called me the love of her life.

That same night, feeling raw and lonely, I broke my rule and joined my client's Christmas party. I'd been avoiding alcohol, and an open bar and welcoming friends felt like what I needed. I downed a few glasses of Chivas with a manager from Humana, who said she had heard great things about my work. We ended up in my room. There was kissing and touching, but when she said no to sex, I respected that. She left, and I passed out.

Back in California, Mila returned, and we headed to Tahoe to ski. On the first day, I got a call from the VP at Humana, who has been a longtime supporter. She told me the woman from the party claimed I had tried to molest her. My champion told me she was about to be fired, but asked, "Do you think this compromises your work?" That question haunted me. The no was stuck in my throat. I felt we had mutually consented to what we did, but the shame and fear hit like a wave. I blurted out, "Yes, I think it does."

I lost contracts worth hundreds of thousands of dollars with a single sentence. Shame consumed me. I walked away from a career I loved—not because I had to, but because I was repeating an old pattern: quitting and running. It was a reflex from childhood that surfaced again when things got tough.

Mila was furious. Her access to the corporate OD world was slipping away. I had just begun teaching 5Rhythms, but it brought in barely enough to sustain us. In a last-ditch effort to keep her, I proposed. She said yes, but the marriage was short-lived.

We built up the 5Rhythms® business together, and while it gained some traction, it was never enough to keep pace with Mila's expensive tastes or emotional volatility. I felt myself unraveling. The stress, the instability, the constant emotional whiplash. It was wearing me down. Less than a year into the marriage, I told her I wanted a divorce. She had just returned from a ski trip, where she'd already crossed the line—into the arms of the man she would turn to after our separation.

Looking back, I see it clearly: I kept attracting partners whose wounds mirrored mine. I began to see that in every failed relationship, the one constant was me.

After we split, I sold my beloved home of thirty years and sank into another deep slump. The shame and self-blame were relentless, a constant echo in my mind. Then came another blow—Mila sued me for half the proceeds from the sale and demanded alimony. Her lawyer managed to freeze the funds for months, leaving me in limbo. In the end, the judge awarded her only $8,000. Out of guilt—or maybe a sense of unresolved responsibility—I added a few thousand more when they asked. It was what I had originally offered her.

Someone later said, "Mila should wear a name tag: Hi, I'm Mila—what can you do for me?" And yeah, love is blind. I had sold my soul to be with someone who, at the core, was seeking the same thing I was: to be taken care of.

RAMONA

I had I had connected with a prominent public figure over our shared passion for environmental and social justice. I'd always assumed she was a lesbian, but one day, I asked if she dated men. Her answer was vague, neither yes nor no. I was drawn to her strength and commitment and invited her out. To my surprise, she accepted.

Initially, we were aligned, fueled by our shared values and activism. Ramona had a powerful physical presence, undeniable charisma, and fierce dedication to her causes. For the first six months, we collaborated, engaged in deep conversations, and had a lot of agreement in our concerns and commitments.

But over time, I began to see a darker side. Ramona thrived on conflict. She framed everything in binaries—right vs. wrong, ally vs. enemy. She stirred controversy wherever she went, alienating even longtime allies. What once felt like conviction began to feel oppressive.

Eventually, I became one of those she turned on. The warmth and laughter disappeared, replaced by tension, judgment, and a growing emotional distance. Then, she stopped returning my calls.

Around that time, I began spending time with my friend, Kathleen. We had a strong connection from the dance community and had dated earlier. I needed clarity. When I ran into Ramona by chance, I asked, "Are we still dating? Someone's interested in dating me, but I need to know where we stand." She didn't miss a beat: "You should date her!" And walked away.

I was stunned—but what followed was far worse. Rumors began to spread that I had killed my wife, molested my daughter, and was a womanizer. I was floored.

These were vicious, baseless lies—deeply personal attacks that struck at the core of who I was. I had always treated Ramona with kindness and respect. I couldn't fathom where this betrayal was coming from.

Eventually, I learned the source: my alcoholic ex-wife, Francis. Though her credibility was shaky, Ramona's public standing gave the stories traction. The damage was swift. Clients and students began pulling away. My income was reduced almost overnight.

Friends rallied to my defense. They called Ramona, reminding her of my long history of community service. How I brought 5Rhythms® to Nevada City, supported local businesses through organizational consulting, hosted a healing-focused radio show for over 15 years, and contributed regularly to the local paper. Still, her only reply was: "I know what I know."

I felt helpless. I considered filing a slander suit, but feared it would only deepen the drama. Every new conversation felt charged—did they hear the rumors? Did they believe them? The uncertainty was suffocating. I could feel trust unraveling around and within me. I pulled inward to protect myself.

In desperation, I turned to shamanic rituals, therapy, and prayer. I cried often. The fear that I might have to leave Nevada City, the place I had poured my heart into for over three decades, was overwhelming. I had helped nurture this community, but now I was cast out and shunned by many.

Ironically, the tagline of my radio show was "healing the wounds that separate, alienate, and marginalize us." And yet, there I was—alienated and marginalized in my own town.

I struggled to make sense of it all. Why would Ramona do something so cruel? The only explanation that seemed to fit was projection. I knew, and she had shared publicly, that her father had molested her. She clearly hadn't yet made peace with that part of her history. Maybe, being twenty years her senior, I became an unconscious stand-in for that unresolved pain—someone to punish, someone to cast out.

Of course, that's just speculation. What I do know is this: I have never hit or sexually forced any woman in my life, and I did not do any of the things I was being accused of. Yes, I've had a passionate and sometimes tumultuous love life and loud arguments in relationships, but those who know me know the truth. They know my heart. And they stood by me.

KATHLEEN

Kathleen was a bright light in our 5Rhythms® dance community—kind, radiant, and deeply committed to spiritual awakening. I had always admired her open heart and grounded presence. Our first date was a picnic at her beautiful home. She had prepared a thoughtful spread, and we spent the afternoon beneath the trees, sharing stories and laughter. There was an ease between us, a quiet comfort in simply being together. Her grace, warmth, and how she moved through life with intention drew me in. I especially loved that she didn't drink—it inspired me to stay sober when I was with her, something that felt like a small act of devotion.

She brought out a bottle of wine she'd had for years. She didn't drink, and when I tasted it and casually poured it out, I realized later how thoughtless and arrogant that was. But she just laughed—

As we spent more time together, our bond deepened. We shared countless adventures—traveling to Hawaii, Mexico, the Ecuadorian rainforest, and the Galapagos Islands. Even simple car rides felt intimate, filled with laughter, teasing, and deep conversation. We studied breathwork and shamanism side by side, exploring healing practices that drew us closer together. Everything with Kathleen felt natural. Even though she kept breaking up with me, she kept coming back.

Cooking together, learning, exploring—it all felt easy and joyful. With Kathleen, life had a gentle rhythm, and I could imagine growing old beside her. But after years of an on-and-off connection, something shifted. I wasn't sure when or why. Maybe it was something I said. Maybe it was the shadow of Ramona's gossip. Whatever the reason, one day Kathleen grew distant and ended things abruptly, without explanation.

Eventually, we sat down for a mediated conversation with a mutual friend. We didn't rekindle the romance, but we managed to restore a fragile friendship. Still, I was left with questions. Why was I again drawn to someone whose father had abused her—a trauma she'd shared publicly and written about? Was there something unspoken between us, a resonance of shared wounds that created the illusion of healing, only to collapse under its weight?

Years later, I visited her in Sedona. I finally asked what had really happened. She told me that Ramona had taken her to lunch and filled her with fear and falsehoods. It made sense now—the strange tension during our mediation, the subtle but cutting innuendos of sexual misconduct that had never happened. Seeds of doubt had been planted, and they took root.

Both Kathleen and Ramona had been abused by their fathers. I believe those buried fears were stirred, and I became an unintended trigger. Kathleen apologized sincerely and asked for forgiveness. That meant a lot. We acknowledged the love and care that still lived between us. For a moment, we even considered what it might look like to try again. But I wasn't leaving Nevada City, and she had no intention of leaving Sedona.

We parted with kindness and clarity—our friendship intact, and a quiet knowing that the love was still there, even if our lives had moved on.

MERIEL

After my breakup After my breakup with Mila, I felt unmoored, restless, and mistrustful amid Ramona's gossiping. My once-cherished foundation in Nevada City now felt shaky. I considered leaving altogether, driven by a longing to get away and be closer to my daughter, Sasha, in Vancouver.

I threw myself into my work to stay afloat—running my conscious dance business, hosting a radio show, teaching shamanic practices through Sandra Ingerman's training programs, and hosting the Shift Network's Shamanic Wisdom Summit. My schedule was full, sometimes overwhelming, but it gave me a sense of purpose and momentum. It also kept me from having to feel.

At a workshop in Joshua Tree, I brought it all together—blending Sandy's wisdom with Gabrielle Roth's 5Rhythms® in early morning movement sessions that pulsed with soul. Something clicked. It felt alive and integrated, as if all the seemingly separate threads of my life were finally weaving into one coherent expression. For a moment, I wasn't fragmented. I felt aligned and alive.

Still, I was searching—longing for direction, for something that felt like home. During a shamanic journey, I asked Spirit if I should move, and where. The message came through clearly, though oddly: "Go north to the sunshine." I laughed out loud. North? Everyone knows you go south for the sun.

Later that day, one of my students approached me after class. "Would you consider teaching a workshop in British Columbia?" she asked. I perked up—my daughter lived there. "Where in BC?" I asked.

"The Sunshine Coast," she said.

I froze. I'd never heard of it before, but there it was—go north to the sunshine.

Then came another sign. The student sent me a photo of a hand-painted sign outside the venue: Bachelor Pad for Rent. As a shamanic practitioner, I've learned to listen when the universe whispers—and especially when it shouts. I called the number, booked the space, and watched as everything began falling into place, as if the path had already been laid out before me.

During a Medicine for the Earth workshop in Gibsons, BC, I noticed a radiant woman named Meriel. She had traveled all the way from Salt Spring Island—three ferries—seven hours, just to be there. At the end of every workshop, I offer a "Walk and Talk" for anyone needing extra support. As the weekend wrapped up, she approached and asked if we could take a walk.

It lasted five years.

As we wandered a driftwood-strewn beach under soft coastal skies, she shared a story of dolphins that had followed her ferry on the way to the workshop. I smiled and teased, "I sent them." We both laughed—but in that moment, something sparked.

Quiet, undeniable, and deeply familiar.

That walk marked the beginning of something beautiful. Five years of love, growth, and shared wonder. And even now, as our paths have shifted, our friendship continues to grow—rooted in respect, touched by magic, and illuminated by the kind of love that never really leaves.

Meriel and I shared a love of dance, Tai Chi, music, nature, and spiritual growth. But there were complexities—she had a long-term partner and an 18-year-old daughter. Though their relationship had faded, her life was deeply tied to theirs. Our connection was instant, passionate, and messy. I fell hard. She eventually moved in, first to my bachelor pad, then with me to a dream home on the beach.

Meriel was 22 years younger than I. We didn't talk about age early on until I asked if she knew my age. She guessed wrong by more than a decade. When I told her, she burst into tears. I sensed then that our relationship might have an expiration date, no matter how strong our love was. Still, we had countless shared adventures. She was athletic and health-conscious—a skier, windsurfer, and jock at heart. I was more of a spiritual romantic. Although I was a dancer and had been a long-distance runner, age was already taking its toll on me.

After five years together, I invited Meriel to join me on a vision quest in the Gila Wilderness of New Mexico. During my solo time in the desert, I found myself confronting old anger—particularly toward my stepmother, who had cut me out of my father's estate just before her death. A final wound I hadn't yet faced. I imagine Meriel spent her solitude reflecting on us.

At the closing circle, she told me it was over.

I was heartbroken, but not surprised. I loved her deeply, and I respected her clarity. She had always been thoughtful and honest. We parted gracefully, and for that, I remain grateful.

Despite the breakup, Meriel and I stayed close. She continues to support my work, and our friendship runs deep. She's now with a good man, and I genuinely wish them well. The truth is, she set the bar so high that I've often wondered whether I'll ever find another relationship like ours.

Looking back, I can see how finances strained us. After relocating to Canada, my income dipped and the debt weighed heavily. It frightened her. I didn't listen—not about the money, or many other things. My relentless drive, once a strength, had become a wedge. I tried to convince her to stay, but her heart had already made the decision.

After we parted, I moved to Nelson, BC, hoping to find community. I loved the Kootenays and settled into a peaceful country home on a farm. But just as I was finding my footing, the world shifted. COVID-19 hit, and connection became scarce. Then came the brutal winter—five long months with my Prius frozen in place, snow so deep I had to buy a four-wheel drive just to reach my doorstep.

And then, I got the call that changed everything—instantly.

REFLECTIONS

Very often, it is the recognition of one another's wounds that brings two people together in a romantic relationship. The unresolved pain of one partner is like a key that perfectly fits the lock made by the unresolved pain in the other.

Thomas Hübl

Imago Relationship Therapy, developed by Harville and Helen Hendrix, teaches that the conflicts we face in intimate relationships aren't just roadblocks—they're doorways. Invitations to heal, to grow, and to rewire the patterns we absorbed in childhood. Our early bonds with caregivers shape who we're drawn to and how we show up in love. Often, we unconsciously recreate what's familiar—even if it hurts. Modern research supports this: dysfunctional relationship dynamics are frequently inherited, passed down through generations like heirlooms of unresolved trauma.

For most of my life, relationships felt like brief, intense dances—fiery beginnings followed by waves of disconnection. Looking back, I can see how closely I mirrored my father's relational patterns. Like him, I married four times, most lasting around five years. Beneath it all, I was guarded—hiding behind emotional walls, numbing myself with alcohol and drugs, afraid to let anyone truly see me.

At the core of it was fear: fear of abandonment, betrayal, death—and most painfully, the quiet, unshakable belief that I was unlovable. That fear made me reactive, defensive. Even the gentlest feedback could feel like an attack. As Terry Real says, "We marry with our unfinished business." And I did—again and again. Each relationship became a mirror, reflecting both the love I longed for and the wounds I had yet to face.

For a long time, I didn't realize it was my wounded child, not my adult self, who was making most of my choices. That little boy, shaped by loss, silence, and emotional neglect, had been left to navigate a world far too complex for his tender and vulnerable heart. His strategies were simple: shut down, lash out, disappear. I dragged him into adult situations and expected him to act like a grown-up—something he never fully became. A part of his psyche had been deeply merged with his younger self.

The turning point came when I stopped exiling him. I stopped trying to fix or silence that hurting part of myself and started listening instead. I began to practice what therapists call unblending—learning to notice when my inner child was in the driver's seat and gently asking my adult self to take the wheel. I began to ask, "Who is speaking right now?" Who is feeling this hurt, this urgency, this fear?

With time and tenderness, I've learned how to reparent myself. To give that boy the love, protection, and presence he needed back then—but never received. My adult self now listens to him, comforts him, sets healthy boundaries, and helps him feel safe. In doing so, my fractured parts have started to integrate slowly. I can feel the difference now—when I respond from wholeness instead of reactivity, choose connection instead of self-defense, and show up not as a hurt child seeking love, but as a loving presence offering it.

I've learned that healing isn't about becoming someone new. It's about remembering who we were before we were taught to forget our worth. Today, I practice walking hand in hand with that little boy. He's no longer alone. And together, we face the world with a tender strength born of love that has been reclaimed.

I remember one night early in a relationship, after a fight that left me hollow, sitting alone in the dark. The wine bottle was empty—and so was I. I had once again tried to control the narrative, sidestep vulnerability, and protect myself from the ache of being hurt. But underneath it all, I wasn't just longing for a partner. I was longing for my mother, the one I lost far too soon. That unhealed wound haunted every relationship, whispering a fear I couldn't name.

I couldn't handle criticism. Even kind, thoughtful feedback felt like a threat. I had learned early that to survive, I had to defend myself by withdrawing, by fighting, or by leaving before I could be left. The closer someone got, the more terrified I became. So I ran. Again and again.

Yet, these patterns weren't uniquely mine. They were inherited—woven into my nervous system through culture, family, and a lineage of unspoken grief. But what is passed down can also be transformed. Once I understood that, everything shifted.

Much of what I once labeled as "my issues" were unexperienced experiences—emotional moments that I had never been able to feel fully or process completely. Healing has meant turning toward those moments with honesty, curiosity, and love, not to dwell in the pain but to allow it to move through me. That movement has been messy, and it hasn't always been graceful, but it has been essential.

I'm learning what it means to love not from desperation, but from wholeness. I'm discovering that authentic connection isn't about perfection—it's about embracing vulnerability, owning my story, and being willing to be seen. That willingness begins to break the unconscious cycles I once repeated—the patterns rooted in old wounds, known in psychology as repetition compulsion. This is how we heal: by becoming conscious of the past we've been trying to resolve through others, and choosing, moment by moment, not to reenact it.

I feel deep remorse for the pain I caused in my past relationships and take full responsibility for the ways I contributed to their unraveling. To those I've hurt, I am genuinely sorry. I can't change the past, but I hope that the work I now do—helping others face and integrate their own unfinished business—serves as a living apology—a quiet gesture of redemption, a ripple of love sent backward and forward in time.

REPETITION COMPULSION: THE UNCONSCIOUS PULL TO RELIVE THE PAST

Repetition compulsion is a deep psychological pattern in which individuals unconsciously recreate situations that echo earlier emotional wounds, often rooted in trauma. These repetitions may appear in relationships, behaviors, or internal experiences and are rarely chosen consciously. Instead, they reflect an inner drive to revisit unresolved pain in hopes of mastering, understanding, or integrating it.

At its core, repetition compulsion is the psyche's attempt to heal by returning to the wound. But without awareness, the cycle often reinforces suffering instead of resolving it.

KEY FEATURES

Unconscious Origin: Repetitions are not deliberate. They arise from implicit memory and emotional imprinting, often outside of awareness.

Trauma-Linked: While not always tied to overt trauma, they frequently stem from early experiences of abandonment, abuse, neglect, or emotional unavailability.

Reenactment Patterns: These can manifest as recurring relationship dynamics, repeated failures, self-destructive behavior, or even recurring dreams and body symptoms.

The Illusion of Mastery: Psychologically, repetition may be a failed attempt to "get it right this time"—to gain control over what once felt overwhelming or powerless.

Resistance to Change: Because these patterns are familiar—even if painful—they often resist therapeutic or personal change, locking individuals in cycles that echo the past.

COMMON EXAMPLES

Choosing partners who evoke the same pain a parent once caused.

Engaging in self-harm, addiction, or risky behaviors was first used to numb early distress.

Repeating emotional roles—caretaker, victim, rescuer—in relationships without knowing why.

Importantly, repetition compulsion is not the same as OCD. While both involve repetition, OCD behaviors are driven by anxiety and attempts to control it; repetition compulsion is driven by the unresolved emotional charge of the past seeking expression or completion.

A PATH TO FREEDOM

Bringing compassion and awareness to these cycles is the first step toward freedom. When we recognize the unconscious pull behind our actions—not with judgment, but with curiosity—we create the possibility of choosing something new. In this light, repetition is not failure, but an invitation: to return to the wounded places, this time with presence, support, and the capacity to transcend and transform.

CHAPTER FOURTEEN:

The Trial: Vindication & Healing

If you spend your time hoping someone will suffer the consequences for what they did to your heart, then you're allowing them to hurt you a second time in your mind.

Shannon L. Alder

After Meriel and I parted ways, I moved to Nelson, British Columbia, in search of a greater sense of community. I had become a Canadian citizen and wasn't ready to return to California, to the shadows of slander and gossip I had worked so hard to escape. A year into my new life, in July 2021, I received a call from Officer Wilson of the DA's office in Salinas, California. They were reopening the case of Sonia's murder.

Shocked, elated, and stunned—I could hardly believe it. Forty-two years had passed since her death. After decades of silence, my daughter's persistence had kept the case alive, and now, for the first time, there was a flicker of hope. The DA's office had received a grant to revisit cold cases with potential DNA evidence. That single call changed everything. It was enough to pull me back to California—back to the place I had once fled. Back to face the past I thought I'd buried.

It took over a year to prepare the case for arrest. The Department of Justice had to review the evidence, authorize the arrest, and conduct DNA testing. Challenges emerged early. One key sample—Sonia's fingernail clipping—had been compromised when the vial of Michael Glazebrook's blood broke, spilling onto the bindle that preserved the evidence. Though it wasn't technically contaminated, the defense would surely pounce. Investigators needed a backup.

Detective Wilson searched tirelessly and finally located the original rape kit, long thought lost. It contained saliva collected from Sonia's breast. The DNA results were conclusive. Glazebrook's DNA matched both the fingernail blood and the saliva. The statistical odds were one in 264 quadrillion that it was Glazebrook. He was arrested.

The judge set bail at over a million dollars, which he quickly posted. He was back on the streets of Seaside within days.

Glazebrook hired a father-son defense team that immediately attempted a plea bargain. When the prosecution refused, they threatened to destroy me instead. Friends began receiving calls from a private investigator hired by the defense. Here was the message:

"This is Virginia Hennesy, a private investigator in Monterey County working on a criminal case involving Michael Stone. I have written permission from Francis Stone to speak with you regarding abuse during their marriage in Nevada County."

Francis—the woman I married about three years after Sonia's death—was the original and only source of the lies, slander, and gossip that began circulating, even though the murder had occurred years before we ever met. The defense later interrogated both her and Ramona, the prominent local political figure I had briefly dated before she connected with Francis.

Despite having no direct knowledge or evidence, Ramona embraced the allegations as truth. I believe she saw herself as protecting the community from some imagined threat.

While I felt some compassion for her, her accusations had no basis in reality. Still, Ramona ensured that these false stories spread like wildfire through our small town and beyond, shaping public perception for over two decades.

The smear campaign reached far and wide. One woman I had just started dating visited me from the Northwest. During her stay, she booked a massage with a local practitioner. When she returned, she was shaken. The masseuse, someone I'd never met, told her to be careful because I was a womanizer and had killed my wife. Terrified, she left early.

I wrote a respectful letter to the therapist, asking her to stop spreading lies and inviting her to meet and hear the truth. She never responded, and the damage was done.

Despite the rumors, many in Nevada County stood by me. I had deep roots there—years of supporting businesses, community service, healing programs, building the 5Rhythms® community, and a beloved radio show that ran for 15 years. But the fear lingered: Was the nightmare starting again?

The defense subpoenaed Francis, her daughter, and Ramona to shift the focus from Glazebrook to me. Ironically, I was relieved. I believed the truth would finally come to light. The prosecution came prepared, with officers ready to testify about Francis's documented history of addiction, fraud, and abuse, including an attempt to swindle an elderly dementia patient.

Meanwhile, Ramona alienated her political base with extremist views, conspiracy theories, and erratic behavior. A local official described her in the newspaper as "the most polarizing figure our town has ever known."

At the pretrial hearing, the judge dismissed the defense's witnesses, stating they lacked credibility and were irrelevant to the case. With their only strategy gone, the defense had nothing left.

My daughter and I sat through an excruciating week in court—graphic police photos, testimonies about the violence Sonia endured, and the weight of decades-long grief and trauma. The defense made one last attempt to point the finger at me. The judge cut them off:

"I didn't let this in the front door, and I'm not going to let it in the back," said Judge Pamela Butler.

In the original trial, Glazebrook walked free despite glaring evidence—thanks to lies from his parents and the suppression of key facts. But this time, the truth had finally come to the surface. DNA does not lie.

While the defense spent most of the trial trying to cast doubt on the DNA evidence, three expert witnesses from the Department of Justice presented overwhelming proof. The two samples—blood beneath Sonia's fingernails and saliva from the rape kit—matched Michael Glazebrook with astronomical certainty. The jury saw through the distractions. After less than six hours of deliberation, the verdict came in: Guilty. First-degree murder and rape.

Glazebrook was led out of the courtroom in handcuffs and sentenced to life without the possibility of parole.

In the wake of the verdict, our local newspaper reached out to do a feature on the case. I was hopeful. Not only would it finally clear my name after decades of suspicion and slander, but it could also spotlight the pro bono trauma and integration healing work I'd been doing in the community since returning from Canada. I had been hosting "hearing circles"—safe spaces for people impacted by violence and trauma to share their stories and find support. The gatherings were well-attended, and I had received many heartfelt letters and testimonials from those who were moved by the work.

When the article was published, I was crushed. Most information about my community contributions had been stripped out and replaced with sensationalized commentary and misleading quotes. Instead of focusing on the healing, the piece gave voice to old rumors. It included statements from Ramona—one of the key sources of misinformation about me—and the woman whose false claims had once caused a home purchase to collapse, resulting in a significant financial loss for my partners.

Rather than feeling vindicated, I was left disheartened. It became clear that not everyone was ready to let go of the old narrative or acknowledge the good I was trying to bring into the world. The article felt like a betrayal.

After reading it, I sat down and wrote:

"The article came out today—the one I hoped would absolve me of the lies and hostility that have haunted me for decades. Even after a unanimous verdict, justice was finally served, but the shadows of suspicion linger. I had imagined this would be the turning point—the moment my name was cleared. Instead, it backfired."

In hindsight, I see where I went wrong. I mistakenly named the two people responsible for the gossip and slander. Still raw from years of defending myself, part of me wanted to set the record straight. I thought naming them might finally expose the truth. Instead, it gave them another platform.

Ramona, who had dated me about six months and then colluded with Francis's story, was quoted as saying, "The judge's decision not to hear testimony from the women of Nevada County has been a mystery. And we are all waiting for the appeal."

Suddenly, two women became "all the women of Nevada County." It was a staggering exaggeration—and a painful reminder that some people would continue to twist the truth to fit their narrative, no matter how many facts or verdicts stood in the way.

Quote from the local newspaper:

"In 1983, at the time of the original trial, there was no DNA testing, so what they were able to do with the evidence from the crime scene was just check it for blood type and those kinds of genetic markers," Monterey prosecutor L'Heureux told KSBW news station. *"The case was reopened, evidence was resubmitted to the Department of Justice Crime Lab, and they were able to extract DNA from under the victim's fingernails and from her sexual assault kit that was taken at the time of her autopsy, and it was a match to Mr. Glazebrook."*

"They arrested Glazebrook again in August 2021 and booked him into Monterey County Jail on a warrant for murder. His bail was set at $1 million, according to officials. The trial lasted eight days, and the jury deliberated for six hours before reaching a unanimous guilty verdict."

"It is true that the defense and those two individuals attempted to introduce evidence into the recent cold case trial," said the presiding Judge, Honorable Pamela L. Butler. District Attorney L'Heureux said that the judge did not accept the evidence because it was insufficient to raise a reasonable doubt against the defendant, Michael Glazebrook."

L'Heureux went on to say that "Michael Stone absolutely did not murder his wife."

I wanted revenge, though I called it "reciprocity and reconciliation." I told myself I was naming names to bring light to the truth, to be pardoned for the things I never did. But the truth is, I wanted someone to pay for the years I'd spent under suspicion, for the torment of knowing people in my community still wondered whether I was guilty. I wanted relief. Vindication. A clean break from the pain.

Instead, when the article came, I felt sick to my stomach. I doubled over, nauseous, like I'd been punched in the gut. I wanted to throw up. I could barely breathe. I went from pacing the floor and yelling at God to curling up and sobbing like a wounded animal.

How had my honest attempt to clear my name only aroused more suspicion? Why did telling the truth feel like pouring gasoline on a fire I had been trying to put out for decades?

I was filled with shame. Remorse. Rage. A thick, heavy self-hatred that wrapped itself around me like a wet blanket I couldn't shake off. I was drowning in it. For three straight days, I beat myself up.

"Oh God, what the f*** was I thinking?"

The question ran through my mind on a loop. I couldn't stop it. I couldn't eat. I could barely sleep. My body was buzzing with adrenaline and despair, stuck in that old trauma state. I kept thinking, I just wanted people to know the truth. I wanted to be seen. Heard. Believed.

I wanted to stop feeling like I had to defend myself every damn day of my life. But instead, I felt more exposed, misunderstood, and alone than ever.

People always believe what they hear first. If they happen, newspaper retractions will be buried where no one can read them. The damage had been done. I had opened my mouth in search of healing, and instead, I had handed my accusers another weapon.

And yet—somewhere beneath the storm, beneath the roar of thoughts and the avalanche of emotion—I kept returning to my body. It was the only place that felt even remotely real. Over the years, I had taught myself to anchor there, to listen to the whispers and screams of my nervous system when the pain became too much to hold. So I sat. I breathed. I trembled. And I let the tidal waves of sorrow, rage, shame, and regret crash through me. The ache in my chest felt like it might cave in my ribs. My gut twisted into knots so tight I could hardly breathe. Behind my eyes, heat pulsed like fire licking the edge of a scream. Each sensation surged through me like an electric shock—flashes of grief from wounds long buried but never healed, each one plugged into some ancient, cosmic current I couldn't shut off. It was all I could do not to disappear like smoke on the wind.

At one point, I thought I might be having a heart attack, but it was a panic attack. My chest was tight, my heart was pounding, and I was gasping for air. I collapsed onto the floor, sobbing, pounding my fists against the hardwood, calling myself a fucking idiot. A stupid jerk. A fool for believing that justice alone would set me free.

And then, somewhere in that collapsed heap of grief and rage, a body memory rose to the surface.

As I lay on the floor sobbing, suddenly a body memory surged forward—so vivid, so primal. I felt my tiny arms lifted above my head, shielding my face—a baby's reflex. I wasn't even old enough to speak, but I remember the sensation—my mother coming at me, or pressing a pillow over my face to silence my cries. Before I had words and could understand the world, I already believed I was doing something wrong. That my very existence, voice, and need for comfort were somehow a threat. I needed to defend myself.

I've never been able to get angry at my mother. I've carried the ache of her absence, the weight of her pain. I still believe, with all my heart, that she took her life to save mine. To spare me from something worse.

That belief lives beside the scars, the ones left by terror I could never name. Even though the threats are long gone, my nervous system was still trying to protect me. It reacted like it did then—guarded, hyper-vigilant, frozen, ready to defend against any real or imagined threats.

What is this ancient intelligence that lives inside me—this fierce, vigilant protector that has stood guard for decades, never once letting its post go unmanned? It's the part of me that knows danger before my mind can name it, that tightens my body, sharpens my senses, and readies me to run or fight. It has kept me alive through chaos, loss, tragedy, and heartbreak. And for that, I honor it. I thank it with all the tenderness I can muster.

But can I rewire, reprogram it? To take that coiled survival instinct—so deeply etched into my being—and ask it to soften. To trust. To evolve. It's like asking a warrior who's only known battle to put down their sword and learn to dance.

There's a grief in that letting go, a fear that without the armor, I'll shatter. And yet, something in me knows: true transformation doesn't come from more protection. It comes from the courage to open, even when every cell wants to contract.

Who will I be if I'm no longer the one who has to defend himself? If I'm no longer the misunderstood suspect or the man who has to explain his pain again and again just to be seen?

How do I reclaim my innocence—not just in the eyes of others, but in the most profound sense? Not just legally or socially, but spiritually? How do I return to that untouched place within—the part that never flinched, never hid, never apologized for simply existing? The soul that only ever wanted to love and be loved?

I don't have the complete answer yet. But I can feel the question reshaping me from within. Maybe reclaiming innocence isn't about going back. Perhaps it's about moving forward with reverence for every scar, every reflex, every collapse—and every rising. It's about meeting those moments with awareness, with compassion, again and again.

Maybe innocence isn't something I lost. Perhaps it's something that's been here all along—waiting patiently, quietly, for me to remember. And now, as I listen more deeply, I begin to hear its voice.

So, where do I go from here?

I walk toward that voice. I keep listening. I keep loving. I let the past become the soil for something new. And I begin again—not from the beginning, but from the truth I now carry.

REFLECTIONS

One thing I've gained from this harrowing passage through the inferno is a deeper, more embodied understanding of betrayal, abandonment, and shame. These are no longer just thoughts in a book or emotions my clients describe—they now live in my nervous system. I know what it feels like to be misjudged, maligned, and exiled from belonging. I know the ache of invisibility. The searing burn of being misunderstood. The raw hum of injustice rings in my bones.

I've wrestled with the demon impulse for revenge—oh, how seductive that siren song can be. But I've learned it doesn't soothe. It doesn't satisfy. It only loops the pain back around like a boomerang with barbed wire, cutting deeper on its return.

Shame is a phantom that clings to the body, a ghost with unfinished business. It lodges in the fascia, in the breath, in the gut. It shapes posture and perception. And if we don't name it, it speaks through us anyway. I've carried shame like a suit of rusted anchor—old, inherited, unspoken. I carried my mother's silence after her suicide, her absence like a rip in the fabric of my being. Her name was erased. Her story is buried. Her grave is unmarked. Our grief has been swallowed. My sense of worth was quietly replaced by the belief that love could vanish without warning.

That ancient abandonment—sharp, silent, and gutting—rose again during this ordeal, like a ghost I thought I'd buried long ago. And maybe, just maybe, this storm—the article, the reckoning, the grief—wasn't punishment, but initiation. Not a breaking, but an invitation: to feel it all. The hollow ache in my belly. The longing to be seen. The hunger for a love that stays.

And the more profound truth: the love I've always craved is mine to give. No one else can fill that place. It's my responsibility now to tend to the younger part of me that still waits—still hopes—for the reassurance and care he was once denied.

There were moments I turned on myself with venom. Called myself names and questioned my worth. I wanted to disappear. Even my dog kept his distance, as if grief had altered my scent. I was soaked in sorrow and rage—not just my own, but the legacy of pain passed down through generations, like a poisoned heirloom handed from one trembling hand to the next.

I fell into a void so vast, so eerily still, I finally understood how emptiness can ache more than pain. Maybe my mother felt that too, grasping for control in a world that kept slipping through her fingers.

Now, I ask myself: Do I have the courage to face the void and not flinch? Can I lay down the old story—the one that said I'm broken, unworthy, destined to repeat the past—and write a new one?

Because healing doesn't erase the pain. It transforms it. And maybe, that's where true freedom begins.

Because right now, I want to hide. I feel shunned. Exiled for a crime I didn't commit. A scapegoat for collective projection. Part of me feels like I'm dying, another feels like I'm waking up.

But I pause. I catch my breath. I say to myself—Stop. Be here. You can feel this. You've spent a lifetime trying to outrun this pain. Now is the time to sit with every jagged edge. Let it rise. Let it burn. Let it break you open.

I place my bare feet on the earth. I feel the chaos in my mind, the pressure in my chest, the tears rising like tidewater behind my eyes. And still, I say yes. Yes to the rage. Yes to the sorrow. Yes to the shame. I let it all move through me like a thunderstorm, not to destroy me, but to cleanse what no longer serves.

And then, a shift. Subtle. Unexpectedly. A stillness begins to bloom. Not the silence of suppression, but a more profound, anchored calm. A knowing. A strength I didn't know I had, built from the rubble of my old narrative.

If I can meet this, I can meet anything. I can face life not with shields and swords, but with an open, undefended heart. No more hiding. No more proving. No more shrinking to fit someone else's story.

I choose love—even when fear roars louder. I choose truth—even when it costs me comfort. I choose to belong to myself, to stand in the light of who I truly am. Not the accusations. Not the projections. Not the shame. I am not the shadows—I am the one who sees them and invites them in to be felt, seen, heard, held, and released. I am the one who turns toward the wound, not away.

My heart is open. My soul is intact. I'm here to heal. To hold. To give. To breathe. And, perhaps hardest of all, to receive.

And I will not be stopped.

BREATH AS MEDICINE: RELEASING TRAUMA THROUGH MINDFUL BREATHING

When trauma is triggered, the body reacts before the mind can respond—tight chest, racing heart, shallow breath. In those moments, mindful breathing becomes more than a wellness practice—it becomes a form of medicine.

Mindful breathing is the simple act of fully noticing your breath. Where do you feel it—belly, chest, ribs? Is it shallow or deep? Bringing attention to the breath shifts your focus from the trigger to the present moment, signaling safety to your nervous system. Let the exhale be longer than the inhale. This subtle shift invites awareness into the body and opens space for calm.

BEGIN HERE:

Sit or lie in a comfortable position with your spine straight and feet grounded.

Bring awareness to your inhale—follow it through your nose, into your chest, and belly.

Exhale slowly. Let it soften your jaw, shoulders, and belly.

As thoughts or emotions arise, gently return to the rhythm of your breath.

BREATHING TECHNIQUES:

Belly Breathing (Diaphragmatic)
Grounds you in your body, eases tension, and helps regulate the fight-or-flight response. Feel the breath rise and fall in your belly.

Box Breathing
Inhale for 4 counts, hold for 4, exhale for 4, hold again for 4. Creates balance and focus, ideal when feeling overwhelmed.

4-7-8 Breathing

Inhale for 4 counts, hold for 7, exhale for 8. Deeply calming, this technique activates the parasympathetic nervous system, supporting emotional release and restoration.

Trauma lives in the body. The breath offers a doorway back to presence. With practice, these techniques can interrupt old patterns, reduce anxiety, and rebuild a sense of safety—one breath at a time.

CHAPTER FIFTEEN

Holding Little Mickey

A Case Study in Trauma Healing

*An unacknowledged trauma is like a wound that
never heals over and may start to bleed again at any time.*

Alice Miller

I was planning to write a case study on one of my clients. That was the original idea. But after this session, I realized: no, this isn't just another intervention. This is my story. My life. My healing. And if I'm going to tell the truth in these pages—the whole truth—then I can't stay on the outside looking in. I have to step into the fire. Tell it from the inside out.

I often sit with people in their pain, gently guiding them into the vulnerable terrain of their childhood wounding. I hold space for their trembling bodies, their silences, and their forgotten parts. But during this session, it was me I who needed the holding. Me, I who had spiraled into the hollow ache of grief, shame, and confusion. I realized that this is what I ask others to do all the time. Why can't I offer the same tenderness to myself?

When we're not witnessed as children, when our emotional world is ignored, dismissed, or too overwhelming for our caregivers to hold, we lose something essential: the capacity to regulate our own pain. We lose the mirror of safety. And without that mirror, we begin to vanish. We adapt in all the ways we must to survive, but at the cost of connection to ourselves, our bodies, and to others.

We were wounded in relationships, and it is only through relationships that we can begin to heal.

That's why I lead trauma circles. I believe in the transformative power of being witnessed. When we allow ourselves to be seen—in our rawness, our sorrow, our rage, our tenderness—we begin to reclaim the parts of ourselves we were taught to hide. The parts labeled "too much" or "not enough." In the presence of compassionate witnessing, those frozen fragments of our past begin to thaw. We call them home. We remember who we are—not just in isolation, but in connection.

This kind of remembering isn't easy. It can hurt like hell. There's nothing comfortable about peeling back the layers we've used to protect ourselves. But in my experience, suppressing our pain is even more exhausting than feeling it. Repression costs us dearly—our vitality, our clarity, our health, and our creativity. It keeps us locked in patterns of contraction and self-protection.

When we make space to feel fully, something shifts. The pain doesn't vanish, but it integrates. It becomes part of our wholeness, rather than a fracture we're forever trying to ignore. And from that integration comes energy—clean, creative, life-giving energy. Insight rises. Possibility expands. The space we once used to hide becomes space we can now use to build, to express, to love more deeply.

In the circle, we witness each other back into being. Not by fixing or advising, but simply by staying present—by holding each other in reverence, not fixing. That, to me, is where healing truly begins.

CHAPTER FIFTEEN: HOLDING LITTLE MICKEY

I arrived at my therapist's office that day, barely able to function. My shoulders were slumped, my eyes already brimming with tears. I felt like a shell of myself, depressed, disoriented, bone-deep exhausted. My legs moved me there on autopilot, but my spirit lagged behind. I collapsed into the couch like I was surrendering to gravity itself.

Tears slipped out before I could even speak.

She didn't rush me. She sat quietly in her chair, feet grounded, heart open, holding space in that way she always does, patient, unwavering, present. Breathing me in.

"What's here?" she asked gently.

I shook my head. Words felt like pebbles in my mouth. I mumbled something about my car, the world, the chaos outside, and "I think I might be allergic to my dog, Buddha." I was rambling, reaching for something to tether myself.

She listened, then offered a soft redirect:

"Let's stay with the inner sphere," she said, her voice soft and steady. "The part you do have some control over."

That landed.

Her tone wasn't clinical; it wasn't trying to analyze or fix me. It was more like someone standing beside you on a dark porch, gently handing you the key to your own front door, not forcing you to go in, just reminding you that you live here, you have the key, but don't have to enter alone.

I inhaled, shaking. My chest felt tight, like I'd been holding my breath for years without realizing it.

Beneath the scattered words and stories I'd come in with, the car, the noise of the world, the spiraling state of everything, I began to feel my body again. I felt the heavy, airless fog of shame.

That thick, metallic stillness I've known since childhood. The old atmosphere of death and disappearance. A kind of emotional smog that clung to the inside of my skin.

I was spiraling. Again. And yet… something about her presence gave me permission to stay. To not flee the moment like I usually do.

"I took a long walk yesterday," I murmured, my voice barely audible, as if the words might vanish if I said them too loudly. "Trying to feel into it… to touch whatever this is."

I paused, blinking back tears I didn't yet understand.

"But nothing came. No insight. No clarity. Just… this kind of nothingness. This ache."

The silence that followed didn't feel empty. It felt scary. My therapist didn't rush to fill it. She just waited with me, her body still, her eyes soft, embracing me with a motherly stillness.

And in that stillness, something stirred. Not a solution. Not an answer. Just a flicker of warmth. The kind that says: You're not alone in this anymore.

She nodded with a knowing that reached beyond her words. "Sometimes that 'nothingness' is actually where the deepest pain lives. The ache without a story yet."

Then she tilted her head slightly, her eyes steady.

"I know you have spent most of your life trying to make a difference. And you have. But I wonder, what was the deeper intent behind that? I wonder if some part of you still feels like you have to earn your right to exist."

Her words hit like a bell tolling in a cathedral of grief.

I was having trouble breathing.

"I wanted to matter," I whispered, my voice cracking. "I didn't want to be a victim. I wanted to do something that would make a difference in the world, something that had meaning and purpose."

She paused. Let the words settle like a trembling net cast over haunted waters, drawing up the sorrow that had drifted, silent and unseen, beneath the surface for years.

"And maybe," she said gently, "that desire came from a much earlier place. Maybe it began the moment you lost your mother."

Suddenly, I wasn't in the room anymore.

I was two and a half years old. My mother was gone. And so was I, lost in the deep waters of grief and longing.

In the earliest years of life, our sense of self is not something we possess. It's something we receive. It's given to us through the caring eyes, the tender touch, and the voice of a mother or primary caregiver. We come to know we exist because someone else reflects us back to ourselves. We are held, seen, and named. We are told, in a thousand nonverbal ways: You're here. You matter. You are safe. You are loved.

But when my mother died by suicide, that mirror shattered. There were no eyes to meet mine. No arms to hold me. No voice to say, "It's not your fault." All I had was silence. A vacancy so total that it swallowed me whole.

This is one of the core wounds of early trauma: not just the event itself, but the response to the trauma, the separation and aloneness that comes with it. The rupture that never gets repaired. The confusion that becomes identity.

"I think that's what you're terrified of," she said, her voice soft but unwavering. "That if no one is there to see you… You might disappear."

And then, like someone reaching across time, she added: "You don't have to do this alone. I'm here. With you."

My body braced. Aloneness was safer. Familiar. But something more ancient in me, older than fear, wanted to trust, wanted to connect, wanted to be seen.

So I let her guide me.

She invited me to visualize my young self, Little Mickey. The boy who had just lost his mother at two and a half, after experiencing a lot of pain from the one who was supposed to protect him. The boy who found her hanging. The boy who disappeared because no one knew how to hold his grief.

"What did he need?" she asked.

And suddenly, I knew.

"To be held. To be told the truth. To be seen. To know it wasn't his fault."

But instead, I had inherited the guilt of the adults around me. The silence. The shame. The secret. The terror that couldn't be spoken, that lived beyond words and stories.

"You don't have to carry that anymore," she said, her eyes moist now, too. "That guilt and shame… it was never yours."

CHAPTER FIFTEEN: HOLDING LITTLE MICKEY

That's when the dam broke.

My body convulsed. I curled in on myself, weeping into my hands. The tears were ancient, older than memory could recall. I sobbed from a place beneath language, as if my bones were releasing the scream they'd held for over seventy-five years.

Still, something inside whispered: It was your fault.

She leaned in closer, not physically, but energetically.

"That's your young self speaking," she said. "But you… Your adult self… knows the truth. Can you come back to this moment with me?"

I nodded. Just barely. But it was enough.

"Let's go to him," she said. "Let's bring him home together."

She guided me into an imaginal realm, part memory, part dream, part soul retrieval.

We returned to my grandparents' home. The place where it all happened. But this time, we weren't there to relive the trauma. We were there to rescue the boy.

I saw him. Alone. Frozen. Sitting in a dark corner, shaking with fear. At my therapist's request:

I reached for him.

I picked him up.

Held my arms around him.

Whispered to him: I've got you now, and held him against my heart.

And then we left.

We walked out of that haunted space, my therapist, my adult self, and Little Mickey. Leaving the adults alone in their silent shame and suffering, we went to the backyard, one of the few places I remembered feeling free. I crawled through the hedges and lost myself in the yellow and purple pansies that I loved so much.

"Let's help him pick some flowers," she said.

So we did.

I watched him gather them in his tiny hands. It wasn't just an image. It was medicine. A new memory, planted like seeds in my nervous system. A memory that said, 'You survived.' You are loved. You can come home now. It wasn't your fault.

That image, of Little Mickey holding flowers, became the cover of this book. Because it's not just symbolic, it's real. He is real.

And he lives in me still.

As the session continued, something softened inside. A quietness settled, not numbness, but presence.

We hadn't "fixed" anything. But we had re-patterned something essential. I could almost feel new neural pathways being formed.

We had offered my inner child a new experience, one where he wasn't alone. One where he wasn't blamed, ignored, or shamed. One where he was loved and treasured.

"He doesn't need to make sense of it all," she said. "That's what your writing has been trying to do: make it all make sense. But Little Mickey doesn't need sense-making. He just needs to be held and loved."

And I can do that now.

Seventy-five years of carrying a child who never felt safe. Seventy-five years of rescuing others, over-functioning, trying to matter, to make a difference, but never feeling enough, or worthy of belonging.

"You have been letting him drive the car, but he's too young. You need to put him in the back seat to play, and you take the wheel. Your adult needs to drive and keep him safe."

For now... I can simply hold him close to my heart.

He doesn't have to search for a mother who is gone. Or a father who vanished into his own wounds.

He has me.

And that... is enough.

REFLECTIONS

This session didn't erase my trauma. It didn't tie everything up in with a neat little bow. But it did something more powerful: it created a moment of repair. A moment of connection. And in trauma work, that is everything.

The core wound of trauma is not the pain itself—it's the aloneness inside the pain. The absence of a regulating other. The experience of being too much, too little, or too invisible for someone else to meet us there.

When trauma happens and we are not held in it, it gets frozen in the body. It becomes procedural memory, an implicit pattern that repeats itself over and over. We reenact the same dynamics, not because we're broken, but because our nervous system is trying to complete what was never finished. An experience from the past, trying to find its way home.

That's why trauma healing isn't about insight alone. It's about somatic experiencing. About having new, embodied, regulating moments that contradict the old map.

In this session, I had one of those moments.

I wasn't performing. I wasn't fixing. I wasn't earning love or trying to prove my worth.

I was simply there, with my younger self. With the mirror of my therapist. With truth.

And that moment became a thread of safety woven into my system.

A thread I can follow back, again and again.

Because healing isn't a destination, it's a relationship—a commitment to turn toward ourselves with kindness, even when it hurts.

Especially when it hurts.

And in that turning, we discover something radical:

We are not broken.

We are healing into wholeness.

We are remembering who we were before the world forgot us.

And we are learning—at last—how to hold the young child who still longs to be seen.

WHAT IS TRAUMA FACILITATION? FOUR PERSPECTIVES ON INTEGRATION

Trauma facilitation is the art and practice of creating safe, attuned spaces where individuals and communities can gently explore, process, and integrate the impact of trauma, whether personal, ancestral, or cultural. It recognizes trauma not merely as an event in the past, but as an imprint carried in the body, mind, and spirit—a disconnection from safety, presence, and wholeness.

Below are four influential perspectives that offer distinct yet complementary approaches to trauma integration. While they share core principles, each brings its own lens and methodology to the healing journey.

1. Collective Healing through Presence: Thomas Hübl's Relational Approach

Thomas Hübl frames trauma as a collective phenomenon that is not only embedded in individuals but also groups, cultures, and entire societies. His Collective Trauma Integration Process (CTIP) is a deeply relational and often mystical journey.

Through group coherence, attunement, and shared witnessing, Hübl invites what has been hidden—intergenerational pain, systemic wounds, and dissociated memory—into a field of presence where it can be metabolized. Healing, in this view, becomes a service not only to the self but to the evolution of collective human consciousness.

2. Compassionate Inquiry: Gabor Maté's Path to Authenticity

Gabor Maté redefines trauma not as what happened to us, but what happened inside us as a result. His Compassionate Inquiry approach fosters a gentle, curious inner dialogue that helps uncover core wounds and unmet needs.

Maté emphasizes emotional safety, mindful awareness, and reconnection with nature and the body. By exploring these inner landscapes with compassion rather than judgment, individuals begin to reclaim their authenticity, vitality, and inner coherence.

3. Somatic Experiencing: Peter Levine's Body-Wisdom Method

Peter Levine's Somatic Experiencing (SE) is grounded in the insight that trauma lives in the nervous system. According to Levine, traumatic energy gets trapped when the body is overwhelmed and unable to complete its natural stress response. SE supports healing through slow, titrated awareness of physical sensations, helping individuals safely discharge stored tension and reconnect with a felt sense of safety, aliveness, and self-regulation. It's a bottom-up approach that honors the body's innate intelligence.

4. Indigenous Healing: Restoring Connection and Identity

Indigenous trauma healing offers a holistic and culturally rooted path, seeing trauma not only as personal pain but as collective, historical, and spiritual disruption. Rather than targeting symptoms, this approach seeks to restore balance by reconnecting with the land, language, ancestors, community, and ceremony. Practices are grounded in self-determination, cultural pride, storytelling, and traditional knowledge. A "two-eyed seeing" model integrates Indigenous and Western wisdom, always centering Indigenous values such as non-interference, communal healing, and deep respect for all life. Here, healing becomes an act of reclamation—of identity, of voice, of belonging.

Trauma Facilitation: A Path of Remembering

Across these traditions, a shared truth emerges: trauma is not something to be fixed, but something to be felt, witnessed, and integrated. Whether in one-on-one sessions or collective circles, trauma facilitation honors the wisdom of the body, the medicine of presence, and the resilience of the human spirit. In a world fractured by disconnection, it offers a sacred path back to coherence, to aliveness, and to the truth of who we are.

CHAPTER SIXTEEN

Relational Intimacy

Real intimacy is a sacred experience.
It never exposes its secret trust and belonging to the
voyeuristic eye of a neon culture. Real intimacy is of
the soul, and the soul is reserved.

John O'Donohue

For the past decade, I've been walking a path I never imagined—teaching and exploring relational intimacy through the lens of trauma. Given the chaos, heartbreak, and ruptures that colored many of my earlier relationships, I often wondered if I was qualified to speak on the subject. But perhaps that's what makes this path sacred: the humility forged by failure, the wisdom born from wounds that no longer fester but inform, and the grace that comes through surrender.

At this or the past decade, I've been walking a path I never imagined—teaching and exploring relational intimacy through the lens of trauma. Given the chaos, heartbreak, and ruptures that colored many of my earlier relationships, I often wondered if I was qualified to speak on the subject. But perhaps that's what makes this path sacred: the humility forged by failure, the wisdom born from wounds that no longer fester but inform, and the grace that comes through surrender.

At this stage in life, I look back not with shame but with reverence. Every failed attempt at closeness, every heartbreak, every misstep has become part of the curriculum. They've taught me not just what fractures connection, but what fosters it—what love requires beyond the romance, the rush, and the fairy tale we're sold.

I've come to see relational intimacy as a sacred, dynamic unfolding—an emergent process by which we reawaken and cultivate our innate sense of connection and deep belonging to ourselves, one another, and the wider relational and ecological field we inhabit.

Many of us walk around armored and defended, shaped by early traumas, heartbreaks, and inherited patterns of behavior. We tuck away our unacceptable parts like contraband—too scared to be seen, too protected to let ourselves be known.

But true intimacy invites us into the holy act of seeing and being seen from the inside out. And that kind of vulnerability feels impossible without a foundation of safety. Safety isn't a given. It's something we must learn to feel and co-create. In my courses, I always start by asking, 'What helps you feel safe?' What do you need in place to stay open, even when you're triggered? What boundaries must be honored, and how can we hold each other accountable with love?

We turn toward embodied awareness because the body tells the truth. Without attuning to our breath, sensations, emotions, and the deep intelligence of our felt sense, we remain distant from our sacred selves and authentic connection with others. We might speak of intimacy, but we're not truly living it without embodiment. Intimacy unfolds in the raw, present-moment experience of being fully here with each other.

One of the most powerful distinctions I've learned is between "relationship" and "relating." The word 'relationship' often carries a static weight, as if it were a thing, a fixed structure made of memories, roles, and agreements. We say, "my relationship with my partner," but we are speaking of is a story based on what has happened in the past. This can trap us in a version of ourselves that no longer fits, grows, evolves, or connects us with our higher selves.

Relating is alive. It's a verb. A pulse. A dance. An emergence from the field of possibility. It's what happens in the moment, between breaths and glances, in the pauses and ruptures, in the courage to ask, "What's here now?" instead of clinging to what was. Relating isn't about performance or perfection; it's about presence. It invites curiosity instead of assumption, Aliveness instead of repetition.

When we relate in real time, we step into the sacred field that Thich Nhat Hanh calls inter-being, the felt recognition that we are not separate. That there is no "me" without "you." The quality of our connection is a mirror for how deeply we've come home to ourselves.

> *My willingness to be intimate with my own deep feelings creates the space for intimacy with another.*
>
> Shakti Gawain

How can we open ourselves to another if we've kept our feelings and sensations locked inside? Even the most tender love can feel threatening if our inner world is ruled by judgment, shame, or silence. We flinch at kindness. We sabotage closeness. We long for connection, but recoil when it comes too near.

This is why true intimacy begins within—with the quiet courage to sit beside our own grief, rage, and longing—not to fix or flee, but to feel. To meet what aches with presence, to turn toward what's hard instead of away. Only from this tender self-communion can we offer something real to another, not from need, not for approval, but from the rooted ground of our own wholeness, woven into the greater web of interconnection.

Embodied relating is the gateway. It brings us home to the body—the original archive of our lived experience. Here, the unspoken stories live. Ancestral echoes, cultural wounds, childhood imprints—all whisper through tight shoulders, hollow bellies, and the subtle tremble in the jaw. The body remembers what the mind has learned to forget or suppress. And when we slow down enough to listen, not just conceptually but viscerally, we begin to thaw the frozen places within us.

Relational intimacy offers us a sacred mirror. Not just of our beauty, but of our shadow—the exiled parts, the raw ache, the places we hide. Time and again, I've witnessed how the steady presence of another can illuminate what I couldn't face alone. And in that brave reflection, something begins to soften. I've come to integrate parts of myself I once believed were too broken, too much, too tender to reveal.

At the root of all trauma is separation, from our bodies, from each other, and from the living Earth. Healing in relationships isn't simply about the connection between two people. It's a deeper restoration of the very fabric of belonging across the field of time. I've experienced moments when being deeply seen cracked open a reservoir of pain held tight in my nervous system for decades, pain that began to dissolve not because it was fixed, but because it was finally felt… and stayed with. Witnessed. Held. Loved.

And here's the paradox: when met with awareness, conflict can deepen intimacy. It exposes our projections, our defenses, and our terror of being abandoned or engulfed. But if we resist the urge to flee, defend, or blame, if we pause instead of collapsing, conflict becomes a doorway —a portal to repair, an invitation to love with greater clarity and compassion.

This mirrors Imago theory, which suggests that we unconsciously choose partners who echo our earliest wounds, not to relive the pain, but to bring it to the surface for healing. It's not always graceful. But it's real. And it's sacred.

Healing doesn't happen in the mind. It occurs in the trembling, tears, and breath returning after years, sometimes lifetimes of being held. Emotions and sensations are the native language of intimacy. When we build the capacity to stay present with our inner world, we stop outsourcing our worth. We stop demanding that others carry what we haven't yet met in ourselves. This inner spaciousness becomes the soil for authentic connection.

It allows us to shift from reflex to response. From fear to compassion. From performance to presence.

I invite you to pause and reflect:

Where in your life are you reacting out of habit instead of responding with presence?

What conversation is waiting to be had, not just with someone else but yourself?

We don't need to fix each other to connect. We don't even need to agree.

What we need is to stay, to feel, and to listen without turning away. Intimacy isn't sameness; it's depth, the courage to let someone be who they are and choose to stay in connection anyway.

Meditation, prayer, and reflection aren't just personal practices. They're relational. They help us soften before we speak, pause before we project, and choose love before we collapse into defense. They return us to the heart, not the wound masquerading as truth, but the heart that remembers who we are beneath it all.

Relational intimacy asks us to show up whole, not perfect. To meet each moment as it is, not as we wish it were. It's a practice of returning—again and again—to the pulse of what's true in the moment.

And in many ways, this is the very essence of healing: a phenomenological unfolding.

Phenomenology is not a theory but a lived experience, felt in the body, shaped by perception, and interpreted through memory. It teaches us that healing arises not in the idea of a moment but in how it occurs in the present: raw, immediate, and unfiltered. It invites us to inhabit our experience more fully, with less distortion and more presence.

And it's in this returning that we become trustworthy. Not because we never leave, but because we keep coming back.

Back to presence.

Back to humility.

Back to love.

> *"The beginning of love is to let those we love be perfectly themselves, and not to twist them to fit our own image. Otherwise, we love only the reflection of ourselves we find in them."*
>
> Thomas Merton

And real love isn't just something we feel, it's something we practice. Moment by moment. In the small choices to stay open when we want to shut down. In the pauses, we choose to breathe instead of react. In the mess of human connection, where nothing is tidy but everything is alive.

Relational intimacy isn't about perfect communication or avoiding conflict. It's about showing up as we are, with all of it—the ache, the beauty, the confusion, the longing—and discovering, over time, that it's safe to be seen.

This kind of connection changes things—not just between two people but in the spaces we inhabit, the communities we touch, and even the systems we live within. When we start to relate from a place of presence rather than protection and projection, we break the cycles of numbing and disconnection that nourish and heal the world's collective wounds.

The unraveling we see around us—climate collapse, political polarization, systemic injustice—isn't separate from our personal pain. It's all part of the same rupture—a collective body that's been bracing, distancing, and numbing for too long, holding too much, and forgetting how to feel.

And yet, when one of us softens, something shifts. When one of us chooses to stay with the discomfort rather than abandon ourselves, we begin to repair what's never really been broken. It doesn't have to be big—a breath. A word. A willingness to remain in the room, heart open, even when it's hard and we want to turn away.

That's where healing begins.

In my own life, I've seen that the most transformative moments often came not through answers, but through presence, when someone stayed with me, and I stayed with myself, when the walls cracked just enough for the light to get in.

And through that sacred light, I began to see that others shared the pain I thought was mine alone. The wounds weren't just personal but part of a larger story. And that story can change. It must change if humanity is to survive these challenging times.

So maybe the work isn't about striving to fix what's broken but about learning how to hold it differently—with more tenderness, truth, breath, compassion, and love. It is about allowing the past to be an integrated memory rather than an unfinished past that keeps arising to be felt, seen, and embraced.

This is how we remember that we belong to each other, to the Earth, to something more profound than the wounds we've carried. We are not separate from the world. We are the world!

In the end, intimacy is not the absence of pain, but the presence of love.

> *Love does not happen where we already love someone. Love happens when we embrace something that was difficult to include.*
>
> Thomas Hübl

TOWARD RELATIONAL HEALING

Relational healing begins with how we listen and speak—with presence, care, and embodied awareness. True intimacy lives in the courage to show up, to speak from the heart, and to meet each other beyond inherited roles and stories.

It takes courage to face our shadows and tend to what we've exiled. But in that turning, we begin to co-create connection rooted in love and shared humanity.

Perception isn't truth—it's a lens shaped by culture, memory, and conditioning. We don't see the world as it is, but as we perceive it to be. A powerful question to ask: What am I looking and listening through?

The Gestalt Paradoxical Theory of Change teaches that transformation doesn't come by striving to be different but by fully embracing who we are. Healing isn't about fixing—it's about remembering our true nature.

What keeps us stuck—reactivity, repetition, disconnection—often stems from what we've been avoiding. We unconsciously recreate old dynamics, seeking completion, but the chase only deepens the split.

Healing begins when we stop running and meet our experience with curiosity and compassion, when we feel what once felt unbearable. When we welcome back the parts we've left behind.

Change arises not through effort, but through presence. Through loving awareness. We don't become someone new—we return to who we've always been.

And in that remembering, change no longer needs to be chased. It simply happens.

REFLECTIONS

One of One of the most profound relational discoveries I've made is this: I don't listen. I never have. And I never will. Of course, that's not entirely true, but holding it this way keeps us awake.

It reveals the illusion that I'm fully present when, in truth, I'm often listening through layers of expectation, defense, and habit. This lens—what I call my "already, always listening"—is where most of us unconsciously dwell: in a bubble of separation shaped by projection, interpretation, and assumption. Rather than truly receiving, we translate. We hear the words, but miss what lives beneath them—the more profound meaning, the felt truth.

By admitting that I don't listen, I stay curious. I keep asking myself:

What am I missing?

What's being said beneath the words?

What truth is living in the silence?

This shift has become a sacred practice. It reminds us to check in rather than check out, pause before reacting, soften the need to be right, and choose to be with instead. It cultivates humility and opens the door to genuine connection, where the unsaid becomes visible and deeper understanding can finally emerge.

This realization didn't come easily. It struck me like a bolt of lightning during a workshop exercise on deep listening. I witnessed two participants—a man and a woman—as they took turns sharing their primary relationships, while I practiced being fully present, attentive, and embodied.

The man spoke about his current partner, describing how difficult she was, constantly questioning, arguing, and pushing back. He compared her to his first wife, who, in his words, was "so easy." They never argued, and she always went along with whatever he suggested. My initial thought was, Why aren't they still together if it was so easy? Then it hit me like a ton of bricks: He wasn't listening in that relationship. No wonder she left.

At that moment, a more profound truth surfaced. My thoughts shifted to Meriel, my Canadian partner, and I felt a wave of recognition: Oh, my God, I wasn't listening to her either. Meriel was naturally easygoing, the kind of person who avoided confrontation and didn't press too hard when things felt tense. I realized I had overridden her quiet concerns and challenges about our finances, living situation, and emotional connection. I hadn't honestly heard her because, at some level, I didn't want to hear, or I was triggered into a trauma response. Her voice had gotten muted, lost beneath my distractions, assumptions, and projections.

The depth of this realization moved me to act. Since Meriel and I had managed to remain good friends after our separation, I picked up the phone and called her immediately. I apologized for not listening to her, for dismissing what mattered to her. She acknowledged that it was true, and while there was no anger in her response, there was a gentle affirmation of the hurt my inattention had caused. It was a humbling moment, but also an opportunity for healing.

The problem wasn't that I couldn't hear. The problem was that by the time her words passed through the filters of my projections, unexamined beliefs, and unresolved trauma, they were distorted. My past hijacked my ability to listen, not just to her, but to my own emotions and my body. Add to that the whirlwind of my

ADHD, a mind constantly leaping from thought to thought like a Mexican jumping bean. It's no wonder I struggled to stay present.

I realized that authentic listening is an act of intimacy, requiring not just ears, but also heart, mind, and body.

Through this exploration, I've realized that listening isn't simply about hearing; it's about presence, connection, and cultivating the inner spaciousness needed to receive another fully. The way we listen shapes not only our relationships but also our understanding of the world and ourselves.

One framework that has deeply supported my growth in this area comes from MIT professor Otto Scharmer, who describes four distinct levels of listening. I've adapted his insights and made them my own. I invite you to reflect on each level, not as a judgment, but as a map. Notice where you tend to operate, and where there's room to expand into deeper, more embodied listening in your everyday life. Below are some of the distinctions from our Relational Intimacy course.

FOUR LEVELS OF LISTENING

1. Habitual Listening (Downloading) – 2D

This is the flatland of listening, reactive, repetitive, filtered through old stories and unconscious projection. We're not really with the other; we're translating and projecting everything through the noise of our mind. This level is like watching shadows on a wall: familiar, but disconnected from the source. There's no depth, no discovery, just the disembodied illusion of listening.

2. Factual Listening – 2D with edges of 3D

Here, the mind opens. We tune into data, track what's being said, and gather information. There's progress—but it's still mostly mental, lacking emotional resonance. I've done this with friends in crisis, listening for what I could fix, while missing the ache in their voice. This level feels like reading a map: helpful, but not the terrain. You're still separate, standing outside the experience.

3. Empathic Listening – 3D

This is where listening becomes a living bridge—relational, embodied, and heart-centered. We drop beneath the surface of words and into the shared field between us. We feel the contours of the other's experience from the inside, letting their reality touch and move us. Empathic listening isn't about fixing or analyzing; it's about being with—fully, vulnerably, humanly.

It brings dimension—depth, resonance, and attunement. We listen not just with our ears, but with our bodies, our breath, our presence. In this space, silence can speak volumes, and understanding emerges not from thought but from felt connection.

This is the listening that heals—not by offering answers, but by offering ourselves. It is here, in the sacred act of truly being with another, that authentic transformation begins.

4. Generative Listening – 4D

This is listening beyond listening—a gateway into what has not yet taken form. Here, we transcend subject-object separation and enter intra-being, where we no longer observe each other from the outside but co-inhabit a shared field of becoming.

Generative listening is sacred receptivity. We engage with our whole being—body, heart, mind, intuition—tuning into what is emerging through us. Boundaries soften. The "WE" space opens, rich with creative potential.

Insight no longer comes from the past—it flows from presence. Words slow, silence deepens, and something holy begins to move. Dialogue becomes a vessel for what wants to be born.

This is not about fixing or understanding. It's about surrendering to mystery, co-creating with the unknown. Listening becomes a prayer and a prophecy—an invocation of new futures waiting to be lived.

Listening as an Act of Love

Authentic listening is love made visible—a way of saying, you matter. It softens walls, builds trust, and invites connection through presence.

As we truly listen—not just to others, but to ourselves—we meet old wounds, unmet needs, and forgotten parts longing to be heard.

As Thomas Hübl teaches, we practice listening to myself, listening to you, listening to me, and the space between us.

In that shared field, something deeper arises: coherence, resonance, connection, integration, and healing.

This kind of listening asks for courage and openness. But when we give it, love moves. We remember we're not alone—we're human, together.

As Ram Dass says, "I am loving awareness."

Listening Gives Speaking

Authentic speaking
doesn't begin with words.
It begins with listening—
not just hearing, but tuning the soul
like a drumskin to what trembles beneath.
Listening to breath,
to the quiver in your voice,
to the hush between us
where truth waits, shivering,
longing to be known.
When I truly listen,
I become a hollow bone—
empty of answers,
of armor,
of the need to be right.
I fall below the noise
into the low, sacred hum
of what's real.
From that stillness,
something raw and radiant finds me—
not polished, not rehearsed,
but pulsing with life.
Words rise like smoke from a fire,
from presence, not performance.
And when they come,
they don't strike—they settle.
They land like soft stones
in the center of the fire,
offerings we can circle around.

This is how listening gives speaking.
It clears the air,
so truth can breathe—
not just mine,
but ours.
When I listen first,
you feel it.
Something inside you loosens.
The air between us
becomes breathable.
And suddenly,
connection isn't a show—
it's a moment.
A shared horizon.
A beginning.
This is intimacy's root:
not fixing, not fighting,
not even agreeing—
but staying.
Holding presence
like a bowl of still water.
Letting each word
be carved by the quiet hand
of truly hearing
one another.

**Because the most powerful words
are born of silence.**

CHAPTER SEVENTEEN

Finding Our Purpose: A Journey Toward Wholeness

"Anything or anyone that does not bring you alive is too small for you.".

David Whyte

For much of my life, I searched—restlessly, relentlessly—for purpose. Like many, I was taught to equate purpose with productivity, to measure my worth by how hard I worked, what I achieved, or how successful I appeared. I chased goals, convinced the next one would finally make me feel whole

But it wasn't failure that disillusioned me—it was success. Again and again, I reached the goals I had set, achieving what I believed would finally make me feel whole. And yet, each time, the celebration was fleeting, the satisfaction thin. Beneath the applause and outer accomplishment, a quiet emptiness echoed through me. It was as though no matter how high I climbed, something essential remained untouched.

I didn't see then how deeply the belief in my own unworthiness had rooted itself in my psyche. I wasn't just afraid of failure—I was uncomfortable with success. It felt undeserved, foreign, even dangerous. So I began to sabotage it, often without realizing it. I'd overextend, procrastinate, push people away, or abandon projects just as they were about to flourish. And every time I did, it reinforced the old narrative: See? You're not enough. You don't belong. You'll never hold on to what matters.

This cycle—reach, achieve, collapse—repeated itself more than I remember. It wasn't about laziness or a lack of will. It was more profound and complex to see: an unconscious compulsion to reenact an old, inherited story. A story passed down through generations, etched into my nervous system long before I had words for it. The belief that love must be earned, that worth is conditional, and that only by doing something exceptional could I justify my existence. Beneath every ambition was a quiet desperation: Am I enough yet? Have I finally proven I belong? Will my father love me now?

This began to shift only through the long, often painful path of healing, one that asked me to stop running and start facing the inner architecture of my suffering. I had to see the habitual structures I had built: the striving, the self-sabotage, the constant seeking of approval disguised as ambition. These patterns weren't just behaviors—they were survival strategies, crafted with care to protect a younger self who didn't feel safe simply being.

At first, I resisted. I wanted transformation without discomfort, change without grief. But healing doesn't work that way. It asked me to sit in the discomfort, to breathe into the ache, and to begin again and again, each time with more gentleness.

Gradually, I stopped chasing purpose as something out there, some future identity that would finally make me whole. I turned inward—not to fix what was broken, but to listen to what had been exiled. The parts of me that had gone silent, shamed, or forgotten began to speak. And I, for the first time, truly listened.

What emerged wasn't a grand revelation, but a quiet truth: purpose isn't something I need to earn. It's not a role, a title, or a measure of worth. It's a presence to live into, a relationship with my being. It's how I meet myself in each moment—with honesty, compassion, and the courage to stay.

Purpose became less about what I do and more about how I do it—how fully I show up, how deeply I feel, how willingly I love. It is an unfolding, not a destination. A remembering, not a reward. And beneath it all, the most radical realization of all: I am, and have always been, enough.

I now see that purpose isn't the light at the end of healing—it is the path itself. It lives in the daily act of turning toward what I once turned away from, in softening the hard edges I built to survive, in making space for the grief I was told to hide, the anger I was taught to fear, and the tenderness I didn't believe I deserved.

Each time I welcome back a part of myself I once rejected, I am living my purpose—not as a performance but as a practice—a quiet revolution of self-compassion. This is how the soul mends—not all at once, but in moments of presence, honest breaths, and the courage to stay with what is.

I've come to trust that there is purpose in every stumble, every return, every whispered truth that rises from within. And I've learned that the most profound transformation doesn't come from doing more, but from being more—more present, more real, more fully human.

This kind of purpose is not measured in milestones. It reveals itself in how I meet the world—with open hands, a grounded heart, and the willingness to let my healing ripple out into the lives of others. With all its scars and awakenings, my story becomes part of a larger unfolding—a sacred thread in the great weaving of collective restoration.

And so I walk forward, not seeking perfection but integration. I am not chasing meaning but creating it—moment by moment—through the way I live, love, and choose to begin again.

I used to think purpose had to be big, loud, clear, unquestionable. I believed it would arrive like a calling, fully formed and impossible to miss. But what I've discovered is far more subtle and sacred. Purpose doesn't shout. It whispers. It hums in the breath. It trembles in the body when truth is near. It rises in the quiet courage to be fully ourselves, even when the world urges us to be anything but.

As Emerson wrote, "To be yourself in a world that is constantly trying to make you something else is the greatest accomplishment." And yet, it's not a one-time act of defiance—it's a daily devotion—a practice of remembering, returning, and releasing the masks we've worn to survive.

The more I trust the language of the body—the heat of presence, the weight of misalignment, the flutter of resonance—the more I live from the inside out.

Purpose ceases to be a goal and becomes a rhythm. Something I am attuned to rather than striving for. And in that shift, something softens. The pressure lifts. I no longer need to prove my worth through grand achievements. My being is enough.

But this isn't a solitary walk. If anything, purpose is revealed through our relationships: the tender gaze of a friend, the vulnerable moment in a healing circle, the wordless recognition between two people who have walked through fire and stayed open. These are the places where my purpose speaks most clearly—where it's mirrored back to me, shaped and refined by love, connection, and community.

I've learned that purpose isn't just about what I bring to the world—it's also about what the world brings forth in me. It's a conversation, not a monologue. A shared breath, not a solo declaration.

And so I keep listening. I keep showing up—not because I have all the answers, but because I'm willing to keep asking the questions, with humility, reverence, and the understanding that purpose is not a possession but a path walked together, one step at a time.

My teachers, friends, mentors, and those I've served have all shaped this unfolding. Their presence taught me what no solitary path ever could—that my purpose is not mine alone. It is woven into a larger fabric of shared becoming. As Thomas Hübl reminds us, our path is braided with the collective. When we heal, we help mend the invisible wounds of our culture. Our transformation ripples outward, offering others permission and possibility.

I see this most clearly in the trauma healing circles I hold. In these sacred containers, something ancient and alive moves through us, beyond individual stories, roles, or identities. Vulnerability becomes a doorway, and as each person reclaims the parts of themselves once left behind, a deeper wholeness emerges—not just for them but for all of us.

Witnessing others heal, I feel my own healing deepen. Offering presence, I receive it. Telling the truth, I hear it echo through the room.

This is co-healing—reciprocal, embodied, real. It's where purpose becomes more than a concept. It becomes contact, a force that lives between us, drawing us back to the sacred ground of connection.

What I've come to know is that true purpose arises not from ambition but from integration. It comes when mind, body, and heart are no longer in conflict but in conversation. This coherence becomes my compass when thought is grounded in feeling and action flows from truth. It doesn't always point to ease, but it always points to what's real.

Purpose, then, is not something to find. It's a way of listening. A way of relating. A way of remembering—moment by moment—who we are, what we carry, and what we're here to offer, together.

Each morning, I understand that purpose is not something to arrive at but something to return to—again and again. It lives not in grand declarations but in the small, often unseen choices to stay present, to stay open. It lives in how I respond to difficulty with curiosity instead of defense, how I speak to the ones I love, and how I forgive myself when I forget.

Purpose isn't static—it breathes with me. It expands in moments of joy, contracts in grief, and pulses through the ordinary rhythms of life. It humbles me with its simplicity: a hand held, a truth spoken, a silence honored. These are not gestures of grandeur, but of grace. And grace guides me back when I wander, which I still do. Often.

A softness comes with this knowing—a release from the pressure to prove or perform. I no longer feel the need to earn my place here. My worth is not measured in productivity, perfection, or praise. It is inherent, inherited, and held.

And as I honor the lives that made mine possible—the women who carried me before I was born, the ancestors whose blood and memory move through me—I also honor the future, not just in legacy but in how I choose to live now. The way I tend to my own healing becomes part of the inheritance I leave behind.

So I walk forward not to achieve purpose but to embody it, to let it unfold through me, to trust that by living in alignment with what is real, tender, and true, I am already doing what I came here to do. And maybe that is enough. Maybe it always has been.

There is beauty in this ongoing journey, which lies in the integration of all that I am. I have learned that true purpose emerges when I stop trying to compartmentalize my life into neat boxes of achievement and instead allow myself to experience the full spectrum of human emotion. In the interplay of light and shadow, joy and sorrow, I find the raw materials of transformation. I have embraced the idea that my purpose is a dialogue between my inner world and the external reality. This conversation is constantly unfolding, inviting me to participate in creating something greater than myself.

Ultimately, I no longer chase purpose as if it were an external prize waiting to be discovered. Instead, I let it emerge naturally through my expression, healing, and relationships. My purpose isn't confined to a career or a singular passion; it is the integration of all that I am, continuously shaped by my experiences, connections, and commitment to healing myself and the collective. Every step I take, every emotion I honor, and every moment of vulnerability I share contribute to a life of profound meaning. This life not only transforms me but also resonates with those around me.

I invite you to join me in this ongoing journey of discovery. Let us embrace our wounds, reclaim our suppressed parts, and allow our true purpose to shine forth—not as a destination but as an ever-evolving movement toward wholeness and connection. In doing so, we participate in a collective healing that transcends our individual stories, creating a tapestry of resilience, compassion, and shared humanity to light the way for future generations.

When freedom does not have a purpose, when it does not wish to know anything about the rule of law engraved in the hearts of men and women, when it does not listen to the voice of conscience, it turns against humanity and society.

Pope John Paul II

CHAPTER EIGHTEEN

Ancestors

Our souls, as well as our bodies, are composed of individual elements already present in the ranks of our ancestors. The "newness" in the individual psyche is an endlessly varied recombination of age-old components.

C. G. Jung

Have you ever felt the presence of those who came before you—not just in old photographs or family stories, but as quiet patterns in your thoughts, emotions, or even the shape and movements of your body? Our Ancestors are our roots. They have been encoded in our bodies since the beginning of time.

Connecting with our ancestors opens a powerful doorway into understanding the deeper roots of our suffering, behaviors, and longings. When I began exploring my lineage, I didn't just uncover inherited pain. I discovered strength, resilience, and hard-won wisdom. My ancestors stopped being distant figures lost in time. They became allies, guides, and messengers from the past, illuminating the path ahead.

I can feel them when I slow down and listen to their subtle energy. Their unfinished stories live in my cells, in the places I ache, in the choices I make without fully knowing why. As I learned to engage in ancestral healing, I realized I was not only tending to my own wounds but helping to complete cycles my ancestors couldn't finish in their lifetimes. That kind of healing doesn't just move backward but also forward. It restores vitality to the lineage and frees future generations from carrying burdens that were never theirs to bear.

There's a beautiful reciprocity in this work. As we bring love and awareness to our ancestors, we evolve. We become the ones who can say, "It ends here," or "It starts here."

We become the physical presence needed to resolve what is left undone. In doing so, we interrupt patterns of harm and unconscious repetition, not just in our families but also in our culture and even in our relationship with the Earth.

Much of our disconnection from one another and nature has its roots in unresolved ancestral trauma. When we tend to these unseen wounds, we remember who we truly are: beings of light, life, and love, woven into the great web of existence.

Our DNA carries more than physical traits. It holds memories, emotions, beliefs, trauma, and wisdom. Thanks to the science of epigenetics, we now understand that our ancestors' experiences, especially unhealed trauma, can affect how our genes are expressed, passing emotional pain and survival patterns down through generations.

Listening to the story in our blood and bones reveals our proper place in the world, our potential, and our role in healing something far greater than ourselves.

This work is not merely personal—it is planetary. It is a call to remember, to listen deeply, and to reclaim the ancestral wisdom that already lives within us, waiting to be awakened.

My healing journey has helped me see the hidden forces that have shaped my life—forces I would never have recognized had I not looked deeply into the past. Understanding the shock of the Pearl Harbor bombing on both my parents gave context to my mother's suicide and my father's emotional absence. That one historical event sent a silent shock wave through our family, creating a void I lived with for decades.

It helped me see the roots of my lifelong yearning—to be seen, heard, and felt—and the armor I built to survive. Like many men in my lineage, I inherited a deep, unconscious drive to protect myself. I found myself trapped in a cycle of victim and perpetrator, repeating patterns I didn't fully understand—until one day, I said, "No more." Breaking that cycle has become a central purpose of my life.

Exploring my paternal grandparents' immigration from Scandinavia revealed the roots of a deeply ingrained scarcity mindset—a belief in "not enough," born from loss, displacement, and disconnection from the land. It helped me understand the part of me that longs to return to something more grounded, more whole.

Looking at my Danish grandfather's and father's patriarchal attitudes helped me confront my struggles with intimacy, emotional neediness, and desire. But these reflections also opened me to compassion for them and myself.

From my mother's early life, I uncovered the source of my tenderness, creativity, and capacity to care—qualities I once feared made me appear weak but now recognize as some of my greatest strengths. Through the story of my maternal grandmother, a woman shaped by fear and feudalism, I traced the roots of the low self-worth and subservience that haunted generations.

Yet even amidst the trauma and silence, I can now see the love that was there, trying to find its way through. These ancestral threads—woven from hardship, resilience, and care—laid the foundation for my healing. They've helped me remember where I come from and who I truly am.

WHO ARE OUR ANCESTORS

> *We are caught in an inescapable network of mutuality, tied in a single garment of destiny. Whatever affects one directly affects all indirectly.*
>
> Martin Luther King Jr.

At first, I saw my ancestors simply as my direct bloodline. But through indigenous and shamanic traditions, my understanding has deepened. I've seen ancestry as far more expansive, encompassing cultural ancestors, spiritual teachers, and even the land itself.

Beyond biology, I'm shaped by spiritual leaders and historical figures tied to my lineage. The land I live on holds its ancestral memory—native peoples, plants, trees, and animals, all part of the living web that sustains us.

For those who are adopted, there are both bloodlines and "milk lines"—the ones who raised and nurtured them. We inherit not only pain and patterns of harm, but also resilience, love, care, and wisdom passed down in many forms.

Even close friends, mentors, and beloved guides who have passed on can become "heart ancestors," offering lasting guidance and support.

Our ancestors connect us with the web of life itself.

Honoring this wider lineage has deepened my sense of belonging to my soul's purpose, my community, and the land I call home. It gently dissolves the illusion of separation and softens the defenses I once depended on. In remembering and honoring my ancestors, I draw from a deep reservoir of strength and guidance that sustains both my healing and the work I offer to others.

I no longer see myself as a separate object in a world of objects. I am a thread in the great tapestry of life—woven into something far greater, and never alone

FAMILY CONSTELLATION WORK

> *Constellations succeed by diminishing the unconscious impulses that drive destructive behaviors. The pattern is released in a heartbeat, opening the heart to reverence for life and compassion for others.*
>
> Bert Hellinger

Family Constellation work, developed by psychotherapist Bert Hellinger, reveals the often unseen influence of ancestral trauma on our lives. This therapeutic approach uncovers how emotional, behavioral, and belief patterns are passed down through generations, surfacing as "core language" in our thoughts, words, and actions.

We inherit more than physical traits—we also carry the emotional and psychological burdens of our lineage. Unresolved traumas from previous generations can entangle us in cycles of pain, even without conscious awareness or direct knowledge of their origins.

By exploring at least three generations of family history, we can trace the roots of suffering to major disruptions—war, immigration, loss, parental separation, or maternal stress during pregnancy. Recognizing the impact of these events helps us bring inherited patterns to light, break free from them, and pave the way toward healing and greater freedom.

Unconscious loyalty to ancestral trauma can bind us to the pain of those who came before, especially when family members have been excluded, forgotten, or cast aside. These hidden entanglements often weigh heaviest on firstborn or only children, who may carry an unspoken duty to fulfill or redeem the family's unfinished stories. When we begin to see these patterns, the door to healing opens. Life-affirming experiences and practices, such as visualization and recalling positive memories, can rewire our neural pathways and cultivate resilience.

But healing asks more than insight—it asks for embodiment. We must feel what was once buried, especially the emotions we inherited but never had permission to express. Reconnecting with our parents, particularly our mothers, can be a profound part of this process. Strained maternal bonds often reflect generational wounds, and healing them enables us to receive life more fully and build deeper, more nourishing connections.

Family Constellation work reveals how our struggles often echo a larger family story. By acknowledging and honoring these inherited wounds, we begin to break the cycles. Even the language we use—our repeated complaints, core beliefs, and emotional signatures—can offer clues, pointing to what remains unresolved. With awareness and compassion, we can disrupt these patterns, reclaim our wholeness, and shape a life aligned with our soul's most profound truth.

CASE STUDY: FAMILY CONSTELLATION AND THE CYCLE OF FINANCIAL SCARCITY

I noticed a troubling pattern throughout my life: I would achieve significant financial success only to experience devastating losses shortly afterward. These losses often coincided with betrayals, breakups, or economic crises. Over time, I became more aware of this cycle of abundance followed by scarcity and felt it was deeply ingrained in my life. To understand and break this pattern, I decided to work with a friend who facilitated Family Constellations, a therapeutic process designed to reveal and heal intergenerational dynamics.

I brought the question to the constellation: "Why do I experience this repeated cycle of financial gain followed by loss?"

SETTING THE CONSTELLATION

In a Family Constellation, the facilitator guides you to select group members to represent significant people or elements in your life, positioning them in the room to reflect those relationships. Each representative tunes into the energy, emotions, and physical sensations they experience in their role, bringing hidden systemic dynamics to light. For example, after a difficult breakup, you might place someone as your ex, standing back-to-back with the person representing you, and then add others to reveal deeper patterns and insights.

First, I chose someone to represent me and my fear of scarcity.

Then, I selected a person to represent money, who intuitively found their place at the center of the room.

I chose a representative for my father, who instinctively positioned himself near the door, as if he were almost ready to leave.

My maternal grandmother and mother were brought in and stood near me, with my grandmother slightly in front of me.

My first stepmother, also my third, who was wealthy and had a significant influence on my father, was placed between my father and me. I believe he married her twice for financial security and childcare despite her alcoholism.

Finally, a representative for my paternal grandfather joined, standing beside me.

As each representative entered the constellation, they naturally found their places in the constellation field. The facilitator tuned into their feelings and movements, allowing the constellation to evolve organically.

EMERGING DYNAMICS

As the constellation unfolded, more profound truths began to emerge:

THE FEAR OF SCARCITY

The representative for my paternal grandfather shared a deep sense of fear and anxiety. He exuded the energy of a man who had immigrated from Denmark, conveying a profound sense of scarcity and survival-based thinking. Both my father and grandfather experienced poverty during the great depression. This fear was passed down to my father and, eventually, to me as a legacy burden.

MY FATHER'S RELATIONSHIP WITH MONEY

My father's representative gravitated toward my stepmother, who stood with the representative for money. It became clear that my father's marriage to her was heavily influenced by her wealth.

His connection to money felt transactional and fraught with unspoken shame and guilt.

MY MATERNAL LINEAGE

My maternal grandmother surprisingly stood protectively before me, representing a legacy of resilience and care.

THE BREAKTHROUGH

The facilitator instructed my representative to address my paternal grandfather and father directly. Through the representatives, I expressed the following:

To my paternal grandfather: "I honor and love you for your sacrifices. I see how hard you worked to improve our family's life. "I see also that the feelings of fear and scarcity I carry belong to you. Holding them was my way of saying I love you, but I now realize that doing so serves neither of us. With love and respect, I give them back to you. I will honor your sacrifices by doing good in the world."

To my father: "I honor your journey and your choices—this fear of not having enough shaped your life and decisions. However, I have chosen to live differently. I release myself from carrying this legacy of scarcity. Please bless me if I choose to live a different life."

As I spoke these words, the representatives shifted positions.

My father's representative moved away from the door, closer to me, while the representative for money moved into an open space between us. The dynamic between my father, my stepmother, and money softened, and the energy in the room felt lighter.

THE RESOLUTION

The constellation revealed that the cycle of financial success followed by loss wasn't truly mine; it was an inherited pattern rooted in my paternal grandfather's experiences of lack and survival. By acknowledging and honoring my ancestors' burdens while letting them go, I created space for a healthier relationship with money and abundance.

As the constellation concluded, I felt a profound relief, as if a heavy weight had been lifted from my shoulders. For the first time, I felt free from the fear of not having enough or not being enough.

This experience is a powerful example of how Family Constellations can illuminate and transform the unseen intergenerational and systemic dynamics that shape our lives, helping us heal ourselves, our ancestors, and future generations.

SHAMANISM

> *Shamanism is a way of life. It reminds us that everything is alive with energy and that we are all connected to and inseparable from a universal web of life.*
>
> Sandra Ingerman

Shamanism is an ancient animistic practice of direct revelation, a journey inward to connect with our most profound truths and access spiritual wisdom to guide our lives. We often turn to external "experts" like priests, doctors, and politicians in modern culture. While these professionals can provide valuable insights, relying solely on them can lead us to give away our power and agency. Shamanism reminds us that these external sources, however helpful, are no substitute for our innate inner guidance and the wisdom of our soul.

Direct revelation lies at the heart of shamanism. The mystical branches of many religions that followed have borrowed from this ancient wisdom tradition. The word shaman means "one who sees in the dark"—a reference to the ability to enter non-ordinary reality and access insight beyond linear time and conditioned beliefs. This realm, often referred to as Dreamtime, provides a trustworthy wellspring of creativity, compassion, manifestation, and profound insight. Here, we reconnect with ancestral wisdom and understand how our everyday thoughts, words, and actions ripple outward, shaping not only our lives but also those of future generations.

When I began exploring Shamanism three decades ago, I realized the extent of my disconnection from my personal story and ancestral lineage. Until then, my sense of self started only at birth, as if I existed in isolation, detached from the intricate web of ancestors that stretched back hundreds of thousands of years. I was blind to this vast lineage, a living "V" fanning backward through ancient times, each life a vital thread in the tapestry of my existence.

Our ancestors are not just figures of the past; they live encoded within us, their experiences woven into our bodies, breath, and bones. Their resilience, having endured wars, slavery, climate shifts, genocide, and the darkest chapters of human history, stands as a powerful testament to life's enduring drive to continue. Through each of us, their strength persists, reminding us that life, no matter the obstacles, seeks to heal, thrive, and evolve.

As my teacher Thomas Hübl says, "Life wants to live, and it wants to live through us." Embracing shamanic practices has helped me experience this truth firsthand. I've come to see my ancestors' legacy not as something static from the past, but as a living force moving through me. I am a vessel for their survival, resilience, wisdom, and hope—each step I take carries their story forward, shaping the path for those who will come after.

Shamanism is the world's oldest known spiritual healing tradition, dating back 50,000 to 100,000 years. It is grounded in an animistic worldview, the belief that all things, including objects, places, and living beings, possess a spiritual essence.

This perspective views the world as an interconnected web in which all beings, including humans, hold a relational role rather than a dominant or separate place within the ecosystem.

Unlike many mystical traditions, shamanism is not confined to fixed forms or rituals. Instead, it is a continuously evolving, earth-centered wisdom tradition attuned to the rhythms of nature and the cosmos. Its essence is alive—constantly moving, growing, and expanding like the universe.

Because of its fluid nature, shamanism resists commodification. True wisdom emerges from the vast inner world that holds the story of evolution itself, free from the limitations of modern marketing and branding.

The basic principle behind shamanic work is that to create change in the outer world, we must first transmute the inner world of toxic thoughts, limiting beliefs, and assumptions into the golden light of loving awareness.

Today's challenges require a transcendental awakening across the planet. Without such an awakening, future generations will likely face increasing hardship and a dystopian future. The following are some key distinctions of Shamanism and Journeying, followed by my journey to find an ally and enter into the web of my ancestry.

KEY DISTINCTIONS OF SHAMANISM AND SHAMANIC JOURNEYING

Journeying offers a gateway to ancestral wisdom and spiritual insight—wisdom that transcends cultural conditioning and ego-driven narratives. These journeys can support healing, facilitate conflict resolution, foster deeper understanding, and provide guidance from beyond the visible world.

Non-Ordinary Reality is the realm accessed during journeying. It is an altered state of consciousness often reached through rhythmic drumming, which helps shift the brain into a relaxed, receptive theta state. Practitioners explore the Lower, Middle, and Upper Worlds, offering unique experiences and connections with spirit allies, nature beings, or wise guides.

The Journey Process begins with a clear, heartfelt intention—this is the thread that guides the experience. Entering the journey requires a relaxed, receptive state of mind, where the chatter of everyday consciousness quiets and presence deepens. Practitioners use vivid mental imagery to cross into non-ordinary reality, often through symbolic portals like tree roots, caves, rivers, or tunnels—natural gateways between worlds. Spirit animals, such as birds, snakes, cats, or raptors, may appear as guides or carriers, helping navigate these unseen realms.

With intention as their compass, journeyers move through these inner landscapes not to escape reality, but to engage more deeply with it—to receive insight, healing, and wisdom that transcends logic and opens the heart to a larger field of knowing.

LOWER, MIDDLE, AND UPPER WORLDS

Lower World – Rooted in the earth, this realm connects us with power animals and elemental spirits who offer grounding, protection, and instinctual wisdom.

Middle World – A spiritual reflection of our physical world, the Middle World reveals insights into current relationships, life patterns, and everyday dynamics.

Upper World – Radiant and expansive, the Upper World connects us with luminous guides and teachers who offer spiritual perspective, clarity of purpose, and higher wisdom

Power Animals and Spirit Teachers: Practitioners may encounter power animals, representing entire species, or human-form guides, each bringing unique lessons and support tailored to the journeyer's life circumstances.

Receiving Guidance – Messages can arise as images, sounds, sensations, symbols, or a deep inner knowing. The key is to stay relaxed, open, and receptive through all your senses. Trust the process, and let go of the need to control or interpret too quickly. Guidance often emerges not through vivid visuals, but through a felt sense or quiet intuition. Surrender creates the space for true insight to unfold.

Preparation and Focus: Practicing meditation or mindfulness beforehand helps improve focus, while a clear, concise question or intention anchors the journey. The process ends with gratitude for any insights or messages received.

ANCESTRAL PRACTICES, RITUALS, AND GUIDANCE

Establishing an ancestor altar in my home has become essential for nurturing a meaningful connection with my lineage. This sacred space holds photographs, heirlooms, and a hand-drawn family tree, a visual tapestry reflecting the generations woven into my life. Offering prayers, flowers, and conscious awareness at the altar forms a daily ritual that bridges time, fostering a deep sense of continuity and reverence for those who came before me. This intentional practice is a way to honor and invite the guidance of my ancestors, creating an energetic flow that transcends generations.

Shamanic journeys are sacred explorations where drumbeats guide me into a theta state, leading to the three realms: upper, middle, and lower realms. I connect with spiritual guides, power animals, and wisdom keepers there. I've learned this ancient practice from shamanic teachers, guided online journeys, and local drumming circles.

Intergenerational healing is a profound commitment to healing inherited wounds and shaping a healthier, interconnected future. By confronting patterns of trauma and limiting beliefs, we can break these cycles and create a positive legacy for future generations. Ancestral healing rituals, tributes, ceremonies, and forgiveness practices form a personal pilgrimage, releasing the burdens of ancestral trauma.

Daily practices such as meditation, journaling, and prayer connect us with our ancestral guides, grounding us in their wisdom and support. This journey to honor and release ancestral trauma is a path of profound healing, unlocking a wellspring of guidance that enriches my life and resonates across the tapestry of generations past and future. I hope this chapter and book inspire you to do your own trauma integration work. Your healing is essential for the healing of this traumatized world.

> *Until you make the unconscious conscious, it will direct your life, and you will call it fate.*
>
> C.G. Jung

MY JOURNEY TO FIND AN ALLY

As the One powerful way to explore our ancestral legacy, patterns, resilience, and areas that need healing and transformation is by finding an ally, a friendly, benevolent ancestor who can act as a guide through the intricate web of intergenerational stories. In my quest to navigate this sacred terrain, I sought an ancestral guide to serve as a gatekeeper who could help open doors to deep connection and support healing for myself and my lineage.

With clear intention, I prepared to enter a shamanic journey. I set aside distractions and opened my senses, ready to move beyond the physical world in search of an ancestral ally. Guided by the steady rhythm of my drum, I slipped into a receptive state, trusting that a wise and benevolent ancestor would appear. This guide would lead me into the ancestral realm, illuminating inherited patterns and hidden strengths woven through my lineage, revealing where healing was most needed. Together, we would begin to unlock the potential for profound, lasting transformation across generations.

In the sacred stillness, a potent energy stirred as I called upon Raven, my loyal power animal who had guided me through countless journeys across the Lower, Middle, and Upper Worlds. I felt drawn to the Upper World this time, seeking a spiritual ally to deepen my connection to ancestral wisdom. As my intention rose, the drumbeat echoed like a cosmic heartbeat, pulling me beyond the veil of ordinary reality.

Raven's wings unfurled, enveloping me in a cloak of shadow and safety. Held firmly in his talons, we soared beyond the Earth, past constellations and into the swirling arms of galaxies. A thick, silver fog enveloped us—silence, mystery, and weightless anticipation.

Then, we broke through into the luminous brilliance of the Upper World. Soft, radiant colors shimmered with life, and the air thrummed with a subtle, sacred hum. It pulsed in rhythm with my heart, weaving my intention into the very fabric of this celestial realm.

I spoke my intention aloud: "Please guide me to a spirit ally who will illuminate the path to ancestral healing." My words rippled outward, absorbed into the glowing atmosphere. A profound stillness followed, as if the realm itself listened.

Then, from the radiant light, a figure emerged. It was a familiar, tender, and vulnerable face with eyes filled with sorrow and love. A soul echo of suffering and grace returned to guide me home.

My heart skipped as I recognized her, my mother, the woman who had, in life, caused both wounds and longings in equal measure. Here, she stood as my guide, enveloped in a softness that transcended the complicated layers of our past. Her presence, gentle and ethereal, reached toward me with open arms, her hands outstretched in a gesture of vulnerability and peace. She radiated a love that felt ancient, unaffected by the limitations of our earthly memories.

Tears welled in my eyes as I stepped toward her, and suddenly, unexpectedly, a wave of forgiveness rose from within me. It wasn't just mine; it felt ancient, as if it had traveled through the hidden folds of time to meet us here. The pain, the fear, the years of longing dissolved into a quiet, breathless understanding. Her hands, soft but firm with something older than words, reached for mine. In that tender touch, something unspoken was healed. Reconciliation didn't need language—it had already arrived.

At that moment, the barriers that had defined our relationship in life dissolved. I knew, with unshakable certainty, that her spirit had come as a guide, carrying the very wisdom I sought for healing the generations that connected us.

As I stood before her, everything within me softened, and the veil of pain between us seemed to dissolve. Our earthly wounds fell away, leaving only a radiant, timeless bond in the luminous vastness around us. There were no spoken words, just a wave of love that poured from her spirit to mine, sweeping through me with a depth and gentleness that brought tears to my eyes. I felt not only the mother I had always hoped to know but also her story, her struggles, and the previously untold traumas she carried.

With her hands extended, she invited me into a space where compassion overpowered resentment, where love dissolved the echoes of hurt. This encounter was not just about her; it was a portal to understanding the maternal lineage we shared.

Behind her, I sensed an array of ancestors—each a quiet witness, their eyes soft, their presence palpable. It was as if they were waiting for me to step forward and join them on a journey into our collective story.

In this profound, serene space, I realized that connecting with her in this way was a beginning, a sacred invitation to continue exploring the wounds, strengths, and resilience within our lineage. The vision of my mother faded as the ancestral figures grew closer, beckoning me into their realm. My path forward was clear; I would travel further into the lineage, weaving together the fragmented threads of my ancestry to reveal the tapestry of intergenerational healing and strength.

REFLECTIONS

It still astonishes me, the depth of that longing. Throughout my life, I have wanted my father to see me, not just with his eyes, but with his heart. I longed for him to speak to me about real things, look beneath the surface, and recognize who I was. I wanted to feel his pride, his love, his presence. As a boy, I didn't make it easy. I acted out, got in trouble, and pushed people away. But beneath the defiance was a quiet, aching hope—that somehow he might see through the noise and find the child who just wanted to be held, known, loved.

I've spent much of my adult life trying to make a difference, seeking purpose, reaching for meaning, maybe still chasing that elusive sense of being enough in my father's eyes. But everything changed when I began connecting with my ancestors—the silence I had carried cracked open. And to my surprise, my father, long gone, started showing up, not in memory, but in presence. He won't shut up now. And I love it.

I feel him around me—courageous, steady, protective—a quiet sentinel watching from beyond the veil. For the first time, it feels like he truly sees me. Once frayed and invisible, the thread between us is being rewoven—stronger, more alive than ever.

One day, I put on his old aftershave—Mennen Skin Bracer, Original—and time folded in on itself. The scent hit me like a memory made flesh. My skin tingled. My heart cracked open. I could feel him—there, real, close—as if that simple act brought us both to our senses. And in that moment, something shifted. A quiet, radiant healing took root.

Since reconnecting with my mother in the Upper World, her presence as an ally has undergone a profound transformation.

For so long, I held her as an untouchable, almost mythic figure—suspended in the sorrow of her death, more a symbol of loss than a living presence. But in that sacred realm, she emerged not as a ghost of grief, but as a radiant, fully embodied spirit—tender, creative, deeply compassionate, and profoundly human. I began to see her not only as the mother I lost, but as the woman she truly was, shaped by war, abandonment, and isolation—wounds that echoed through our lineage, not unlike my own.

Now, I feel her alive in every cell of my body. The old ache to be held and mothered has softened into a quiet knowing—her love is here, and it moves through me. She has become my trusted guide, not only in spirit, but in navigating the tangled threads of my ancestral field. Where I once felt alone in the task of healing, I now feel her at my side—clear-eyed, fierce in love, helping me sense what needs attention, what wants to be remembered, and what is ready to be released. I am no longer the boy who lost his mother. I am the man who carries her forward, the one who listens, the one who holds her love and lineage with reverence, and knows how to pass it on.

These reflections, rooted in ancestral connection, have helped me reclaim and integrate the parts of myself I once believed were lost or beyond repair. I've shifted from reactivity and woundedness toward presence and responsibility. Healing, I've learned, isn't about erasing pain or rewriting the past. It's about weaving those fragmented threads into a more complete, embodied whole.

By learning to listen across the veil, to my father's voice, my mother's love, and my lineage's deep, pulsing rhythm, I've found the guidance I once sought in living experts. I'm no longer waiting to be seen. I am witnessing myself. I'm no longer aching to be held. I am holding myself.

This is the quiet miracle of ancestral healing: it alchemizes grief into wisdom, longing into love, and separation into a sense of belonging. It reshapes our relationship to the past and our ability to meet the present with tenderness and courage, walking into the future with roots deep in wholeness.

CHAPTER NINETEEN

Collective Trauma, Technology, and Post-Truth

We continue to have this illusion that things outside of us aren't driving what we think and believe, when in fact so much of what we spend our attention on is driven by decisions of thousands of engineers and product designers.

Tristan Harris

SEEING THE WATER WE SWIM IN

Trauma isn't just personal, it's collective. We are born into an ecosystem shaped by war, genocide, colonialism, racism, and oppression, not as distant history but as living imprints in our societies, relationships, and bodies. It's the tension in the air, the way people yell at and blame each other, and the cycles of violence and disconnection that keep repeating.

Most of us don't realize we're swimming in trauma—it's like wearing tinted glasses from birth, never knowing the world has other colors. Collective trauma becomes the lens through which we perceive everything: relationships, conflict, even reality itself.

It sculpts our nervous systems to expect danger, making us highly reactive to fear, shame, and outrage—the emotions that media algorithms are designed to exploit.

When trauma goes unhealed, it loops. We find ourselves reacting to wars, injustices, and divisions as if they're happening inside us—because in a way, they are. Our nervous system can't distinguish between past and present, so we respond to today's events through the lens of old wounds. But healing is possible.

Through therapy, somatic work, spiritual practice, or deep relational witnessing, we begin to reintegrate the parts of us that were once fragmented or frozen in time. Gradually, we create more space within space to pause, to choose, to respond rather than react. We're no longer hijacked by headlines that echo our unprocessed pain. Instead, we meet the moment with clarity, grounded presence, and a sense of choice.

Healing reconnects us to compassion, curiosity, and nuance. We stop seeing others as enemies. We begin to hold complexity and bridge divides. This is how personal healing becomes collective medicine. The more we tend to what's broken inside, the more we help heal what's broken outside.

Yet in our tech-driven world, this healing is more complicated than ever. Social media amplifies our trauma, locking us in echo chambers of fear and outrage.

The ancient survival wiring in our brains is being hacked—exploited by platforms that profit from our pain. We're not just inheriting trauma now; we're consuming it, sharing it, monetizing it.

To heal, we must first step outside the distortion and see how our attention is manipulated and our nervous systems are overwhelmed. Only then can we reclaim our connection to ourselves, to each other, and the deeper world beyond the algorithm.

CHAPTER NINETEEN: COLLECTIVE TRAUMA, TECHNOLOGY, AND POST-TRUTH

*The medium, or process, of our time—electric technology—
is reshaping and restructuring patterns of social
interdependence and every aspect of our personal lives.*

Marshall McLuhan

Looking back, I see how much my undiagnosed ADHD shaped my relationship with technology. Even as Director of Sales and Marketing for IMSAI Computers—helping launch the first commercially available personal computer—I struggled with attention, impulsivity, and restlessness. At the time, I had no idea these were symptoms of ADHD. It wasn't until I got fired that I realized how incompatible traditional jobs were for me. In my late twenties, I declared myself "terminally unemployable" and shifted to consulting, sales, and entrepreneurship—paths that gave me freedom and flexibility.

However, as technology became increasingly embedded in daily life, it brought with it a new kind of stress—one I wasn't prepared for. It didn't just change how we communicated or worked; it rewired the very fabric of how we connect, relate, and exist in the world. It evolved relentlessly—faster, more complex, more invasive—like a language I never quite learned, but was expected to speak fluently. And the pace left no time to catch up.

What made it harder was the disappearance of live, person-to-person support. Simple human interactions—the reassurance of a voice, a kind face across a desk—were replaced by chatbots, passwords, and automated systems that seemed indifferent to the human on the other side. As a senior, I feel this loss acutely. There's a growing sense of alienation, as if the world has moved on without me. The digital realm often feels cold, disembodied, and unrelenting, offering convenience, perhaps, but stripping away warmth, nuance, and the safety of being seen.

There's fear in that—fear of making a mistake I can't undo, of being locked out or left behind. It's not just about frustration with devices or apps. It's about the more profound anxiety of becoming invisible in a world that no longer values lived experience, relational presence, or the slow, thoughtful pace of human connection.

A recent experience with Stripe made this painfully clear. They failed to pay me over $1,500 in class fees. I spent days trying to reach a real person, trapped in automated loops, each directing me to a website that couldn't help.

After 45 minutes on hold with a robotic voice repeating the same message, I snapped. I started screaming, "I need a person! A real human being!" Tears streamed down my face. I was yelling at a machine. I felt humiliated, helpless, like I might have a heart attack.

Eventually, I had to contact each student individually, explain the situation, cancel their payments, and ask them to resend fees months after the course had ended. It took hours of exhausting follow-up—one more tech nightmare in what's become a daily grind.

We're living through a "techno-stress" epidemic. Studies confirm what many of us feel: tech overuse is linked to anxiety, depression, and chronic stress. Social media, once a tool for connection, now fuels comparison, distraction, and overload. Research suggests up to 90% of illness is stress-related. No wonder so many people are burned out and sick.

It's a strange irony. I helped launch the personal computer—and now I often feel alienated by the very technologies I once championed. This isn't just personal. It's cultural.

SOCIAL MEDIA

> *Modern technology, particularly social media, is significantly harming society by "downgrading" human capabilities through its design that exploits our psychological vulnerabilities, leading to issues like addiction, polarization, misinformation, and a decreased ability to focus and engage in meaningful interactions.*
>
> Tristan Harris, Technology ethicist

In the Netflix documentary The Social Dilemma, Tristan Harris and other social media insiders reveal the hidden mechanisms of "surveillance capitalism." This eye-opening film pulls back the curtain on tech giants, exposing how these companies manipulate user behavior and exploit data to fuel profits, often at the expense of mental health and social cohesion. It describes how the design of modern platforms leverages our psychological vulnerabilities, contributing to addiction, mental illness, polarization, misinformation, and a diminished ability to focus or form meaningful connections.

As Harris notes, every online interaction is tracked. Every post, email, location, and conversation is stored in databases tied to our identities. The product isn't the app or service we use—it's our attention, sold to the highest bidder through personalized ads and content to steer our thoughts and actions. This data-driven influence enables companies to predict and subtly shape our behavior, affecting everything from purchasing decisions to political views.

I've experienced firsthand how technology's design captures attention and shapes habits. In the middle of concentrated writing the other day, I instinctively reached for my phone, drawn by the urge to check a meaningless notification. The device had me. Every beep, buzz, and vibration felt urgent, pulling me out of my flow. Even when silent, I check for updates as if my brain has been rewired to anticipate interruptions.

The cost of these minor distractions is far greater than we realize. Research from the University of California, Irvine, found that after a phone interruption, it takes an average of 23 minutes to regain focus fully. So a glance at my screen doesn't just steal a moment, it fractures my concentration, scattering my attention for nearly half an hour. Multiply that by the dozens of times we check our phones each day, and it becomes clear: our capacity for depth, whether in our work, our relationships, or our inner life, is slowly being eroded.

The algorithms behind social media also exploit a psychological phenomenon known as negativity bias—our tendency to pay more attention to negative information. When we encounter alarming or emotional content, we're more likely to engage with it, making us more susceptible to misinformation. Negative or sensational headlines capture our attention, and platforms are aware of this; they amplify such content to boost engagement. As a result, fear and outrage spread rapidly online, often unchallenged, because we're less likely to question content that resonates with our pre-existing anxieties or beliefs.

For example, research from MIT shows that misinformation spreads faster and more widely than the truth on Twitter. Fake news is 70% more likely to be retweeted than accurate stories, reaching a cascade depth of ten to twenty times faster than the truth. This rapid spread skews public perception, influencing beliefs and fueling societal divides. Social media algorithms prioritize content that generates engagement, meaning that fear-driven, emotionally charged falsehoods are often magnified, reinforcing echo chambers and isolating people within narrow views. Because of these algorithms, we are fed information that supports our preconceived beliefs. What you receive in your feed will likely be very different from what I accept if you already think differently from me, reinforcing the divide between us.

This issue extends far beyond personal distractions—it has profound global consequences. In crises like climate change, pandemics, and political instability, misinformation erodes public trust and distorts scientific facts.

The rise of visual misinformation—including deepfakes (a video of a person in which their face or body has been digitally altered so that they appear to be someone else, typically used maliciously or to spread false information) and AI-generated images—further manipulates public perception, as people are likelier to believe content with visual elements. These technologies are evolving rapidly, making it increasingly difficult to separate truth from fiction.

The speed at which misinformation spreads makes the problem even more alarming. A recent study found that fake news spreads six times faster than accurate information. In a world where false narratives can sway elections, shape health policies, and fuel social movements, this isn't just an inconvenience—it's a fundamental threat to our collective understanding of reality.

Post-truth threatens more than just facts—it undermines the very fabric of our shared reality. We live in an era where objective truth feels fragile, contested, and increasingly shaped by biases, algorithms, and polarizing forces distorting our perceptions. In the past, truth was something we could at least strive toward collectively—through shared experiences, open dialogue, and the accountability of trusted institutions. However, in the 21st century, truth has become increasingly subjective, shaped to fit personal beliefs, with individuals and groups inhabiting entirely separate realities.

This isn't just about political debates or disagreements over facts; it's about the erosion of our ability to agree on what is real. Society begins to fracture when there is no common ground and no shared language for truth. Without a foundation of collective reality, our ability to connect, empathize, and make meaningful progress is deeply compromised. If we can't agree on what's true, how can we solve the world's most pressing issues?

In a post-truth society, facts are no longer grounded in evidence but in emotional appeal, often amplified by technology that learns precisely what we'll respond to and feeds us more.

Social media algorithms prioritize sensationalism over accuracy, amplifying polarizing views and dividing us into echo chambers where misinformation proliferates unchecked. This doesn't just distort individual perspectives—it fragments entire communities, erodes trust, and undermines the cohesion that holds societies together. It creates fertile ground for extremism, where even the most outrageous claims gain traction, feeding off our most primal fears and insecurities.

As we lose the ability to agree on what's real, we face a dangerous potential for authoritarianism, violence, and societal decay. Suppose we are to transcend this post-truth crisis. In that case, we must actively seek ways to restore integrity to our shared understanding of reality through transparency, media literacy, and the conscious choice to engage in difficult conversations with an open heart and mind.

Ultimately, Harris captures it best when he says, "How can you wake up from the matrix when you don't know you are in it?"

AI — ARTIFICIAL INTELLIGENCE

> *By far, the greatest danger of Artificial Intelligence is that people conclude too early that they understand it.*
>
> Eliezer Yudkowsky, computer scientist and Researcher

Reflecting on the immense influence of social media and AI in my life, I can't deny the benefits these technologies have brought. They've made it easier to connect, share ideas, do research, access information, and support creative ventures and small businesses. But beneath the surface of convenience lies a far more disturbing and consequential reality—one we ignore at our peril.

The downsides are not merely inconvenient; they are insidious. And they're unfolding faster than we can comprehend. With AI evolving exponentially—doubling its capabilities in shorter and shorter cycles—the very pace has become destabilizing. I feel it in my nervous system: the relentless pings, alerts, algorithm-driven headlines, and curated content create a sense of constant interruption, a kind of internal fragmentation. This "techno-stress" leaves me anxious, depleted, and increasingly disconnected from my capacity to focus, feel, and think deeply.

On a collective level, the stakes are even more alarming. These technologies now shape public discourse, polarize communities, and confine us to digital echo chambers where truth becomes subjective and outrage becomes a currency. Social media algorithms don't elevate wisdom—they amplify what keeps us scrolling: fear, conflict, novelty, and dopamine hits. Misinformation spreads faster than facts, eroding our ability to discern what's real. Meanwhile, AI harvests our data—our clicks, habits, fears, and desires—not just to serve us, but to influence us, shape our choices, and even steer our political beliefs. It's chilling to realize how subtly our sense of agency is being hijacked.

Now, with AI-generated images, audio, and video reaching levels of near-indistinguishable realism, we face a more dangerous frontier. These synthetic creations can forge identities, fabricate events, and spread lies that look and sound like truth. They're not just illusions—they're tools of deception, capable of fooling both people and machines. The line between the real and the artificial is dissolving, and with it, our trust in what we see, hear, and believe. This isn't some distant threat—it's already happening. If we don't pause to question, regulate, and rehumanize our relationship with these tools, we risk a world where reality becomes optional. The cost of that confusion is our shared humanity.

We're already witnessing the collapse of a shared reality. Where we once agreed on basic facts, we now fracture into opposing belief systems. Conspiracy theories, misinformation, and "alternative facts" have undermined trust in science, journalism, and democratic institutions. Look no further than the climate crisis—how denial, doubt, and disinformation have stalled collective action in the face of planetary urgency. This erosion breeds fear, deepens division, and fractures our ability to cooperate, even when our survival depends on it.

We stand at a tipping point. It's no longer enough to be passive consumers of technology—we must become conscious stewards of its influence. That means setting boundaries with our devices, demanding transparency and ethical oversight, and restoring the stillness, presence, and wisdom that hyperconnectivity erodes. The future isn't predetermined. It's being shaped by how we show up now. Let us meet this moment with courage, discernment, and a fierce commitment to protect what makes us most human: empathy, truth, connection, and the ability to choose love over fear.

Yes, AI holds extraordinary promise—it could revolutionize medicine, accelerate climate solutions, and democratize education. But that promise carries a warning. For every dollar invested in AI safety, a thousand are spent on capability. Without regulation, ethical guardrails, and a moral compass, we're building tools that could easily outpace our ability to control them. The question isn't whether AI will reshape our future—it's whether we will guide that future wisely, or become casualties of our own unchecked invention.

So, the question is, how do we reclaim control and create a healthier relationship with technology?

Here are some questions I'm exploring for personal and collective action:

How can I limit the impact of technology on my mental health and productivity? Are there specific habits I can adopt, such as restricting notifications, scheduling screen-free times, or practicing mindfulness, to counteract the anxiety and distraction that technology can create?

What role do I play in fostering a more mindful digital culture? How can I encourage meaningful interactions and reduce the spread of misinformation or reactive content?

How can society reclaim agency over technology? Should we advocate for more transparent regulatory policies, such as transparency in algorithms, data privacy protections, or restrictions on manipulative content?

How can AI development be aligned with societal well-being? Could international collaboration help establish ethical guidelines, similar to an "AI Bill of Rights," to govern the responsible growth of technology?

These questions remind me that, even in a digital landscape designed to capture our attention, we still have the power to shape our relationship with technology through personal choices and collective action.

COLLECTIVE TRAUMA

> *Trauma constrains evolutionary development, delays progress, and inhibits innovation, manifesting a negative feedback loop of stagnation, systemic breakdowns, and cultural collapse.*
>
> —Thomas Hubl

Thomas Hübl describes collective trauma as a deep-seated, shared response to historical harms that affect entire societies, cultures, and classes. When left unresolved, it can manifest as a destructive cycle—repeating unhealthy behaviors and sustaining a collective shock that stagnates innovation, restrains progress, and even drives cultural collapse. This "shadow" of unresolved trauma not only blinds us to the present moment but also keeps us trapped in a cycle of aggression, exclusion, and fear-driven responses, creating a dangerous feedback loop of denial, numbing, and stagnation.

In today's interconnected world, social media and AI exacerbate collective trauma by amplifying disconnection and polarizing perspectives. Unchecked, these technologies fuel division and apathy, clouding our ability to embrace diversity, creativity, and democratic principles.

When people are continually exposed to trauma-activating content and negative feedback loops, they can lose the capacity for genuine empathy and open-mindedness. This detachment from present reality creates a fertile ground for authoritarianism, exploitation, and an erosion of democratic thinking. Furthermore, it fosters resistance to addressing pressing global issues, such as climate change, systemic violence, and corruption.

When trauma remains unprocessed, it shapes how we see the world. Our nervous systems stay on high alert, scanning for danger, making us more susceptible to content that triggers fear, shame, anger, or helplessness—the very emotions that sensationalized media and polarizing narratives are designed to provoke. Social media algorithms thrive on this activation, feeding us content that confirms our biases and reinforces our pain, keeping us trapped in cycles of reactivity.

But healing is possible. Through therapy, somatic work, inner child healing, spiritual practice, or deep relational witnessing, something shifts. We begin to create space within—space to pause, reflect, and respond instead of react. No longer hooked by headlines that mirror our wounds, we become discerning. What is true? What is manipulative? What calls for our attention—and what can we release?

As we integrate trauma, we reconnect with the deeper intelligence of the heart: compassion, curiosity, and nuance. We stop seeing others as threats and start recognizing our shared humanity. We become more resilient, more capable of holding complexity, and more willing to bridge divides. Personal healing becomes collective medicine. The more we mend what's fragmented inside, the more we can help restore what's fractured in the world.

Yes, we need media reform and ethical technology, but the deeper revolution begins within. When our wounds no longer rule us, we stop being pawns in someone else's algorithm. We reclaim our attention. We reclaim our choices. We reclaim our humanity.

Let that be our call to action.

Just like personal trauma, collective trauma is an evolutionary response—an expression of protective intelligence designed to help us survive the unbearable. When entire communities or societies endure overwhelming experiences, the collective nervous system fragments, suppressing pain to maintain functionality. But what helps us survive in the short term can cost us dearly over time: emotional numbness, chronic anxiety, and a profound, pervasive disconnection from ourselves and one another.

In this numbed state, we struggle to inhabit the present fully. Unresolved trauma lingers in our systems and is often passed down through generations. Rather than consciously engaging with life, we react from inherited survival patterns—unconsciously reenacting the past. Without integration, trauma energy becomes toxic, limiting our capacity to feel, relate, empathize, and create. This disconnection dulls our collective imagination and impairs our ability to collaborate, innovate, and heal.

The social crises we face—racism, inequality, violence, ecological collapse—are not just political or economic issues. They are symptoms of widespread disembodiment. We live in a culture shaped by a mechanistic worldview that sees people as separate units rather than as interdependent beings. We've grown over-intellectualized, hyper-individualistic, and cut off from the wisdom of our bodies and hearts. As long as we refuse to face our personal and collective shadows, we will keep accelerating toward crises of our own making—eroding democracy, destroying ecosystems, and feeding systemic injustice.

And yet, signs of awakening are all around us. Across the globe, people are turning toward practices that restore connection, including trauma-informed care, somatic healing, meditation, circle work, and collective truth-telling. More of us are beginning to understand that the work of healing isn't just personal—it's planetary. Even the deep divisions we see may serve as a wake-up call, urging us to slow down, feel more deeply, and remember that we belong to one another.

Nature teaches us that regeneration is possible. Our ancestors knew how to live in rhythm with life's cycles, and that wisdom still lives in our bones. If we can tap into that resilience through presence, compassion, and the courage to integrate what we've inherited, we can co-create a future rooted in wholeness, not fragmentation.

This is our moment. The path forward is not about perfection, but participation. If we each do the inner work, show up in relationships, and stay committed to healing, we can transform systems, rebuild trust, and shape a world where everyone and everything has a place.

Let us meet this moment with humility, truth, and fierce love. Let us reclaim our humanity—and with it, our future.

CHAPTER TWENTY

The Light of A Dying Star

*Your vision will become clear only when you can
look into your own heart. Who looks outside, dreams;
who looks inside, awakens.*

Carl Jung

I'm lying on the deck of my friend's villa in Rocky Point, Mexico, relaxing on the outdoor bed, gazing up at the darkening sky and anticipating the night's starscape. I have spent the past few weeks here working on the manuscript for this book. Buddha is lying beside me, relaxing on his back, anxiously awaiting his nightly belly rub. We are both getting old. We are the same age, 11 in dog years. I don't feel old. I feel more vibrantly alive and awake than I have ever felt. My hair has thinned, my nails are chipping, my skin is dry and spotted with age, and I have to pee several times at night. I'm no longer running marathons, skiing, or racing around the world, searching for something I can't define. I love my life. After all the years of struggle, shame, self-doubt, and searching, I have found a place of inner peace that I never thought possible. I feel that my life has meaning and purpose.

Looking up at the star-strewn canopy of the night sky above me, I wonder which stars still shine even though they may have collapsed in a supernova 20 million years before we even saw their light. Will my own light, the conscious awareness of my soul, continue to shine after I've been released from this aging skin suit? Will I be able to continue my work from the other side? Will I be reincarnated and continue my work in a new body, perhaps one that is black, brown, or yellow? I don't know. And that's part of the beautiful mystery of life. I've let go of trying to control life and am learning to embrace not knowing. What a relief.

Sleeping under the stars, listening to the restless movement of the turbulent waters of the Sea of Cortez below me, I am at peace. The waxing Cancer moon filters through the swirling cloud formations, and I can feel the power and pull of Grandmother Moon. Her gravitational pull is so strong that my nose bleeds, which often happens during a full moon phase. I am a moon child and have always been sensitive to the lunar cycles.

Gazing at the bewitching fullness of the moon, I'm reminded of what it feels like to look into the faces of my students and clients. I don't just see the surface—I sense the glow behind their eyes, the silent presence of their ancestors standing at their backs, and the vast, untapped reservoir of resilience stirring just beneath the skin.

Like the moon, we reveal only a sliver of who we are. But beneath that visible curve lies a whole world of mystery, memory, and light—a world of possibility and potential waiting to be seen, felt, and remembered.

The moon doesn't generate its own light, yet it illuminates the night sky with a brilliance that captivates us, inspires poetry, pulls tides, and stirs something ancient in our bones. Its power is subtle but profound. We don't question whether the moon matters—we feel it. We sleep differently under its glow. Our dreams change. The tides rise and fall, whole oceans answering to a celestial pull we can't see.

This is the mystery and majesty of the unseen. What's invisible often moves us more deeply than what's visible. Gravity, emotion, intuition, spirit, and the magnetic forces of connection, love, and longing are the currents that shape our lives.

I've learned to see more than the body sitting before me. When I look into someone's eyes, I glimpse inherited dreams and quiet sorrows, soul fragments calling to be gathered home. I sense the potential not yet embraced, the path not yet walked. I see who they might become if they dare to trust their own light—even when all they know is darkness. I feel their longing to become, to belong, and the beautiful obstacles waiting to be embraced as teachers.

Just as the moon reflects the light of the sun, we reflect the light in one another. Sometimes, all it takes is for one soul to be seen, deeply seen—for someone to hold the mirror of belief before another—and healing begins. That is the gift of true presence: the quiet, unwavering witness to what others may never notice.

This, I believe, is our sacred work: to attune ourselves to the invisible forces that shape us, to speak the language of soul, to revere the unseen as holy. It's not the outer form that transforms the world, but the radiance that shines through us. The moon reminds us. So does love. So does healing.

And so we remember. We remember our place in the greater web of life: the stars above us, the wind weaving through the trees, the pulse of the sea, the moon's silent glow, the steady ground beneath our feet. We are more than skin and story—we are energy in motion, a thread in the cosmic loom. Life is not happening to us; it's moving through us. We are the witness and the composer, dancing with the great unfolding. This knowing—this embodied remembrance—is a gift we all carry in our bones.

The call of a western screech owl slices through my thoughts, leaving a hush in its wake. I pause, letting the stillness settle in.

I remember Owl as guide and guardian—bringer of insight, seer in the dark. Her cry stirs something ancient within me, asking not just what I must see, but what we are being invited to illuminate—together—in the shadowlands of our becoming.

Maybe she's simply reminding us to slow down… to rest in the vast stillness and let beauty have its way with us. I never imagined stillness could be this alive, this generous, this full. After lifetimes of running, of striving and doing, what a wonder it is to be here, now—in this breath, this body, this unfolding moment.

What a fantastic gift this life is.

I've faced many challenges in my life: death, suicide, slander, betrayal, loss, murder, war, and abandonment. The weight of fear, shame, self-doubt, grief, and anger that burdened me for most of my life has dissolved into a peaceful settling into a work and life that nourishes me and supports others. Amidst the chaos and disorder, it has mostly dissolved into a strange and miraculous undulating flow state. Mostly, I find myself completely absorbed in what I'm doing, with a sense of energized focus and enjoyment that I never thought possible. Everything else fades away, and I become fully present in my activities, thriving despite past hardships. I trust life and love being alive.

It's not that I don't face challenges, get triggered, or feel the sting of regret from time to time. These experiences still arise—like waves crashing on the ever-changing shore of our evolving lives. But I've come to witness them differently. I feel them fully, then let them pass, dissolving back into the vast ocean of infinite possibility.

Like the sacred hydrological cycle—evaporating, condensing, falling as rain—our struggles too are part of a greater rhythm. They rise, move through us, and return, cleansed and transformed, to nourish the roots of our becoming. Each surge and retreat is a necessary pulse in the greater heartbeat of life.

We are not separate from these cycles. We are the cycles—living, breathing expressions of nature's intelligence. We belong to the systems that hold us, the transmutations that shape us, the sacred movements that carry us forward on the long arc of evolution.

I've made peace with my mother's suicide, not by forgetting the pain, but by transforming it into something sacred—a bridge between worlds. In spirit, she has become my ally, my muse, my confidant. I feel her presence in moments of tenderness and inspiration, and I'm profoundly grateful for the beauty, sensitivity, and love she passed on to me—gifts that continue to shape who I am.

And yet, as I reflect on the darker strands of our shared story, I recognize a difficult truth: her suffering could have ended not only her life, but mine.

My mother, deeply scarred by the aftermath of war, carried burdens far too heavy for her tender soul. I know she loved me. But her pain often eclipsed that love, spilling into moments of frustration, fury, and sometimes abuse. When I look back now, I see a woman trapped in a storm of despair, doing the best she could with what little inner resources she had. As her pain deepened, so did the volatility of her outbursts.

There's a truth I've come to accept—one that lives in paradox and is still hard to hold: had she lived, her escalating anguish might have destroyed me. And so, in a strange and unfathomable way, her decision to end her life may have saved mine.

It's a heavy truth—but one that has brought unexpected grace. Whether this memory is factual or symbolic, it helps me hold our story with greater compassion. It helps the child in me understand what once seemed incomprehensible. And in that understanding, I find forgiveness, not only for her, but for myself—and a profound sense of peace.

Through the long arc of healing, I've learned to honor my father too—for the life and light he and my mother passed on to me, and for the resilience seeded deep within our lineage. I've come to recognize the courage it must have taken for him to navigate his own trauma-shadowed path.

In tracing the patterns of inherited pain—of trauma passed down and repeated—I've encountered the concept of repetition compulsion: that unconscious drive to recreate the wounds we know, hoping this time they'll heal. I see how easily these cycles perpetuate, and how vital it is that we interrupt them.

The healing work I've done is not mine alone. It feels like a gift offered back to my ancestors, a quiet acknowledgement that says, I see you. I carry both your light and your sorrow. I trust that the ripples of this healing reach backward through time as well as forward—mending old fractures and laying down a more whole foundation for those yet to come.

My mother's memory is no longer defined by her suffering. Now, I carry her light. I feel her presence not as a wound, but as a whisper of wisdom and love. I am grateful for the gifts she gave me—and for the lessons we continue to share, soul to soul, across the veil.

Letting go of that need to defend myself has been like releasing an old, heavy cloak. For most of my life, the instinct to protect and defend became my armor, forged in the fire of my past, shaped by both childhood experiences and the sudden, brutal loss of my wife. That event reinforced the walls I'd built around myself as if an unspoken contract with my younger self had been signed to keep out pain at all costs. But in recent years, something has shifted. Forgiveness, though difficult, came to feel like the only way forward, so I began to release my grip, piece by piece.

This wasn't just forgiving those who had hurt me; it was understanding, on some deeper level, why they acted as they did. For my stepmother, who'd been put in an unwinnable situation she never asked for, I began to find compassion. I saw the roles we'd both been cast in, and it softened something in me, turning rigid memories into something fluid and more human. Even my father, who'd always felt more like a distant dream than a present figure, began to rest in my mind more peacefully as I let go of my need to be seen by him.

But this story, I've realized, isn't just mine. It touches something much more significant. Our collective story seems to cry out for an evolutionary shift—an urgent transformation that speaks to the whole of humanity. I feel humanity is at a crossroads, and the choices before us aren't simply about overcoming or forgetting our own personal challenges. It's about honoring the collective wisdom of our nervous system and tapping into the resilience of our ancestors. What if we approached every challenge with curiosity, acceptance, awe, and respect instead of trying to erase our pain, transcend our difficulties, and eliminate our fears? Those memories and triggers are the echoes of a time when shutting down was the only way we saw to survive. They're like silent witnesses to a past when life seemed too overwhelming to bear.

Our ancestors carried their defenses in their blood and bones, forged through lifetimes of survival, war, and loss. They passed them down to us—not as burdens, but as sacred inheritances, entrusted to our care. Perhaps they weren't meant to be carried forever but held only until we became present enough to feel them fully… and then lovingly let them go.

I believe this may be our great task as a species: to awaken to the intelligence embedded in our pain and recognize the adaptive beauty in the parts of ourselves we've learned to resist or hide. What if our wounds aren't weaknesses but invitations to an evolutionary awakening? What if our defenses, rather than enemies, are loyal messengers—guardians of unprocessed grief, unmet needs, and ancient fear?

This could be our evolutionary turning point: a collective willingness to meet those parts with reverence, thank them with gratefulness for how hard they've worked to keep us safe, and gently lay them down—not because we no longer need protection but because we're finally ready to live in a new way—open-hearted, undefended, whole. Maybe, just maybe, we are ready now to live without them.

How can we transcend the myth of separation and actively seek to heal the wounds that separate, alienate, and marginalize us? There is no separate self. The universe was designed for cooperation, connection, and compassion. When I take the time to heal and integrate my wounding, I cultivate an understanding of those whom I have distanced or absenced and held as an enemy or a threat.

Faith in life's grand design is not passive surrender—it is a courageous trust that allows us to meet the unknown with open hands. It is the balm for fear, the soft unraveling of our need to control what was never ours to manage. The idea that we are in charge of this vast, mysterious unfolding is a myth born of disconnection. We are not separate from creation—we are creation, participating in an evolving, intelligent, and inherently benevolent universe. Our thoughts, our actions, our very presence ripple outward in ways we can't always see, but they matter. They always matter.

And at the core of it all—beyond the stories we tell, beyond the striving and struggle—is love. Not the fleeting emotion, but the deeper current of radical acceptance, of being fully here in this moment, without dragging the past behind us or reaching anxiously toward the future. Love is what heals us, binds us, moves us. It is what restores our humanity and reminds us of our divinity.

May we live as a prayer for Buckminster Fuller's vision—a world that works for everyone and everything, where nothing and no one is left behind. Not as an abstract ideal, but as a living, breathing reality we help shape with our choices, our voices, and our willingness to feel.

If we are to create a different future, we must stop abandoning the present. We must come home to the now—not just intellectually, but viscerally, in our bodies, in our breath, in our hearts. For too long, the mind has ruled like a tyrant, cutting us off from the wisdom that lives in our emotional body, from the sacred intelligence of the heart.

But life is calling us back. Calling us to remember. Calling us to reclaim what we've exiled.

This is not just healing—it is a revolution. A revolution of the heart.

And we don't walk it alone.

I hope you'll join me—fellow travelers, truth seekers, soul rememberers—in restoring the heart to its rightful place as our compass and our bridge to the divine. When we reclaim our hearts, we reclaim our wholeness. We come back into alignment with the rhythm of life itself.

And from that place of love, the world transforms.

> *You never change things by fighting the existing reality.*
> *To change something, build a new model that*
> *makes the existing model obsolete.*
>
> Buckminster Fuller

ABOUT THE AUTHOR
Michael Stone

Michael Stone's healing journey began even before birth, carried in the womb between the dropping of two atomic bombs, born into a world steeped in fear, scarcity, and war. His early life was marked by profound and formative trauma: the suicide of his mother when he was just two and a half, an absent father, sexual abuse, and the accidental death of his beloved dog. From the harsh discipline of military school and the U.S. Army to years of chaos and grief, Michael's path has been one of reclaiming life through presence, courage, and deep inner work.

A turning point came in 1972 with the est Training, where he glimpsed a radical truth: he could either remain a victim of his past or step onto a path of healing and transformation. That moment set in motion five decades of personal evolution, spiritual practice, and service to others. He immersed himself in the teachings of Werner Erhard, Pema Chödrön, Eknath Easwaran, Sandra Ingerman, and Gabrielle Roth, becoming a certified 5Rhythms teacher and guiding conscious movement journeys for over 40 years across North America and Europe.

Michael holds advanced degrees in Psychology and Organizational Development and has spent over three decades consulting with global organizations. Through his signature course, Presence, Power & Performance, he helped pioneer the integration of somatic awareness, trauma-informed facilitation, moving meditation, and embodied leadership into corporate and nonprofit cultures.

In 1981, tragedy struck again. His wife was murdered in Carmel, California, and for the next 42 years, the case remained unsolved, leaving Michael under a cloud of suspicion and the crushing weight of silence. When DNA evidence finally exonerated him and revealed the actual killer, a new layer of healing became possible. Throughout it all, he raised his daughter as a single father, remained committed to his community, and walked his path of transformation with integrity.

For seventeen years, Michael hosted Conversations, a weekly radio show exploring the frontiers of personal and collective healing. As a faculty member of The Shift Network, he produced the Shamanic Wisdom Summit, amplifying the voices of indigenous elders and spiritual visionaries from around the world. His two decades of shamanic practice opened doors to soul retrieval, ancestral healing, and deep engagement with the spiritual dimensions of trauma.

In 2015, his journey took another decisive turn when he met Thomas Hübl. Hübl's teachings on Individual, Ancestral, and Collective trauma expanded Michael's lens and deepened his work. Since then, he has trained extensively with Hübl, Gabor Maté, Peter Levine, Arielle Schwartz, and other pioneers in trauma healing and somatic integration.

Michael Stone's life is not a story of escape from pain, but of walking through it—honoring the past, reclaiming presence, and helping others do the same. His work continues to weave together ancient wisdom, modern science, and embodied practice to serve individual and collective healing and awakening.